My Father's Will

An heir must satisfy the terms of her earthly father's will
without violating her Father in Heaven's will

MAGDEL ROETS

Since 1978

Publication Consultants

PO Box 221974 Anchorage, Alaska 99522-1974
books@publicationconsultants.com—www.publicationconsultants.com

ISBN 978-1-59433-619-5
eISBN 978-1-59433-618-8
Library of Congress Catalog Card Number: 2015960029

Manufactured in the United States of America.

Table of Contents

CHAPTER 1. Sad News 5

CHAPTER 2. The Reading of the Will 15

CHAPTER 3. The Past 19

CHAPTER 4. Childhood 27

CHAPTER 5. Young Adulthood......................................35

CHAPTER 6. A New Life...45

CHAPTER 7. Terrence 59

CHAPTER 8. The Other Siblings....................................65

CHAPTER 9. Terrence Again 75

CHAPTER 10. Mother...83

CHAPTER 11. More Deaths 91

CHAPTER 12. Making Changes 103

CHAPTER 13. Time to be Creative................................109

CHAPTER 14. Enjoying Life 119

CHAPTER 15. Restless 123

CHAPTER 16. Francois Verduyn 133

CHAPTER 17. My Great Day...143

CHAPTER 18. Big Spending Begins 145

CHAPTER 19. Emigration...155

CHAPTER 20. Terrence and Stacy 159

CHAPTER 21. Some More Spending.............................169

CHAPTER 22. Time to Go Home 181

CHAPTER 23. A Losing Battle 191

CHAPTER 24. Surprise..201

CHAPTER 25. Beginning of the End............................215

CHAPTER 26. Starting Over 225

CHAPTER 27. Closure 235

CHAPTER 1

Sad News

My dad died this morning. Andrew phoned as I was packing my bags. In two hours, I have to be on the plane, but it is too late. He is gone. I sit down on my bed and start sobbing. 'Daddy, why didn't you wait for me! Couldn't you last a few more hours? Couldn't you...?' I grab a pillow and hug it tightly; burying my face in it. After a few minutes, it is soaked.

I chuck the pillow aside, go to the bathroom to wash my face and redo my makeup, especially around my red and swollen eyes. Quickly I finish packing, grab my car keys, lock up and drive away. I'm in a hurry now praying that the traffic will be light and the flight won't be delayed. At O R Tambo I park my car in the long term parking garage. I thank the Lord that it took me less than an hour to reach the airport safely.

I call Gerald as soon as I have checked in:

"Gerald, hello. Darling, I have bad news. My dad died a few hours ago. I was about to leave for the airport when Andrew called."

"Oh, Francine, I'm so sorry. Honey, where are you now? Shall I come over?"

"No, actually I'm at the airport. I've just checked in. It's a good thing you got me such an early flight. Unfortunately it's still too late."

I struggle to keep my composure. We say goodbye and I promise to call again as soon as I have arrived. Then I call Aunt Emma to tell her I'm on my way.

The flight is delayed for five minutes waiting for some dignitary to board. To me it feels like fifty. 'Try to relax,' I tell myself. It serves no purpose to be in a hurry now. It's over. He is gone and nothing will change that. If only I could have a chance to say goodbye. The plane slowly taxis out towards the runway. We are on our way. High up in the sky I start to think about the consequences for me. And I am terrified. How will I manage? I am not ready for this. I cannot do it! Daddy why couldn't you live forever? Yeshua, You have to help me.

My thoughts turn back to Andrew's call early this morning. He did not sound heartbroken, and why would he? None of Dad's children loved him deeply. I will probably be the only one who will mourn him. Perhaps a few loyal employees will mourn a generous boss, some business people might mourn the loss of a worthy rival. Even a few friends might sincerely miss him, but most relatives and friends are probably already rubbing their hands together in anticipation of a possible mention of their names in his will.

Two minutes before eleven o'clock I park the rented car in the circular driveway in front of the house in Pinegrove, Constantia. Aunt Emma opens the door before I can turn the knob. We hug each other, cry a little and then she takes me through to the small family room next to the kitchen.

"Sit down, my dear, I'll get Simon to take your bags to your room. Would you like something to drink?"

"*Rooibos* would be fine, thanks." I sink deep into the comfortable cushions of the big armchair by the window. She spends a few minutes in the kitchen talking to the staff; then joins me in the family room.

"Tell me everything, please". My dad's younger sister starts telling me about the massive heart attack my dad had late last night. How she followed the ambulance and how she felt when the doctor told her there is little hope. At that moment, Andrew arrived and heard the news first hand from the cardiologist. He then immediately made phone calls to all of us. My dad never woke from the deep coma. He passed away in the early hours. But it's all so sudden. I knew he was having health problems, but I did not realize it was that serious. Perhaps I did not want to believe it. He did inform me, didn't he?

"Has there been any indication before that he was having serious trouble? Anything like that in the family?"

"Our family had had its share of trouble. You know my father, your granddad was barely seventy when he became ill and in a few months, it was over. Your father was not as energetic as he used to be. Come to think of it; he was always tired. And he went to the doctor without telling me."

"How did you find out?"

"The receptionist at the doctor called one day to confirm an appointment. Coincidently I was near the phone and answered the call. I could not understand it, because he saw the doctor two weeks before. 'Just for a check-up,' he told me."

"Did you ask him about it?"

"Yes, and he mumbled something about checking up on something. He was very vague about it, did not want to go into any details." Typical Hammond.

Late afternoon both Aunt Emma and I decide to lie down a bit. I do not think I would sleep, but emotional exhaustion takes over and I actually dose off. An hour later I wake up refreshed, realizing the music I am hearing comes from my cell phone.

"Anita, hi."

"Hi Francine. When are you coming?"

"I arrived this morning and I just woke up from a blissful nap."

"Well, sorry to disturb you. I am coming over right now. I hope it's convenient."

"Of course. I'll wait for you down stairs."

"See you, bye."

Half an hour later, my elder sister arrives. I am waiting for her in the family room. A tray with two pots of tea - one with *rooibos* for me and one with green tea for Anita - and biscuits is sitting on the coffee table. As always she is dressed stylishly and as often, in black, adorned with modest gold jewellery, her hair in an attractive short, feathery style and freshly coloured black. Her make-up is noticeable, but not overdone. It suits her. She trots delicately on stilettos into the family room. I get up from my chair and we cheek-kiss carefully not to transfer lipstick.

"You look well, Anita."

"I have picked up half a kilo since last you were here. I quit smoking, you see, and now I have to give up sugar too, otherwise I will roll down the mountain soon." She pours herself a cup of tea and has it without sugar. She does take a biscuit, though.

"I am very proud of you. I knew you could do it. And I really don't see the extra kilo."

"Half a kilo!"

"Sorry, half kilo. Don't worry about it." She grabs a piece of skin below her ribcage half a centimetre thick: "It's right here, see?"

I just shrug because I really don't see one gram of fat on her body.

"Were you with Dad when he died?"

"Were you? Of course I was not. Andrew phoned me last night, but I was out and I did not think it was all that serious." I cannot think of a single thing to say to that, not without stirring up an argument. I can hardly believe her callousness. Doesn't she feel anything? Doesn't she even..."

"What do you think is in his will for us?"

"Really, Anita, aren't you ashamed of yourself? He is hardly cold and you think of what he might have left you."

"Now don't you get all sanctimonious here. You must be hard up for a little money like everyone else. Living in that dump, I bet you will come back right here to the Cape where you belong the moment you receive your inheritance. You will have enough money to maintain this old house, staff and all."

"I doubt it. I am quite happy where I am. I live comfortably with enough money of my own. I really don't care about the money. Right now, I'm mourning a loss that can never be replaced. I don't even want to think about anything else. I'll miss him. I really cared about him, you know."

"That's why I thought you might know something about his will. You were quite chummy with him lately. Perhaps he gave you a clue."

"We never talked about money except when he advised me on some investment possibility or managerial matter concerning my own affairs." If I am overreacting, trying too hard to hide the truth from her, she doesn't seem to notice.

"Don't tell me you never had the opportunity to hint in that direction?"

"Why on earth would I do that? I was never interested in his money and I am not now. Even if he cut me out of his will or cut you all out and left me his entire fortune does not bother me. I might hand it all over to you, but you will probably squander it and be broke again in a few years…" I bite my tongue not to say more. Too much said already.

"Oh come on! Aren't you just a little bit curious? Wait a minute, what do you mean 'cut us out'? What do you know that I don't?"

"No, I'm not curious and I don't know anything you don't." I hesitate for a second praying in my thoughts: 'Please, Lord, forgive me this lie.'

"It's just a way of letting you know I don't care. I'm not going to say it one more time."

"Well, maybe your needs are not as big as mine. Maybe you like to live the way you do. I certainly don't want to live in relative poverty for the rest of my life."

"If you lived within your means, you would have coped well enough. Debt is not a good thing, but you have always wanted more than you could afford."

"With such a rich father I should have been able to have everything I want."

"He worked hard and smart and invested well. Nothing fell into his lap. He did not start on top. He was no better off than you and I when he started his business. And his mother did not leave him a small fortune to begin with." I can't help hinting about our mom's money.

"Why did he do it? Why did he work so hard and build a prosperous business? Wasn't it to take care of his family?"

"Of course, and he did take care of us very well. He also taught us to work hard and earn our way through life. Even thought he was not as present in our lives as much as we'd like him to be, it was his influence that made us work during school holidays. Mom encouraged us and showed us how to save, but Dad urged her to see to it that we don't grow up taking money for granted and expecting everything to fall down from heaven". She obviously failed with you, I thought to myself. "Now you have your own family and you must take care of it. Any inheritance is a bonus and not an earned one. It's a blessing from above. We should not sit back, live in debt and then expect our problems to be solved at the death of someone rich that can leave us his fortune. If that's the attitude, how long will the fortune last?"

Anita rolls her eyes: "What a speech. You're just trying to be difficult. And please don't preach to me."

"Well, can we please talk about something else? I have no desire to argue."

"What else is there to talk about?"

"How are your kids doing? Chanté is getting married soon, isn't she? And what about Donny? He is final year varsity, right? Is he already looking out for a job to start next year? Is he looking forward to being independent?"

All of a sudden, Anita is in a hurry. She gets up and yells "bye, Aunt Emma," in the general direction of where Aunt Emma might be. Then she is out through the door and gone. I know she will be back tomorrow night.

After supper, Andrew arrives with his wife, Marie and teenaged daughter, Delia. Their son, Justin stayed home with a child minder to study for a test. Andrew greeted me warmly and as we settle in the family room, he starts to tell everything that happened the previous night. I have already heard most of it from Aunt Emma, but sense he needs to talk, so I listen with interest at his version. It is obvious that he is not as unaffected as Anita.

"Is there a date for the funeral yet?"

"No, I spoke to Edwin today and he will let me know when he can be here. I will finalize the arrangements tomorrow."

"Will Enid be coming?"

"I think so. Edwin said she is much better after her last operation."

"Glad to hear that. I would like to see her. It's been a long time."

"Yes, it has. They will probably bring the children too. Enid would not like to leave them behind."

****

In spite of all the calls, the day drags by as if time is waiting. I take Aunt Emma shopping. She does not have anything appropriate to wear to the funeral. The outfit she wore to her husband's funeral three years ago is just not good enough for the Hammond-family. Her husband was a government worker in the department of Public Works. He tried his best to provide for his family, but one can stretch a government salary only so far. Especially when there are four ambitious children to see through university.

We have lunch in a small, cosy coffee shop. Over coffee, she raises for the first time her concern about her future. What will happen to her and where will she go if my dad did not provide for her in his will. She does not want money - and I know this is true. She has not one greedy hair on her head. Her husband did not provide for her. That is why my dad took pity on his only sister and took her in three days after she became a widow. If she could only stay on in the house and manage the household as she has been doing these past three years. But what if the house must be sold?

I can't believe nobody told her the truth about the house. This is so typical Hammond. No one talks about anything to anyone.

"Dear Aunt Emma, you have nothing to worry about. It does not depend on Dad's will whether you can stay or not. I own the house and I will never expect you to live anywhere else. The house belonged to my mother. After Dad left her, he transferred the house to her name, and when she died, she left my siblings cash, but I got the house. So there. You can stay as long as you want to. Of course, you can always come and stay with me in Johannesburg. The house is big and whenever you feel lonely, you can visit me and I'll show you my city."

"You are so kind. I did not know all this". Emotion overtakes her and she struggles to keep the tears from flowing. As soon as she composes herself, she asks:

"Don't you have any plans to move down here and move in? Since the house is yours, what is keeping you? It will be nice to have you around."

"I haven't given it any thought. But perhaps I should. My life is still going well up there, but things are changing. I just might want to give up everything there sooner or later". Except of course Gerald, I am thinking. As long as he stays there, I'll stay.

"I pray it'll be sooner. I can see why your mother chose you to have the house. Gwendolyn was a good woman and so are you."

"Yes, well, she probably chose me to lure me back to Cape Town," I said with a smile. "The others have houses and they intend to stay close by. Perhaps she just wanted me to have a home whenever I visit. I'm not sure what motivated her to give the house to me."

At home Aunt Emma takes a nap again, but I am restless. The rain has stopped and although it is still cloudy and cold, I wander around in the garden avoiding the dripping leaves for more than an hour. I cannot wait for evening to come so that Andrew can inform us about all the arrangements; on one hand. On the other hand, I do not want the day to end; I do not want to hear about the arrangements. It will finalize something I am not ready to deal with, yet.

Like yesterday, Andrew arrives after supper. This time his son, Justin is with them. I ask Justin how the test went. With a grin, he tells me he probably did not pass. He might even be kicked out of school for some answers he wrote. Surprised I ask him what he means, to which he replies:

"There was a question about Darwin and his theory, you know, all that junk about evolution."

"So what did you answer?"

"I wrote that Darwin was the world's greatest comedian. His best jokes were published in a book titled 'Origin of the species'." I pat him on the shoulder:

"Good for you. If they kick you out you can always apply for home schooling. More and more children do that these days."

"Gee, that'll be cool."

Soon to follow them, is Anita with her daughter, Chanté and half an hour later Terrence and Stacy turn up. There is a sharp contrast between the appearance of Andrew's family and Terrence's. Andrew is as always well shod, perfectly tidy, his thinning, greying, light brown hair well kempt. His wife, Marie is dressed like yesterday in super conservative woollen shirtdress and court shoes, the daughter much the same while Terrence and his family are very casually dressed in clothes obviously bought with the groceries at the clothes department of the nearest grocery store. Terrence did not have a haircut in months, his face covered in week-old stubble. My youngest brother and his wife are glad to see me. Hugs and kisses and then we all settle in the family room to be enlightened by our eldest brother.

"The funeral will take place next Thursday. I wanted it sooner, but Edwin can only be here on Tuesday."

"My goodness, is he coming by bike? London is only eleven hours away."

"He has things to take care of, dear Sis," snaps Andrew. "I thought to give them a day to recover from jetlag. Is everyone happy with that?"

"When will we see the will?" Anita is not too shy to ask.

"Err, I, err... I think we must get Father's lawyer to come over directly after the funeral. We can have the service early, say ten o'clock and have the reading of the will at two-thirty." He raises an eyebrow inviting comment but there is none.

"That's settled then. I did not expect any objection, so I have already made the arrangements."

I go to the kitchen with Aunt Emma to make coffee. She carries the cake and biscuits, I the tray with cups and coffee. As we enter the room, the cheerful chatter suddenly stops and the delighted faces change. They all return to being serious and solemn. My insides almost turn upside down. Later in bed, I allow the tears to flow once more. I can hardly believe it. Everyone is cheerful. Only Aunt Emma and I are tearful. What are these people thinking? 'Put the old man in the ground so we can get to the money?' And to think I thought Andrew was different. Or maybe he just mourns fast.

Like the day I arrived, the phone would not stop ringing. Dad was well known and friends, relatives and acquaintances call, if not by phone, then in person, to convey their condolences and offer comfort and help. The house has become a beehive. Two days later, I suggest we switch the phone to silent in the afternoon so that we both can have a break. Any calls coming in can use the message service and we'll pick it up in the evening after the last visitor has left. Six days in a row people keep coming, or calling by phone. Then it stops, except for the occasional call or text.

CHAPTER 2

The Reading of the Will

I t is a cold and miserable day. Rain is pouring down as my brothers and sister and their families shed their raincoats and umbrellas on the front *stoep*. Dad is in the ground and now we are all gathering here to listen to the reading of the last will and testament of Stephan Howard Hammond.

The grandchildren have not been invited to attend the event. Those who are present are all escorted into the games room. My dad was passionate about all sorts of games. In this room, he and I spent most of our time together. The grandchildren should not be bored. Simon's son, Ephraim was asked to help keeping an eye on the younger ones. Katrina made sure there is enough to eat and drink for them all. Little Stevie, Terrence' two-year old, is trusted into the hands of his cousin Debra-Ann.

As expected, Enid insisted on her children coming with them. Howie, now almost sixteen, Debra-Ann, twelve and Tamsin, seven, did not know their granddad well. They saw him only once a year when the whole family came over for Christmas.

Andrew's daughter, Delia, not yet fifteen sits down in a corner and does not want to mix. Whether she believes it would contaminate her, or whether she feels out of place because of her super outdated clothing no one knows. She was dressed like her mother, not in anything any teenager would be seen dead in.

Her brother, Justin always enjoys his cousins at family gatherings. He chats with everyone, challenges Howie, more than three years older, to any game that caught his attention. Debra-Ann, a real caring little motherly type, took charge of her little cousin, Stevie who utterly enjoys all the attention and affection poured on him. Tamsin had to keep herself busy. The only one in her own age group she is the odd one out and no one is interested in her. Of Anita's two children, Chanté and her brother Donny, young adults by now, only Donny is present. Chanté is probably with her fiancé out house-hunting. Donny keeps himself occupied listening to music, chatting a little in between with the boys and watching the youngsters at play. He did not have to come, but would not miss it for the world.

The atmosphere is heavy with anticipation. Big money is about to be distributed. The chairs and sofas are arranged in an open-ended V-shape with the open end at the fireplace and spreading out towards the table where the lawyer will be sitting. The table is facing the huge fireplace where the friendly flames are dancing to the crackling tune of the fire, sending bright sparks up the chimney in the big formal living room. Together with the flames, the brown tiles of the fireplace repeat the autumn colour scheme of the room. Against one wall of the room is a large coffee table laden with all sorts of savouries, cakes, tarts and pastries. I recall Katrina and her daughter having a ball in the kitchen yesterday and the day before.

Andrew and Marie take place on the two-seater to the left of the fireplace. Edwin and Enid sit down on the opposite side of the fireplace. Anita takes a seat on a single armchair next to Enid, her back to the window. Like with her previous visits she had the good sense to come alone. Her latest toy-boy was told to stay put. Terrence and Stacy seat themselves next to Marie, who half-turns her back on them. Scattered through the room are loose chairs for a few relatives, an old friend and some employees who the lawyer insisted be present, including Simon and Katrina. Aunt Emma and I sit down on the easy chairs on both sides of the table provided for the lawyer. Gerald stays at my side.

Everyone seems a little on edge not knowing what to expect. Dad often had surprises up his sleeve and you never knew what he was up to. Some quickly start eating; others peck on a pastry; some only sip coffee or tea, too nervous to eat. Edwin continuously touches the top of his head where the light brown curly hair is thinning out. Marie dabs her eyes every so often while Anita turns the many rings on her fingers round and round changing positions in her chair every twenty seconds.

Silence falls on the room when the lawyer, a middle aged, balding and bespectacled man named Daniel Denton enters the room at precisely two-thirty. He introduces himself, makes sure everyone who needs to be here, is present, declines the offer of refreshments and gets down to business right away. The Receiver of Revenue is neither present nor invited, but everybody knows he will take the biggest piece of the pie.

****

The door closes behind Daniel Denton. The staff members who have benefited have been excused. There are smiles showing teeth all around the room, except Aunt Emma. She rests her head on my shoulder and weeps as if she is the one who is disinherited. Dad left her one million in cash and another five million in a trust. I already told her she is welcome to stay on in the house as long as she likes, so her future is secure. Better than this, she could not imagine.

The business, a private company, Hammond Holdings, will remain unchanged. Ownership has already been transferred; therefore, it is of no consequence here. The identity of the new owner will be revealed soon.

Terrence and Stacy are in a hurry. They need to get out and celebrate. Or so I thought. No need to hang around among the snobbish siblings who, except I, never wanted anything to do with them. They both hug me warmly. Discretely they excuse themselves, collect Stevie and then they are gone.

The others linger just long enough not be impolite, not to look too eager to start living the good life. Except Edwin. He complains - as usual - about the huge amounts that Dad gave away to the various different charities and missions that he supported all his life. He feels the children should have received all of it. And what about the company? Where will the profits be going? Dad must have had a reason why he left me out of the will and no one is going to change that, convinced that he speaks for everyone in the room.

"So don't expect anyone of us to share," he says, piercing me with his bright blue eyes, Dad's eyes. Enid just turns her head away and I know that apart from Aunt Emma, she might be the only one who does not agree with him. She pats him on the arm trying to calm him down. They all shake their heads in disbelief. How could Dad do this to Francine, his own flesh and blood. And to think she was so close to him all this time, they whisper among themselves. Just shows you how far "sucking up" can get you in the end. At this moment, I have some nasty thoughts to deal with. Do they think I'm deaf?

Anita looks at me as if to say 'so, who's disinherited now?' But she doesn't say anything. She pecks me on the cheek like she would a distant cousin and leaves shortly after Terrence and Stacy. I can imagine them giving each other high five, low five and whatever five there is, the moment the door closes behind them. I'd like to give them each a kick five were my toes not in my shoes. If these people someday will need taking care of, it will not be done by me.

If Andrew is upset because Dad did not leave him the business; place him in charge of the company, he does not show it. Only once does he mention to Edwin that he would very much like to know who this mysterious person or persons are who now own Dad's company, to which Edwin explodes once more about the unfairness of the company having been given away like that instead of sharing it among us all. Andrew and Enid manage to calm him down reminding him of the generous amount of money they have just received making them rich beyond expectation. So, why worry about a company none of them would want to run. They leave together with their families in tow. Let the good life begin. After tax they are each thirty-seven-and-a-half-million Rand richer and on their way to celebrate. All those heavy debts can be cancelled; new things can be acquired. Mourning time is over or simply forgotten.

The house is deadly quiet after everyone is gone. Even Simon and Katrina who received one million each, kept in a trust for them until they retire, are nowhere to be seen. Aunt Emma has to take a nap to recover from the shock and that leaves me all alone to contemplate my dad's will. I slip out into the garden; under the grass roof of the *lapa* is where Gerald finds me. I ask his opinion of the will. He just shakes his head, smiles and wraps his arms around me, holding me close to his heart.

CHAPTER 3

The Past

I cried until my pillow was wet, turned it around and cried some more. My daddy was gone and he was not coming back. I cried until it hurt and fell asleep from exhaustion. In the middle of the night, I woke and heard my door opening. Mommy appeared in the dim moonlight shining through the curtains. She sat down on my bed, took me in her arms and hugged me tightly. I started crying again. From the tremor in her body, I knew she was crying too.

I woke up with the sun shining brightly through my yellow and orange curtains. I quickly jumped out of bed and ran to my parent's room. There was no one. Clearly, the bed was not even slept in. I ran down the stairs to the kitchen and found Mom sitting on a stool, clutching a steaming mug of coffee and staring out of the window. When she saw me, she smiled that beautiful smile:

"Would you like some coffee?"

"Yes please." I could hardly utter the words with quivering voice. She poured me a cup and I sat down as close to her as I could.

"Would you like us to pray?" she asked, looking down at me. Taking a sip, I just nodded. She put her arm around me and asked the Lord Yeshua to help us through this difficult time, to ease our pain and to show us what to do to remain in the will of Abba Father. I said 'amen' and Mommy's words: 'the will of Abba Father' stuck in my mind. I started sobbing again. Mommy held me close.

After a while she held me by both shoulders away from her and looked me in the eyes: "There, there now, let's drink our coffee, it's getting cold. We're going to grow up nicely and not cry anymore ... not much." She smiled and wiped my tears. I tried my best to smile back.

Outside the sounds and fragrances of spring were dancing for the joy of fresh new life, but did not enter the house.

One by one, my siblings came down and gathered in the kitchen for coffee and rusks. On Saturdays we never had a big breakfast. We usually got up late and had coffee and rusks, biscuits, cereal or toast, each one older than ten helping himself. Mom hugged them each. Andrew was sixteen, and not in the hugging business anymore. He acted grown up as if nothing out of the ordinary had happened.

Edwin the complainer - three weeks from his fifteenth birthday - moaned about everything: Coffee too cold, rusks not his favourite flavour and:

"Anita, what are you staring at?" At what point Anita, thirteen years and one month old, started to cry.

Anita, usually chirpy and cheerful, had turned overnight into a teary, sulking child, restless and unfocused. Andrew had changed from being a boy to being the man in the house. Edwin's being competitive and hate of losing, intensified in every way getting more aggressive, angrier.

I did not make these observations at the time. It was years later that I realized what strong effect that Dad's departure from our house had had on each one of us. I was not yet six years old. I used to be quiet and liked to play dolls with Anita, but enjoyed more and more being creative all alone in my own room. Terrence, the youngest, was the cute, adorable toddler, three years old whom everyone cooed about. He grew to enjoy all the attention and soon learned how to make the best use of it. He became a charming little manipulator early in life.

Terrence. What more can I say about him? Tall and lean like Mom, curly brown hair and brown eyes, unlike Andrew and Edwin who had Dad's slightly stocky built but both a little taller than Dad, but with the same light brown hair and bright blue eyes. He tested more intelligent than any of us, but barely made it from one standard to the next. Early in his standard eight year he saw a movie about lawyers and made up his mind to become one. He started applying himself and matriculated with four distinctions and three B symbols.

Then came university. There he was introduced to girls, alcohol and drugs. Somewhere in his second year, he dropped out and joined a commune at a time when the hippy culture was almost extinct and forgotten. The family turned their backs on him. All but me. But I could do nothing about it. I was still studying with no means of helping him. Dad cancelled the deposits from his trust fund.

At some point, Terrence picked up an old guitar that belonged to someone in the commune. He started strumming and realized he could get some tune out of the instrument. Hey, man, this is great. I didn't know it was so easy. It always looked so difficult, he thought. He asked around:

"Is there anyone that can show me more?" Someone who knew some showed him how it was done. Practicing all day long between puffs of pot, he really got the hang of it, became better and better, wondering why he never before realized there was some talent in him.

"I think I like this, man, show me more."

"You have talent, dude, how come you never played before?" Terrence just shook his head, shrugged and strummed on. He always did love music, just never thought of trying his hand at it.

He hooked up with a girl barely seventeen. She fell pregnant and they both believed he was the father.

"Are you sure, Baby? How far are you? We've been together only a few weeks. You sure it's mine? You were with Marty a month ago."

"I broke up with Marty almost two months ago, Baby. Don't do this to me. I'm sure it's yours, finish *'n klaar*." All through the pregnancy, they drank cheap wine, smoked pot and lived the true, free hippy life. The commune broke up and Terrence took his pregnant girl and the guitar with him. He found a place to stay, a room in a slum area paying the rent with money he earned playing guitar on street corners and backward gig venues.

The baby, a little girl, was born premature. Tiny and week, neglected from her first moment, she just made it past the age of four months. One morning, after hours of silence from the makeshift crib, they realized something was amiss. They found the little girl dead. She had passed away in her sleep.

Terrence was shocked almost sober. For a while, he tried to clean up his act, but it did not last. He soon fell back into his old habits. It was only after his girl died of an overdose a year later that Terrence got to his senses. Like the prodigal son, he went home and begged Dad to help him. He promised to clean up the bad habits. Somehow, he convinced Dad to avail the trust fund again so he could go back to university and finish his studies. He was going to be an exceptionally good lawyer.

He finished among the top three of his class and everyone was proud of him again. Then came the bar exam. He passed that too with honours and celebrated through the night as soon as the results were made available.

"Yeehaa! Life has just begun. Come on, guys," he waved over a bunch of his fellow students, "let's go celebrate." He had passed the bar, but not the pub. The next morning the sun woke him through the bars of a police cell. With throbbing headache, he remembered he had smashed his car as well as his short legal career. Andrew bailed him out because Dad had washed his hands of his youngest son. Mom also felt he should learn a lesson the hard way.

Half past ten one evening there was a knock on my door. It was Terrence. He had hitchhiked all the way to Johannesburg. He needed a place to 'crash' and knew I would take him in. He was right. How could I not help my baby brother knowing every other family member had kicked him out.

****

Andrew tried to follow in Dad's footsteps. He was probably talented in many other areas, but believed he was placed on earth to do the same things Dad did, maybe become Dad's successor in the business. To win his approval he had to show Dad he could match if not beat him at his own game. However, he lacked Dad's imagination and perhaps motivation too; he knew that one day he would inherit much. So why break oneself?

The company he managed to put up was fairly successful, but would never be the multi-million-Rand company Dad had built. He also lacked Terrence's charisma. He could not convince Dad to employ him in any senior position. As the owner's son, he was not willing to start at the bottom where Dad expected every employee to start. So he rather went his way and did his own thing.

Family was always important to him. He played 'dad' to us younger ones from the day our father departed and always felt we were his responsibility. He married young and transferred his sense of responsibility over to his own family. He chose a girl from an old-money family with high social standing. Marie, an attractive dark haired, dark eyed, fair skinned girl, fell pregnant within a year after the wedding, but miscarried at seven weeks. Four months later, she fell pregnant again and miscarried at five weeks. During the next seven years, she had four more miscarriages and then stopped trying.

Andrew was devastated, but kept his emotions mostly to himself. He poured all his energy first into caring for Marie's emotional well-being, and secondly into his business. For years, they did not mention children. They both accepted that there would not be an heir unless they adopted. Marie did not like the thought at all, but realized it would be better than being childless. Knowing the importance of children to her, Andrew had already started looking into the matter when Marie announced that she was pregnant.

Seven months later a beautiful baby girl was born. Twenty-two months later the little girl became elder sister to a brother, a healthy four-kilogram boy. The family was complete, all the relatives were elated and Marie's reputation among her super-snobbish family, of being a proper woman, was restored. Educated women do not talk about their children, but they have to have some.

****

Edwin, being competitive, like our dad, and a sports lover, aspired to become a professional in some line of sport. While at varsity he played rugby for the first team, cricket as well, and took up squash, road running and golf for pass time activities, everyone was convinced sports would be his future. He went on to play provincial rugby.

Then came selection for the Springbok jersey. Edwin was going to be a Springbok at all cost. The cost was a broken collar bone to a teammate and a broken neck to an opponent. The opponent survived but spent his days in a wheelchair. He partially regained the use of two fingers on his right hand. Edwin was barred from rugby for life.

In all other games of sports, he was frowned upon, pushed out or ignored.

"This is just miserable," he complained. "No one can just study. How can I relax without some activity in my life? Between study sessions I need to be physically active to cope with the stress, something to take my mind off and get away from it all for a while."

"I warned you a hundred times to deal with your anger and to think about someone else. You just think about yourself and what you want. You got what you've asked for. There is still golf. No one can forbid you to play golf. How about a round with me on Saturday?" Andrew tried his best to make Edwin see that his own actions had consequences that he had to accept and live with.

"Sure, thanks, it'll be nice. But golf is not fast enough. We can play golf every Saturday, but I need energetic action. You know what I mean?"

"Yes, Brother, I know what you are trying to tell me. I suggest you jog to the golf course. That enough action for you?"

"Don't mock me, Andrew. See you on Saturday. And next time we can play squash." He slammed down the phone. Why bother to talk to anyone? He thought. No one understands. At least Andrew is willing to play golf with him. He fully understood that his isolation on the sports fields was the result of his own wrong doing, but refused to admit it to anyone. Perhaps he should give Wallace or Frankie a call. His two best friends might not reject him. If they do, he thought, then all I have, is Andrew.

His only option was to concentrate on the academic side of university life and made sure to prepare himself for a career. He excelled in chemistry, won a scholarship at a university in England to complete his doctorate. When he was offered a teaching post, he accepted and decided to make his stay permanent.

****

Edwin swore never to marry. He intensely threw himself into everything he did. No time for family. But love often comes unexpectedly. During a long summer holiday - winter in the Cape - he met a girl eight years younger than himself. It was at a party of an old student friend, one of a few who kept in contact with him.

Enid, a beautiful honey-blond girl; eyes the colour of almonds, had just broken up with her fiancé for cheating on her. Her elder brother, Wallace, an overprotective, aggressive kind of person, took her under his wing, after breaking the ex-fiancé's nose and cheekbone. He took her everywhere he went and made sure only men whom he approved of, dared look in her direction.

Being the same kind of man as Edwin, Wallace was quite a close friend of Edwin's, introduced him to his baby sister, and that was it. Love at first sight. Edwin married her after a month and took her with him back to England. The honeymoon was a tour through Europe on their way to their home in the U.K.

CHAPTER 4

Childhood

Our childhood experiences were quite different from each other. Consequently, we grew up to become individuals with complete different personalities. .As I mentioned earlier, Anita used to be a cheerful child, playful, loving and lovable; active but not competitive; energetic but not sporty. She played hockey and tennis and she swam just because her friends did. At home, she kept herself busy with macramé, origami, scrap booking, skipping rope on the back patio, playing with the dogs, chasing butterflies and a thousand other things. Then Dad left and she withdrew.

She was probably hit hardest of us all. She was Daddy's girl and she was in the middle. The elder boys were busy with their own things. I still needed a lot of mom's attention but was able to keep myself busy at times. Terrence needed Mom most of the time. Somewhere among us all, Anita was forgotten.

She became temperamental, her moods swinging from angry to silently sulking. She was either restless and whining about everything, or listless and lethargic. For a time she still enjoyed playing dolls with me, but our times together grew shorter because she got bored faster. Before the year was out, she had grown out of it altogether. Her favourite tree in the back yard, a huge pine increasingly became her hiding place, her sanctuary. Under its branches she would spend hours dreaming about whatever girls of her age dreamt about.

After graduation, Anita got a job in the human resources department of a big company. She was average in everything she did. Everyone knew she could do better if she tried. Even marriage. She could have had a successful, ambitious man, but felt herself unworthy and married the lazy womaniser who was a low ranking colleague at the time. The only reason he proposed to her was that he knew who her father was, hoping to benefit financially from the union. They had two babies in quick succession; the first was conceived before the honeymoon was over.

After three short years of verbal and emotional abuse and numerous affairs on his part, she chucked him out and married a wealthy man, a widower - twice her age - less than a year later. Thomas was decent and the family liked him. He was a heavy drinker, but never misbehaved and never mistreated Anita or the two young children from her first marriage. It was a happy marriage. The children liked Tomas and he treated them well.

The marriage deteriorated after his junkie daughter, Jolene, four-and-a-half years younger than Anita, returned from America where she'd spent several years, after her mother's death, doing nothing of value. She went out of her way to make Anita's life miserable. Thomas could not handle the two most important women in his life fighting like ally-cats. He tried his best to maintain peace but dared not take sides.

The girl would neither work nor study; refused to do anything worthwhile with her life. When Thomas refused to give her money, which he knew she would use to buy drugs, she simply stole anything from Anita that she could lay her hands on, sold or pawned it for cash to satisfy her addiction. She even at one time stole Anita's credit card, bought a lot of jewellery, sold the pieces separately for cash and paid her supplier who was getting impatient.

This went on for almost five years. Anita, on the brink of a nervous breakdown, told Thomas to choose: "You either kick out that daughter, or give me a divorce. I simply shall not stand for this any longer. Jolene does whatever she wants and there are no limits to what she is capable of."

"I'll talk to her. I'll put an ultimatum to her. Then she will listen."

"She might do what you ask for a while, Thomas, but she is addicted. She cannot help herself. You have to get her into a rehab program where she can get cleaned out. Only after that will she listen to what you or anyone else has to say. But I will no longer stand for this nonsense. It's your choice: your junkie daughter, or me."

He loved Anita and was heartbroken. He promised to get the girl into rehab. After ten days in a state-of-the-art-dry-out facility, Jolene ran away. No one knew where she was until she was picked up for shoplifting. Thomas bailed her out and let her come home. She promised to behave. But junkie's promises don't last; she was back in her old habits in no time. Thomas came home early one day to find Anita packing her bags.

"I thought I'd be gone by the time you came home," she told him. "I didn't want you to find me packing."

"Anita, but why? What's happened?"

"That brat of yours emptied my purse. I had two thousand rand in there. And the money wasn't even mine. Tilly, who works with me, gave me money and asked me to make a deposit for her. She is in hospital and can't pay her bills herself. Now I have to tell her the money she trusted to me is stolen."

"How did she draw money if she is in hospital? And why didn't she pay her own debt when drawing money?"

"She drew the money, then fell on her way to her car and broke her hip. That's why. But what has it got to do with Jolene? Tilly's money, my money? What's the difference? The money is gone and your little girl is responsible. You promised to do something about it and you failed. I cannot take any of this anymore. So I'm going, bye." He pleaded but she was adamant. Thomas had a heart attack and died two hours later.

At the funeral, Anita was quiet; hardly spoke to anyone. At the gravesite, she stood next to the sobbing stepdaughter. As soon as the casket touched the bottom of the grave, Anita 'accidentally' stepped with her stiletto on her stepdaughter's foot, 'overbalanced,' knocking her down and fell on top of her. Following this, Anita 'accidentally' kicked soil into her face while getting up, dusted herself, and briskly walked away. No one saw her or heard from her for three days. Mom took her children home with her.

Anita came back in a fighting mood. Her husband had left her the house and everything in it. He also left her a fair amount of cash. The rest of his assets were shared among loyal employees, some charities. An enormous sum of money was put into a trust for his only daughter who was kicked out of the house summarily at Anita's return.

Jolene came home in the small hours, stoned as usual, to find her clothes and personal belongings strewn all over the pavement in front of the house. All the locks were changed, no access to the property. The day the estate was finalized Anita moved out before the estate agent could put up the 'for sale'-sign. There were just too many sad memories. I loved Thomas more than I have loved anyone in all the lonely years after Dad left, she whispered to herself. She looked back at the house one more time before leaving the driveway: I cannot stay on in this house and be reminded of what could have been, she thought, and drove off.

She found a duplex townhouse in Table View and soon after, resigned her job for a better one in the city. She lived quite contentedly with her two young children where they could watch the waves from the balcony and hear the sea roaring at night. Anita vowed never to marry again. Marriage just is not for me, she told herself. I have to do what it takes to protect myself and my children. Protect us from the hurt of losing the man in the house.

****

Like many children in similar circumstances, I blamed myself for the separation. I firmly believed it was my fault that Daddy had left us. I must have been a very naughty girl. When Anita lost interest in playing dolls with me, it just confirmed this belief. So, I tried to be extra good. I tried to 'remain in Abba Father's will' as I recalled Mom's words in prayer.

That made me often withdraw into my own world where only my imagination could run free. I would never allow myself to be free; then I could not be naughty. If I did not do anything, I could not do anything wrong. I stayed in my room most of the time drawing pictures of happy things, happy events from the past when Daddy was still with us.

If it were not for Mother, we would turn out a bunch of unbalanced dropouts. She helped us through the worst, but she could do only so much, having her own pain and regret to deal with. Anita needed her more than I did, but she did not realize that. She somehow felt closer to me. Perhaps I was more receptive. Anita totally closed off, became more and more self-absorbed and shut Mom out. Her pain manifested in ways that was often unpleasant, like her constant sulking and periodic spitefulness. Mom did not know what to do about it, so she just turned her attention increasingly to Terrence and me.

****

By the time I finished school, I was self-reliant and independent. Mom encouraged us to get ourselves a job and start earning our own pocket money when we were teenagers. As soon as a child in the house turned sixteen, Mom made a big fuss of the birthday, let him or her have a big party and then it was time to find a job. Andrew was very proud to announce a week after his birthday that he found employment at the local grocery store as a packer. He worked for seven months, then quit. He tried to find another form of income, but did not succeed. He was not lazy, just picky.

Edwin loved the outdoors. He had quite a struggle, but after two months of being sixteen years old, he met a man on a golf course who needed a caddy. Edwin convinced the man he was just the right one for the job. He kept his job for fifteen months, then quit. His excuse was that he needed more time to study for his matric exams.

Anita, so knowledgeable about fashion, got a weekend job as shop assistant in a boutique. She loved the work and held on to her job even through her varsity years. Her earnings paid for clothes, make-up, toiletries; entertainment; never for books or any study related matter. For those she depended on the trust fund provided by Dad. She never made an effort to see him, but was happy to receive money from him.

Edwin's income exceeded Anita and Andrew's by far. By the end of every month, though, he was as broke as they were. None of them ever bothered to put something away for a rainy day. Blow the money; next month you earn some more, was their motto.

Mom registered all of us at a casting agency that provided extras for film productions. Andrew did not like it but agreed to take the one casting job he got. Edwin could not get it right and Anita was too fidgety. Only Terrence and I actually did some work more than once.

But Terrence spent all the money he earned. He bought everything he saw, treated his friends on movie tickets or tickets for sporting games.

When it was my turn to find a job after my sixteenth birthday I went straight to the mall. I loved doing the filming jobs, but the income was not reliable. I kept my money in the bank and decided I needed a regular income. The day after my sixteenth birthday I started working at a coffee shop, 'The Coffee Cup and TTO' in our nearest shopping centre. I started as a dishwasher and was soon promoted to potato peeler and onion chopper. During peak hours I helped waiting on tables.

After a few months the owner, Monique, noticed that I was good at handling money. When the girl doing the cash register at the 'take-out' station reduced her working hours to mornings only because of changed circumstances, she asked me to do the afternoon shift. Another two months passed before I was promoted again. I learned to place orders for stock at the take-out station where the racks holding crisps, sweets, chocolates, soft drinks, magazines and newspapers, biscuits, nuts and dried fruit lined the side wall.

I worked hard every afternoon and Saturday enjoying every moment. By the time I left school I was a well experienced all-rounder knowing pretty much about every aspect of running a coffee shop from preparing the food to doing the banking. It was not always fun. More often than not I had to grab a mop and clean the floors for lack of hands. But it was worth it. Apart from earning good pocket money I gathered valuable experience and learned to love the business. Later in life this knowledge and fondness of the coffee shop-business came in quite handy.

I used my money to buy necessities and saved the rest. As I was under eighteen, Mom had to help me to invest my savings. Slowly but surely my assets grew securing a future of independence. It was satisfying to know I was in control of my life and that I could take care of myself.

Terrence had an interest in horticulture. He used to cut twigs and leafs off plants to see if he could make them grow. He had success a number of times and started buying plant pots with his pocket money while mother still gave him his allowance. Long before he was sixteen, he had a thriving business selling small potted plants. He advertised in the school newspaper and later in the local newspaper as well. But same as the others he was broke soon after every sale that he had made.

Andrew studied business management, Edwin was interested in science. They did well academically. While Edwin furthered his studies, Andrew was satisfied with his Bachelor's degree and started interviewing for jobs as soon as the final exams were over, starting at his own dad's company. The interview did not go as he expected. He applied for a managerial position. No one freshly out of varsity with no experience was appointed in such a position. He was indignant, confronted Dad and was shown the door.

After many interviews, he realised he would have to start at the bottom and work his way up. It did not sit well with him, but after seven years of work in a small company during which he was promoted once, he resigned to try his hand and started his own business when Dad refused him again a higher position than what he was qualified for. He learned the hard way that it was not as easy as it looked. A year later, he was job hunting again. Another small company employed him in a senior position this time. The salary was nothing to get excited about. By now he was already married a few years and realised he had responsibilities still hoping to someday have a family.

At this job he lasted three years before getting restless again. This time he did his homework well, found a reliable partner and together they started a company that would grow and provide an income that was acceptable even for his wife, Marie, and her family who had great expectations of him. He worked hard although his heart was not in it. What was it that he really wanted? He asked himself this question more than once. There was no answer. He did not know.

CHAPTER 5

Young Adulthood

Since I hadn't chosen a career or study line at the end of my matric year, I decided to explore the world. It was still fashionable at that time, to backpack through Europe. Although I was not one to follow every fashion or trend, the idea appealed to me. Mom was shocked and tried her best to talk me out of it, but eventually she had to see my point: I did not know what else to do with my life and travelling just might help to widen my perspective and give direction. She still tried to convince me to stay till after my birthday in April, but I was impatient. I knew if I waited, I might be talked out of it altogether. Three days after Christmas I boarded a plane and flew north.

I landed on Heathrow in icy weather with only one shoulder bag. After two days in London I decided to tackle Europe from the south, so I flew right down to Barcelona in search of warmer weather. I knew I would not meet with summer temperatures. The few degrees extra were welcome nevertheless. My tour of the northern countries started with excited anticipation.

Going slowly, unhurriedly through the less freezing parts of Spain, I had many experiences, pleasant and less pleasant. To keep expenses low, I did as everyone else and stayed in youth *pensions* and worked my way through wherever I could find a little something to do however humble the wages. I made many friends, even fell a tiny bit in love, but guarded my heart, knowing I would not stay and remembering Mom's words: "remain in Abba Father's will". I saw many things, some of which made lasting impressions, some soon forgotten.

By early spring, I was ready to leave Spain and crossed the border to France. I loved the countryside more than the cities. Tranquil, peaceful, altogether beautiful. The people I met were friendly down-to-earth and hospitable. Many made me promise to keep in contact. If I did not guard my heart knowing that my future can never lie there, I could easily have fallen seriously in love. There was more than enough opportunity for that, like Enrique, the Spaniard, Friedel, the Swiss, not to mention Hans, the Hollander. But, I had decided beforehand that I would not stay, neither would I go home with a broken heart. I intended to remain in the Father's will. Father never intended me to get to my wedding night second hand and all used up. That is how I managed to go home in September of the following year, still a virgin.

The common denominator of all the cities of Europe that impressed me, was the galleries and museums with their breath taking works of art. I think I spent more time admiring paintings than sleeping; I could not get enough. I became completely consumed. From the 'Golden Triangle' in Madrid to the numerous galleries and museums in Barcelona. From the Louvre and a dozen others in Paris and Nice to the overwhelming quantity and quality of what the Netherlands had to offer. Not to mention Italy. On to the galleries in Germany, too many and too good to mention in one paragraph. It would fill an encyclopaedia to record everything I saw. It would take a year or two to digest it all.

I walked the streets, wide and narrow, neatly paved or cobbled, alone or in a group, of every major city in every European country. I took trips by bus, by train or by boat exploring a world that I knew of, but knew nothing about. A picture in a book gives you colours, shapes, light and shadow; it does not give away the smells, the wind in your face, the attitude of the people. It does not show the shifting of the shadows neither the sounds of your shoes on a cobbled street surface nor the change in temperature as the sun rises. Those have to be experienced by being there.

Experiencing Europe helped me understand something of the paintings in the galleries. Street scenes made sense because I was there.

I walked down some of them taking in the sounds and smells, listening to the people talking. I ate at street cafes portrayed in some paintings. I was part of it. I was part of the painting. I might as well be one of the undefined figures in a painting, casting a shadow on the pavement or a reflection in a puddle on a rainy day.

Blending in felt like being one little piece of a big puzzle. Me, Francine Hammond from Cape Town, South-Africa right here in the big puzzle picture of Europe was a thought so overwhelming, it made my head spin. I was only barely eighteen years old and here I was, building my own puzzle, painting my own picture with me in the centre. Yet I felt small.

Often I was reminded of my own little pictures I drew as a child; more often of those I would have liked to draw, but was not skilful enough. Soon I got myself a sketchbook, some pencils and started to sketch things that caught and kept my attention. I still did not know what I was doing and how to do it, but something was born inside me: The desire to learn all there is to know. Everywhere I met artists, I would ask questions, watch what they were doing and how, and ask why they did it the way they did it.

I planned to stay abroad one year. I simply could not go home. I survived another winter and enjoyed another summer. Only when the leaves started falling again, did I finally allow the thought to go home surface in my mind. This thought was sealed by Mom when I called her one evening.

"Honey, I know you'd like to stay, but you must come home, at least for a while."

"Why, what's wrong?"

"Nothing's wrong. Something's right for a change. Edwin is here for the holiday." "Well, what's that got to do with me? I saw him a couple of weeks before he left." "He, believe it or not, is getting married."

"What! I can hardly believe my ears. How, when did that happen?" Mom told me in short how he met Enid and fell in love instantly. We said goodbye. I immediately started making arrangements to get home as quickly as I could.

I felt like a stranger as I stepped down at D F Malan in a typical early-September shower. It was good to be home. Excitement rose up in me when I saw my mother. All I had to tell her, all she probably had to tell me! We hugged tightly for long seconds before I picked up my bags and followed her to the car. On the way home Mom told me in detail all she knew about Edwin, Enid and the wedding that was to take place that coming Saturday.

She also told me my dad had come to know Christ. He was full of remorse about the way he behaved in the past. They had forgiven each other and a new friendship was beginning to develop with great caution. They talked on the phone often and met for lunch once in a while. He asked about us all the time. His interest seemed sincere. I told Mom flatly that my disinterest was just as sincere.

It felt so good to be home as I stepped onto the front *stoep*. Simon was ready to greet me at the door, smiling broadly. He took my bags up to my room while I went through to the kitchen to greet Katrina. She was equally happy to see me. I waited until Simon joined us before I took their gifts from my shoulder bag: "Just to show you how much I missed you both," I said, smiling. They were our most faithful employees. Simon, the butler was there since I got my memory; Katrina came to work as housekeeper before I finished primary school.

Mom went upstairs with me chatting about nothing in particular. On the landing she told me to take a bath if I wished to wash Europe's dust from me. If I wanted to rest a bit that's fine. Otherwise, I could join her for coffee in the family room in an hour or so.

"I'll see what I feel like after the bath," I replied already loosening the clip from my thick, reddish brown hair.

As I sank beneath the thick layer of foam, my eyelids grew heavier and soon I was fast asleep. Half an hour later, the water had cooled so much that I woke up, topped up with warm water and dosed off again. Reluctantly I got out of the bath after another twenty minutes, dried and dressed. I emptied my bag on the corner table in search for Mom's gift. Finding it right at the bottom, I went down to meet her in the family room.

I handed her a small, flat parcel that I had purchased in Paris several weeks before. She took the wrapping off carefully and was speechless. I knew she liked France, I knew she appreciated good works of art. Still I was not prepared for the way she was awestruck at the sight of this simple French landscape. It was as if her thoughts travelled a thousand miles an hour back into the past. Then she smiled: "How beautiful... thank you."

"Glad you like it."

"Have some coffee. The cake was baked especially for you." I helped myself to a large slice of coconut layer cake and sat down.

"Mom, I have decided what I want to do with my life. I am going to study art; painting; oil painting." I told her how the decision slowly sort-of crept up on me over this period of almost two years. She did not respond in the way I expected. She just sat there looking at me and I wondered whether she even heard what I had said. But, then I looked at her eyes where I saw something that was, at that time, completely incomprehensible to me. There was a bright sparkle, that could be the result of moist building up, but somehow I got the impression that there was more to it. I just did not know what it was. She did not look at me when at last she said: "I'm very happy that you found direction."

****

Edwin's wedding was simple, cosy and very beautiful. Enid's family was greatly opposed to such an impulsive move, but still went out of their way to make the day special for her. Her father was friendly, her mother teary and her brother Wallace strutted like a peacock as if it was all his doing alone. Enid was a most pretty bride and Edwin smiled showing more teeth that I knew he had.

****

I applied at all the universities that offered a degree in fine arts and was accepted at them all. Difficult choice. Eventually I decided to stay at home, find a simple part time job to finance my studies - I was not willing to use the trust fund my dad had put up for me - and registered at the University of South Africa. I liked this course best of all those I had considered. Immediately I jumped into my studies with all I had.

I finished my degree with flying colours. But it was not enough. I simply had to go further. After I had acquired the Master's degree, I entered for the diploma in education. Only after that did I feel it was time to take a break. Shortly after the April graduation-ceremony, I jumped onto a plane again to Europe. I needed a holiday.

I stayed with Edwin and Enid for two weeks getting to know Enid well. We grew quite close. I enjoyed taking the little toddler off her hands for a few hours every day so Enid could have some rest, as she was seven months pregnant. My nephew, Howie, and I had lots of fun together. He was a bouncy, energetic little boy who loved all sorts of ball games, not unlike his father.

From Edwin's I toured Europe visiting all the places that had impressed me most the first time I was there. Looking up the friends who had made an effort to keep in contact with me, I renewed and consolidated some friendships at a more mature level. Being still single I was, of course, introduced to several available men. I made it clear, though, that I was not going to get involved since I still believed my life was not in Europe. To get involved at any level more than platonic friendship was going to complicate things. I preferred life to be simple and straightforward. So I did the Joseph-act, I ran from every man who made my heart beat a little faster. Potiphar's wife was probably attractive and Joseph could easily have fallen for her charm, but he ran; so did I.

Like the day well-meaning friends from my back-packer days in Venice set me up for a date with no other than Enrique whom I met on my first visit to Europe. No harm in having coffee, I decided. I met him in a cosy coffee shop close to the water. Smiling broadly when he saw me entering, he pulled a chair out for me and helped me sit down. What a grown-up gentleman he had become. Years earlier, although a bit older than most of us, backpackers in the *pension* in France where I first met him, he was a boy, a little bit vain and ego-centric, yet likable in his own way. The man that sat across the table from me that day in the coffee shop in Venice, was mature, more handsome than before, well kempt and very charming. Everything about him set the red lights flickering.

While we were waiting for our order he toyed with my fingers. I should have kept my hands in my lap. While delicately eating the exquisite cream cake, he blotted some imagined speck of cream on the corner of my mouth. I should have ordered a biscuit. Over espresso he took my hand in his, stroking it gently with his thumb telling me how excited he was when he learned from our common friends that I was in Venice. How he often thought of me during his gruelling medical study years in England. He leaned in closer and said:

"Francine, I met many girls during my travels and also in England. I went out with many, but you always returned to my thoughts. None of those glamorous girls could manage to drive you out of my mind." It was when he looked into my eyes as if he could see my very thoughts, that same moment, did I realise it was time to run. I could feel how the fire in his dark eyes started melting my heart. Slowly, discretely I pulled my hand from his. He smiled and nodded when I excused myself for a visit to the rest room.

When I went back to the table my heart was back in its place and thoroughly cooled off. To his suggestion of a romantic gondola ride through that beautiful city, just for sightseeing, I had an excuse ready. He was disappointed, tried to fix another date, but I had answers to every suggestion. It was very difficult for me to turn him down since he looked so sincere. Whether he was or not, I could not risk starting something I knew I could not possibly finish. Something that would undoubtedly end in heartache.

Outside the coffee shop we said good bye, cheek kissed, promising to keep in touch with a 'perhaps someday' hanging in the air between us. I turned and walked without looking back, blinking away embarrassing tears. Lord, this is painful. He is really nice, but I know he is not the one. I know this is not right, this is not it. I know You have something better, someone better. Help me to keep focussed on You and to stay committed to do Your will.

****

The galleries still held the same attraction for me and even with an added dimension now. I understood so much more, appreciation went so much deeper. The questions I used to ask I could now answer for myself and elaborate. In fact, I could ask questions that might be hard to answer by some of the people who in those days loved to enlighten me.

Two weeks before I intended to go home, I phoned Mom from Milan. I told her I planned to leave for home shortly after Enid's baby was born. It's expected to happen in a week or two. I was on my way back to England. I cannot remember many instances when Mom acted on impulse. It was the rare exception when she did something that she hadn't carefully considered from all angles and weighed at least twice before making a decision. Thus was I rather surprised when she told me she was coming to join me and hope to be in time for the birth of her sixth grandchild not counting Terrence's little girl, whose paternal origin will forever be in question.

Edwin was pleased to have us both at this time in his life. He and Enid both appreciated our presence and assistance with Howie and the little girl whom they named Debra-Ann, especially because Enid was physically not strong. She needed help and lots of rest. Mom considered it a privilege to help out and to get to know Howie better. She really enjoyed being involved in this way.

Debra-Ann saw the light five days earlier than expected. Mom was just in time. She landed on Heathrow at nine in the morning, and three-thirty that afternoon, Enid gave birth. A week later, I reluctantly announced my plans to return home soon. Mom told me to wait a day or two. She wanted to show me something. Early the next morning we said goodbye to the family. Without Howie noticing, I gave Edwin a gift to keep for the boy's forth birthday in two months. Mom and I boarded a plane to Avignon.

We booked into a quaint little guesthouse on the outskirts of Avignon. The landscape reminded a lot of the one in the painting I gave her on my first return from Europe.

"What a pretty place! When did you discover it?"

"It is pretty, isn't it? And it's the right time of year too." I looked at mom's face and recognized the same faraway look she had when I handed her the painting and again when I told her I was going to become an artist. Only this time there was a fraction of sadness added to the already complex expression on her face. "It was a long time ago, a very long time." She smiled, took my hand, gave it a little squeeze and said:

"Let's go for a walk." We walked, we talked and all the while, I got the impression she wanted to say something, but lacked the conviction that she should say what was on her mind. The next day after breakfast we went to the little village on the riverbank, did a little shopping, had coffee; ate croissants; talked of nothing in particular.

After a light lunch we went back to Avignon, caught a plane back to Paris where we said good-bye. I boarded the flight back to South-Africa, she went back to London where Edwin would wait to take her home for a continuation of her visit. As we embraced, I could feel she is more relaxed than when I greeted her on her arrival in England. I looked into her dark brown eyes:

"Do you need to say something to me?"

"No," she said with confidence, "except that I love you, always have and always will. Thank you for coming with me to Avignon. And the village."

She walked away; back straight, slender shoulders pulled back, her slightly curly, shoulder length dark hair swaying attractively with every swift step. I did not understand the meaning of it all, not even years later when I went through her most personal belongings and found the postcards. I sensed it had to be packed to capacity of something meaningful to her, but to no one else. It would be many more years before I discovered the place of Avignon in the puzzle; and how it affected our lives, all of us, the whole Hammond-clan.

CHAPTER 6

A New Life

I stepped off the plane in the middle of winter. No rain, not even a cloud in sight, only a freezing wind blowing from the south to remind me I am in Johannesburg. There must be snow on the Malutis. The temptation was strong to turn in my tracks, re-board the plane and fly all the way down to Cape Town. What the heck was I doing here? As soon as I had collected my baggage, I went straight to the restrooms. Searching my bags for something warmer to put on, I found a lightweight sweatshirt that I put on over the long sleeve summer blouse I was wearing; then put on my jacket again. It may not be enough, but it will have to do.

I rented a car and with a new map of the city, I set out and found a place called Bruma where I booked into a hotel. As I unpacked my bags, I realized I have not much to wear that was appropriate in this weather. I would rest of the jetlag and the next day I'd have to go shopping. First, a long, warm, foamy bath and then I would decide how to spend the rest of the day. The warm water made me drowsy and relaxed. I let my thoughts wander. I deliberately sent them away from yesterday in order to plan tomorrow. "Lord, am I doing the right thing? What if this little adventure turns out to be a rotten egg?"

Before I completely fell asleep, I got out of the bath. Dressed in sweat suit, hair dried, I took a glass of wine and switching on the TV, I sank down into a soft, inviting easy chair. Nothing showing on TV that interested me, I flipped from channel to channel. What about the Christian channels? Let's see... aha, there's something... The Club; Matt and Jerry. I closed my eyes. Just before I fell asleep, I heard Matt saying: "Be bold, don't be afraid to start a new thing or take a new direction..." The remote control fell from my limp hand. The channel changed. Did I dream or did I hear Jesse say: "Go for it, girl..."?

It was mid-afternoon when I woke up. Well rested I was hungry and needed fresh air. I put on everything with long sleeves under my sweat suit and set out for a walk. The wind had abated some and the temperature was several degrees higher than that morning when I arrived. To the west though, there were curdy clouds, which told me some more foul weather was to be expected soon. This convinced me I should go on with my plans to buy winter clothes the very next day.

I briskly walked in the direction of some shops nearby, just to see what Bruma was all about. I found all sorts of interesting shops, mostly Chinese. On the near side was Game and I walked through just to see what was new, or what was different from the stores in Cape Town. I found very little difference. They all looked the same, which was not unexpected. I bought an energy bar to keep me going until supper; then headed back to the hotel.

I had an early supper in my room and went to bed directly afterwards, as the jetlag was not yet completely out of my system. I woke very early, took a shower, dressed again in everything I had that was warm. After a hearty breakfast, I consulted the receptionist on nearby shopping centres. She recommended Eastgate and Bedford Gardens. Eastgate was the nearest. In my room, I found the way to Eastgate on my street map and as it was time for the shops to open, I set out immediately in my rented car.

By noon, I had not exactly emptied the shops, but I had what I needed for the time being. I always enjoyed shopping for clothes, but it is tiring and it makes me hungry. I decided to put my parcels in the boot of the car before I set out to find a place where I can have a bite since I did not feel like going back to the hotel yet. I am here to explore, after all.

Hands free I walked back to look around a bit before I found a restaurant or a coffee shop. I found the movies, some nice boutiques, take-away shops and a confectionary. I got to know where the banks were and my favourite department store. Most importantly was the art supply store that I just happened to notice, walking by. This would have to be investigated thoroughly very soon.

In search for the groceries stores, I turned a corner too sharply and bumped into a woman. Parcels flew thought the air and we both nearly landed on our backsides. I got hold of myself quickly, apologized and helped her pick up the parcels that fell from the overfull shopping trolley. Her companion just stood there saying:

"It's okay, don't worry, we'll be okay," repeating herself over and over again.

The one called Eileen frowned angrily at me, the other one continued soothing both of us as if I needed soothing. Eileen mumbled but her voice grew louder as she talked.

"Come on Eileen, leave the lady alone," the other one said, "can't you see she did not mean to bump into you? Anyone can have an accident? And she said she is sorry. Come now, let's go". She took Eileen by the arm and led her away. "*Ja*, sure, I just wish people would watch where they go!", I heard Eileen say before they disappeared round the corner. Round the next corner, I found a restaurant that appealed to me.

While waiting for my order, I noticed the two women in front of the restaurant. It seemed they were undecided where to have lunch. Then the one called Eileen turned and asked for a table for two. She pushed her trolley into a corner and followed the waiter. They both sat down at a table in the next row near the entrance.

Silly girl, I thought. I'm going to show her something she's not going to forget easily:

"Waiter, you see the ladies at table seven?" The waiter nodded. "Don't give them a bill. Bring their bill to me; I'd like to pay for them. But don't tell them now. Wait till they ask for the bill."

If they noticed me they did not show it. All through the meal I watched them, listened, but could hear only Eileen talking. The other one, Maggie, did not speak loud enough. I took my time eating so that I would not be finished and have to wait too long before they asked for their bill.

As I took the last sip of my second cup of coffee, I sensed someone close by my table. When I looked up, I saw the one named Maggie standing in front of me.

"Thanks for the lunch."

"Hope you enjoyed it."

"Are you a Christian?"

"Sure I am, are you?"

"Yes."

"And your friend; is she a Christian?

"My neighbour." Maggie shrugged: "Err, no. She's Jewish."

"Would the two of you like to sit down and have another cup of coffee with me? Maggie motioned to Eileen to join us at my table. Reluctantly she came. We introduced ourselves.

"I am Francine Hammond, and you are?"

"Maggie Roux, and this is Eileen Whiteman." They sat down to get better acquainted. Eileen led the conversation asking many questions and giving lots of information about herself, Maggie and life in general in the area where they both lived. It turned out that Maggie usually drove them, and sometimes other friends they had in common, to do shopping, but Maggie's car, an old, red BMW they told me, was in the workshop for repairs of some sort. That day they came to the shops by means of meter-taxi.

"Would you like a lift home?" Why I offered I did not know, but I could not possibly turn back now. So we all got into my rented car and drove off, Eileen sitting next to me directing the way. The territory was completely unfamiliar to me as I have never been to Johannesburg before. We drove through middleclass, then higher middleclass suburbs before the scene changed to simpler and then 'sub-middleclass,' but not slum areas. I parked in front of a huge building in Berea. We exchanged phone numbers and promised to keep in touch.

As I drove away, I decided to look around a bit. At some point, I turned left, went downhill and found myself in a suburb called Yeoville. The main street looked interesting with lots of little shops selling everything imaginable, from used clothes to works of art, from jewellery to pot plants, a coffee shop on every corner. This place really needs further exploring. 'Tomorrow I'll be back,' I told myself.

Back at my hotel, I ordered something to drink and then started unpacking my shopping. Though I did not overspent, my budget was stretched and I'd have to slow down or make use of the money in the trust fund Dad put up for my education like he did for all five of his children. That was something I avoided as far as possible. Independence was very important to me even now while I did not have an income, which I'd have to do something about very soon.

What I needed was a place big, light and airy enough to put up ten or twelve easels at one time. More importantly even, was to find a gallery willing to exhibit my paintings. Me, a well-educated nobody in need of establishing a reputation, which was at that point in time still non-existent. Where would I find a gallery interested in a no-name?

The next day I drove through the surrounding areas of my hotel, dropping in at big and small shopping centres to see what was available, spoke to a real estate agent or two, spoke to gallery curators here and there all the while feeling I was wasting my time. 'LORD, am I missing something? Did not YOU confirm this?' Did I not pray and fast and seek direction from YOU? And did YOU not show me clearly this is where YOU want me to be? Exhausted I returned to my hotel in the late afternoon, asking myself what was I really looking for?

Many galleries reacted with enthusiasm at the prospect of taking on my work. My qualifications were good, but of course, they needed proof thereof, as well as my portfolio. The Johannesburgers seemed more relaxed about qualifications than the Capetonians. Still, I could not shake off the feeling of dissatisfaction nagging at my insides. What am I missing?

Early the next morning, I resumed my search...but for what? I took out my city map and paged through as if inspiration was to come from the pages filled with white stripes isolating tiny grey blocks in neat rows. I got in my car and drove aimlessly in widening circles around the starting point. Another day wasted, I decided to have lunch in Melville, as I was there at the time, and go back to the hotel early. I really needed a plan. I could not afford to waste another day looking for something I could not even put a name to. It may come up and look me in the eyes and I might not recognize it. When I did see it, I recognized it as if I knew all along it was there.

It happened on my way back from Melville. I drove through Berea, passed the building where Eileen and Maggie lived, remembered the main street of Yeoville and turned left like I did two days before when I discovered it. Since it was still early, I parked my car in the main street and walked along the sidewalks soaking in the atmosphere. I stopped for coffee in one of the many coffee shops. I felt so relaxed as if I had come home. Reluctantly I got in my car and started uphill. And there it was. How could I have missed it the first time I drove by! I parked the car and got out. I scanned the place from side to side, from top to bottom. This is it.

Rummaging through my handbag, I found a pen and my little notebook. Quickly I jotted down the telephone number of the estate agent advertising the place, as if the number might disappear if I did not hurry up. I walked up to the front door, tried the knob, it was locked, went to a window to catch a peek. I walked right around the house, peeked through every window, examined the garden and got more excited as I went. This was my house, I decided as I pulled the gate close behind me. Hope the price is right. "I'll buy it even if I have to use Dad's money," I said audibly.

The moment I entered my hotel room, I called the estate agent and made an appointment to view.

"Nine o'clock tomorrow?"

"Perfect." That night I hardly slept. All sorts of ideas kept churning around in my mind. The place had so much potential. I could make all my dreams come true on one premises. Art school on the top floor; gallery on ground level; reading room and bookshop in one side. Maybe even a coffee shop in the back room leading to the garden where there was enough space for quite a few tables and a sandpit and jungle gym for the youngsters. In the early hours, my ideas mingled with my dreams. When I woke up before dawn, I could hardly distinguish one from the other.

I had little knowledge about buildings, but I was convinced I knew enough to recognize serious structural problems if I saw them. This house was as solid as they came. Inside I inspected every nook and cranny. My excitement grew as I went. The top floor had five enormous rooms, two with built in cupboards. There were also two and a half bathrooms. The full bathrooms had huge built in cupboards of solid oak. The fifth room on the sunny side of the house was en-suite with a step-in-dressing room. Downstairs were two large reception rooms, dining room, family room, games room guest loo with a washbasin, and an enormous old-fashioned farm style kitchen with separate pantry, scullery and laundry.

It needed a little care, but once renovated, it could well be the place I had dreamed about all night, a gem in a fine setting. After an hour I told the agent, Betsy Bennett that I'd seen enough, when and where could I sign the documents. She cocked her head and looked at me curiously because I did not ask what the price was.

"Well, what is the price?" She mentioned an amount which seemed about right, but I pretended to be shocked, not wanting anyone to know I had money. "Are you sure the owner won't come down a bit?"

"He already dropped the price with seven thousand. He won't go any lower. It's a good, solid house and won't need any serious repair work."

"All right," I said hesitantly, "I'll give you a call tomorrow." Betsy Bennett said neutrally that it would be fine if I called her the next day, not believing I would. I spent the rest of the day calculating, making phone calls and calculating again.

Betsy sounded happy to hear my voice as my call came through the moment she stepped into her office the next morning. I asked where her office was and promised to see her in fifteen minutes;

"Have the papers ready, I'm coming in to sign". That afternoon I visited my new friends in Berea to tell them the good news, and to say goodbye, as I was to fly back to Cape Town the next day. As it happened, Maggie was having coffee at Eileen's place. Two more friends were also there; a German lady, Greta and an Indian lady, Shri. They were all glad to meet me as Eileen had already told them all about me there was to tell.

Back in Cape Town, I started to get my things in order for the big move to Johannesburg. Of course there was a lot of noise from my brother, Andrew and fierce comment from Anita. Did I lose my mind? What would I do in a dump like Johannesburg? How will I make a living? What will Mother say? And so on and so on. I did not heed their warnings and I did not bother to tell them about my plans; they simply would not listen. So I merrily went about my business, did what needed to be done. I would not let them put me off. Sorry, but my decision was final.

I met my mother at the airport on a bright and sunny day:

"Let's hurry home so I can change. We cannot waste such lovely weather. We simply have to go for a walk, get the blood flowing after all those hours sitting on my butt in the plane." Excellent, I thought. I can tell her about my plans on neutral ground. I did not say anything then, but had to comment on her language:

"Mom, when did you get to use words like that? I've never heard you use the word 'butt' before."

"Well, you teach your children to use proper English, and then come along your grandchildren and you learn a completely new version from them. Howie use that word all the time." I just smiled, recalling the many times I heard him saying it.

People probably wondered about those crazy creatures walking in the middle of winter on the beach, but neither mom nor I ever worried about what people thought. It was a lovely day and not to be wasted. We talked about England, Edwin and Enid, Howie and baby Debra-Ann, who was doing very well. Our trip to France was never mentioned.

Good weather seldom lasts long in Cape Town, especially in winter. As the north-westerly wind picked up and misty grey clouds started rolling in, we headed for the nearest coffee shop. We got seated in a corner by a window overlooking the bay the moment the rain started falling.

"So, tell me what made you decide to move to Johannesburg." Surprised, I asked her:

"Who spilled the beans, Andrew or Anita?"

"Andrew phoned me and earnestly asked me to talk sense into you. I phoned Anita to get her version and she gave me a proper earful, but neither could give me any detail or tell me why you want to do this".

"Of course they could not, because they never asked me and they never bothered to listen to what I had to say."

"I'm ready to listen". I told her I felt isolated in Cape Town; that I needed all different kinds of stimuli to be really creative, to bring out what was inside me: "Johannesburg is different. It has the cosmopolitan setting and atmosphere most European cities have, a vibrancy that kick-starts the imagination. I already have four friends there, an Afrikaans lady, a Jewess, a German and an Indian lady, can you imagine, all of them in one friendship circle". I went on and told Mom how these friendships started.

"Do you think you could settle there, stay for good? Capetonians are not good transplants, you know. They always come back".

"I know I may be a little idealistic, but yes, I'm planning to stay. I'll make it work". I noticed the same expression on her face that she had in Avignon, that unfathomable, almost Mona Lisa-kind of smile.

"Are you all right with this?"

"If this is what you want, if it is what it takes to make you happy and fulfilled, then you have my blessing".

"Will you visit me?"

"If you can think of anything that might keep me away, don't tell me about it".

"Thanks, Mom. I don't want to make you unhappy. I'm very pleased that you support me in this".

"When will you leave?"

"My affairs are in order. I'll spend a day or two with you. Thursday. I'll leave Thursday in the morning".

"Will you drive all the way?"

"No, you know how sleepy I get behind the wheel. I'll spend the night somewhere along the way".

Wednesday Simon washed and polished my car inside and out and Katrina outdid herself in the kitchen. Mom had ordered a special dinner for the family. I had spent the previous weekend saying goodbye to all my friends and relatives. That Wednesday our close little family group would enjoy each other's company for the last time in many months. Even Terrence would tear himself away from his law studies to come and say good-bye to his sister.

I arrived in Johannesburg at three o'clock on a crisp, cold Friday. Betsy Bennett met me at my new house with the keys. She helped me carry my bags into the house and asked if there was anything more she could do for me or get me. I said no thanks. She had been a great help and I am sure her other clients needed her. That suited her. She was not to hang around after a job had been done. And this job had been done well.

With the money I deposited for her, she had ordered a bed, had it carried up to the main bedroom, bought bedding and put it in the bedroom. Without asking her, she even supplied my kitchen with a few necessities like bread rolls, butter, an assortment of cold meats, lettuce, two tomatoes, coffee, creamer, sugar, a mug, paper plates and a plastic fork, knife and teaspoon and an old, unused electric kettle from deep inside her own kitchen cupboard. Now this is more than service.

This is walking the extra mile. She also made sure that the electricity was connected.

I was not hungry after the good and solid lunch I had somewhere between Bloemfontein and Kroonstad. I put the kettle on for coffee, though. With a steaming mug of coffee, I wandered through my house, looked through every window, this time from inside to the outside. This was mine. I could still hardly believe it. Tomorrow it might start sinking in. Right now, things were all too new to me and I was too tired. As soon as I had finished a second cup of coffee, I went upstairs. Time to unpack.

With everything fairly in place, I made the bed with the bedding I had brought along. I soon realized it would not be enough to keep me warm on a Highfeld night. Thankfully, I spread the new blanket and the thick duvet that was purchased by Betsy, over the bed. It was almost dark by the time I was finished and only half past five. I took a quick shower and went down to the kitchen. Being hungry from the work, I was now ready to tackle those rolls and cold meat. How I would appreciate a hot meal prepared by Katrina. Satisfied after the meal, thoroughly tired, relaxed and sleepy, I got into my new bed and with a prayer of thanks giving on my lips, I fell asleep almost instantly.

The following weeks I spent sorting out business rights and trade licenses, cleaning and furnishing my house, equipping and decorating it with the help of a free running imagination. My first priority was the classrooms where I would teach classes. One room would be for beginners, the other for advanced students. These two rooms were equipped with shelves; cupboards, lots of drawers to provide storage space for every possible kind of equipment and material needed to run a school on oiled wheels.

Secondly, I concentrated on the galleries downstairs. I used the largest of the two reception rooms for this purpose. Here I would exhibit the best works, my own as well as the best of the advanced students. The smaller reception room would be used for the best works of the beginners. No furniture except a few small tables would be needed in the galleries, only the right kind of lighting.

The living room was turned into a reading room and bookshop. I provided two small tables and chairs and two deep, soft sofas, arranged in an L-shape with a low, square table inside the "L" in the centre of the room. The small tables were put in one corner, back-to-back behind some bookshelves, which I meant to fill with used books. The new books and magazines, for sale only, would be available in the opposite corner near the door and the cash register. There would be no chairs in this corner.

The games room was fitted with low bookshelves. Those I filled with children's books. I also provided drawer chests which I filled with scrapbooks, colouring books, crayons, pencils, toys and all kinds of things that might interest small children and keep them occupied while their parents browse.

Last but not least - as they say - the dining room. Converting this room into a coffee shop was not difficult. It was connected to the kitchen in such a way as to make access easy, yet it was separated enough to prevent disturbance. The patio doors would be opened on good weather days, which, I believe, are numerous here in Gauteng. Tables under the shade trees provided a sort of outside extension to the coffee shop. I bought solid cast iron furniture for this purpose. No umbrellas would be needed, which was just as well. I would not want my garden umbrellas to be caught by the wind and carried up and away to be set down kilometres away in someone else's tree as if Mary Poppins had come to town. It might sound unbelievable, but I had seen it happen. The local August winds, though not as fierce as the Cape winds, were still strong enough to wreak havoc among my umbrellas, should I decide to have any.

Toward the end of August I experienced a strange something in the atmosphere. It was an undefinable feeling of joy waiting to burst forth, to explode and fill the air; a bubbling feeling that permeated the soul of every living thing. Everywhere a green haze spread over the sepia landscape that announced the approaching spring. Flowers, colours, fragrances, grass and trees. Everywhere spring was announced in a way more spectacular than anything I have experienced. When the first spring rain fell six weeks later, I drew deep breaths of the fresh air that smelled of wet soil and grass. If only Anita could be here to experience it.

The Bible says plant your fields before you build your house, I think. Somewhere in Proverbs, I think, is it chapter 14, or is it 24? I'll have to check. Or is it the other way round? Well, anyway, my fields were ready and waiting for rain. Now it was time to fix up my private living quarters. I never liked clutter and preferred a simple, modest life style.

My bedroom was furnished and equipped with the bare necessities, tastefully, beautifully decorated, but simple. One of the two empty rooms upstairs I furnished to be a living room and office, the other to be a spare bedroom for visiting family members. Between my own living quarters and the classrooms, I had a security gate installed to separate work area from living area.

My flyers and advertisements in the local newspaper paid off: "Eats 'n Reads opening soon". Before my work upstairs were completed, the first visitors came to investigate, first the coffee shop and soon the bookshop. I had to wait until the next year for the first art students to come knocking, but that was all right. The other two divisions were making money. Business was slowly building up.

As promised, my mother came visiting in November. She was pleasantly surprised to see my place and how attractive and efficient the whole set up was. She even helped serving and chatting to customers a few times especially in the book and reading department.

"I think you just might make a nice living here".

"Sure. Business will pick up and I am confident that soon I'll be so busy that I'll need more staff. Tell everyone at home if they want me to spend time with them when they visit, they better hurry up or they might have to entertain themselves while I work or else roll up their sleeves and help out". My mother smiled at this. I recognized in her looking at me, that she was proud of me.

During the rest of her stay I showed her the city and all that was good in this 'dump' as Anita called it. It was a beautiful spring and the trees provided lush greenery all over the city. I took her to all the different places that I got to know in the short time I had been here. Places like Emmerentia Dam and the botanical gardens. Jacaranda trees were in full bloom everywhere. The lookout on Munro Drive offered a spectacular view of the purple splashed city right up to Sandton City and beyond. We went for walks at Zoo Lake as often as we could.

Mom's sister lived in Pretoria. She suffered from multiple sclerosis and found it hardly possible to buy her own groceries, let alone travel. I did not remember my mother going to Pretoria to see her sister regularly. Tuesday I asked my mother:

"Mom, wouldn't you like to visit Aunt Francis? I really don't mind taking you."

"Actually I was going to ask you about a trip to Pretoria. I've come all the way from the Cape and to leave again without seeing my only sister, would be kind of awkward."

"Well, what about tomorrow. Would you like to go tomorrow?"

"Perfect. I'll give her a call and find out if it is convenient."

"Do that. We can leave early and perhaps have lunch with her."

So the next day we set out for a visit in Pretoria. Aunt Francis was so happy to see us. She had not seen her only sister in years. While she was semi-immobilised, and Mom too busy to travel to Pretoria often, they seldom saw each other. My cousin, Stephaney, the eldest of Aunt Fran's three daughters never married. She stayed with her mother and took good care of her. The sisters talked, exchanging news, enjoying each other's company while Steph and I got to know each other better. We left in the early afternoon with promises from both to visit more often. Mom had convinced her sister it was not impossible for her to fly to Cape Town. A wheelchair would be waiting upon her arrival.

I had discovered a friendly church in Joubertpark - Maggie introduced me there as it was where she attended - and took Mom along on Sunday. She was warmly welcomed and enjoyed the service more than I thought she would. After church, we went to Eastgate, found a nice restaurant and relaxed at a cosy corner table being waited on, instead of waiting on others. Later that Sunday afternoon we said goodbye at the airport with promises from both of us to visit often.

****

Early in the next year, the gallery and art classes took off with a bang. I neither imagined there would be such interest nor the eager talent, young and old. The struggle I anticipated, to get started never happened. Within a short while, I had more students than I could handle. I employed a final year university student part time to take the beginners classes while I took the advanced students.

For the bookshop, I got a lady to help at the cash register during the afternoons and weekends and two extra waiters over weekends. A fulltime cook took over the kitchen. So, against all expectation my life in Johannesburg flew high like an eagle.

CHAPTER 7

Terrence

It was less than two years later that my youngest brother, Terrence knocked on my door at ten thirty one evening. I took him in, of course, it was what the Father expected me to do, gave him the spare room and allowed him one week to rest, get nourished, since he almost starved on his way here, then sat him down for a sincere sisterly talk. I was not willing to let him lie around for the rest of his life and pay for his leisurely life style. No substance abuse allowed under my roof, he would have to get a job, go to church with me and eventually find a place of his own. If he were interested to study anything, I would help him financially.

"No thanks," he told me. He had had enough of academic matters during his law studies. While he tried his best to find some form of employment, he sat in my coffee shop entertaining my patrons. As a joke, someone one day flung two twenty Rand notes at him. That started it. People started coming to the coffee shop not only for coffee, but to listen to my brother playing his guitar, singing cheerful songs of joy and ballads, sad and nostalgic and paid him for it. Being the charmer that he always had been, he now turned out to be a real entertainer becoming more popular as time went by.

There were regular customers of whom many became friends over a period of time. One I especially noticed was a man named Gerald Crompton. Every time I saw him, my heart leapt. Terrence and I both often joined him at his table for a quick cup of coffee. When he stopped coming, I felt a tiny bit dead inside. I kept watching the door on Saturdays wanting to see him enter.

Terrence was reluctant at first, to go to church with me. Great was his surprise when he realized that it was not the traditional kind we grew up in:

"Goodness, if I knew there were churches like this, I'd have become a Christian long ago". I knew he did not mean to ridicule and was glad that at least he had enjoyed it.

After about two months of church and home-cell attendance, he grew serious and realized church was more than singing nice songs played by an excellent band and listening to a preacher entertaining the congregation on all sorts of interesting stories. He got a grip on what the stories were all about: Life and the best way to live it. One Sunday evening, without flashes of lightning or claps of thunder he stood up out of his pew in answer to the altar call and gave his heart and life to the Lord.

It was good to have my brother nearby. We grew to be close, understanding each other well. Whether it was the shared artistic environment or the way he blended in with the 'scenery' I did not know; we just happened to communicate on a level neither of us were able to do before. Those were happy months for both of us. Life was busy, but simple and relaxed yet at some point I sensed Terrence becoming restless. He was beginning to hope for something more solid, something that could secure a future for him.

****

The offer came out-of-the-blue, from someone who had heard of Terrence through the grapevine. It was a struggling club owner, who desperately needed an injection into his business. Something that would draw people back to his club and make it prospering like it used to. That was all we knew. I was convinced there had to be more to it: Why was his business dwindling; why did he want Terrence, why not someone else?

Terrence and I had an argument about this matter. I wanted him to investigate before he made a decision. There were many sleazy clubs where the main attraction was the availability of drugs. He was doing so well now, I did not want him to re-enter an environment where drugs and alcohol were as normal as afternoon tea. It was far too soon to test him.

There was no stopping him. Terrence had made up his mind. He played on Wednesday afternoon at my coffee shop for the last time. On Thursday afternoon, he went to the club to acquaint himself with the rest of the band members, the equipment and whatever else had to be checked out. He had a practicing session with the band. Friday he played for the first time as the new full-time member of the five-man band.

It did not take long before the drug trade found Terrence. An old buddy from his commune learned about him, told the club owner and Terrence was considered an excellent contact man between supplier and customers. The previous contact man was being watched and life became too hot. He had to disappear, thus the need for Terrence to continue the flow of traffic.

It happened on a Friday night. The club was usually quite busy on Fridays. Terrence was not feeling well and was not playing his best. He played two songs, had to go to the bathroom; then played two more. Close to midnight the club owner, Manny 'something' complained and told Terrence to pull himself together or go home. Terrence, by the grace of God, chose to come home. He was hardly out of the parking garage and round the first corner when the police stormed in. There was a shooting, Manny was fatally wounded; everyone else was arrested. Terrence was unemployed once more and did not even know it. We read it in the newspaper the next day.

My brother was shocked to the core. He realized how close he came to getting himself into big trouble. The customers were already getting to know and trust him. His first contact with the supplier was scheduled for Saturday. Although he was not willing to do it, he felt intimidated and agreed, but was all the time trying to find a way out. God gave a way out, a second chance. He was not going to blow it. He told me these things later and I believed him.

The following days, Terrence was quiet, contemplative. He stayed in his room, studied the Bible and prayed whenever he was not helping me in my business; either in the reading room and bookshop, or in the gallery. Sometimes he waited on tables. He even chopped onions in the kitchen to relieve the cook. His guitar stayed in its bag deep inside his cupboard. When I asked him when did he plan to play for my customers again like he did before the club job came up, he just shook his head:

"No, Sis, I don't think it is wise. It might attract the wrong people to your place. If they are looking for me, it would be easy enough to trace me without my drawing attention. Maybe I should just leave Jozie and go someplace else. I don't want to expose you". I was touched by his concern, but would not hear of him leaving me. He had no money, no job, nothing to fall back on. I made it clear that he should stay until his circumstances changed radically for the better. It felt as if time stood waiting, but when things started happening, it happened fast. But not before Terrence had some things sorted out in his heart and mind.

Days went by without Terrence saying much. He seemed withdrawn, even depressed. When I asked him about it, he said he could not believe he could be so stupid to fall into a trap like that, before, perhaps, but not after he met Christ. He was obviously plagued by feelings of guilt. I suggested he talked to the home-cell leader.

The following Tuesday he did. He told him exactly how he felt and why. "So, if I confess...and repent as you say, I needn't feel guilty anymore?" "We all mess up from time to time, Dear Friend. We're not perfect, just forgiven". "Pastor said two weeks ago if we know something is wrong and we still do it, it is sin".

"Yes, of course it is sin. But if you confess and repent, God is faithful to forgive you. Ask Him to help you in His strength not to repeat this stupidity. You cannot do it in your own strength".

"Oh, I see. Was that my problem? Did I try to do it all in my own strength?"

"It appears to be the problem".

"Yeshua took your sin, your sickness as well as your guilt on him to the cross. Guilt feelings are natural, but they do come from a lack of fully trusting Yeshua. He did it all for us, it really is finished. So what remains to feel guilty about?" With these words we all lay hands on Terrence and prayed to the Father to take away the feelings of guilt, since they were mere feelings - and unreliable as feelings were, they were just baggage that needed to be discarded - and to help him depend on Yeshua for every move and every decision he had to make in future. Terrence was so sincere, he tried so hard to be a good Christian, but he still had so much to learn.

The very next, day things started to happen. Terrence were fiddling about, helping in the kitchen and did my banking. While he was out to the bank, a man walked in, browsed through the gallery, then ordered coffee and cake. The waiter came to tell me he wanted to see me. As I was finishing a class upstairs, I quickly washed the paint off my hands, dismissed my students and went down.

The man looked very familiar and as I approached him, I recognized him as a former customer. He was no taller than the average man, but a lot more handsome, dark blue eyes, dark, curly brown hair and the cutest Tom Selleck-dimples. We were happy to see each other. He used to come almost every Saturday for coffee and cake. I smiled and my heart danced. Gerald Crompton was back.

I had a few minutes before I had to take the next class, so I sat down with Gerald for a chat. He told me he was suddenly called back to Cape Town to take over a branch of the company he worked for. He did not have time to come and say good-bye. Currently he was in town to finalize his personal affairs before he moved back to Cape Town permanently. Then he asked about Terrence. He told me he remembered him playing guitar and singing some of his own songs just before he went back to the Cape. He was quite impressed. Such talent was rare and he was hoping Terrence would make the most of it.

Just then, my next students walked in, Terrence came back from the bank; I showed him to Gerald's table and excused myself to attend to my next class. Terrence sat down at Gerald's table and the two men chatted, Terrence, glad to have a break. I quickly set the students to work and went down hoping to join Terrence and Gerald again, but as I was descending, I met Terrence on the stairway on his way up to his room. Gerald had already left and sent his regards. My disappointment was greater than I was prepared to admit.

Three days later, there was a phone call for Terrence. It was Gerald's cousin Tim Tanner from Cape Town. Gerald had told him about Terrence and would he be interested in coming down for an audition. Tim needed a guitarist for his own band. Gerald sounded so enthusiastic that Tim decided to give him a chance before making a final decision. Two days later Terrence jumped onto a plane to Cape Town believing this could be his breakthrough. I had a hunch he might be right; he would not be coming back.

Four days later Terrence called. It was a big band. They played at Christmas parties for big companies, weddings at grand venues and so on. Tim was as impressed as Gerald. He had already practiced with the band twice. Tim had a look at his songs and promised to work some of the songs into the next practicing session. A contract for six months will be signed later that day. He promised to find a nice church and join immediately. I told him I missed him, but that I was very happy for him.

Once again, I was alone. Terrence had moved back home with Mom using her car whenever he needed it just like he used my car when he stayed here. Now at least he would soon be able to buy his own ride again. Life would soon return to normal. I was really happy for him. But, my heart was empty knowing that Gerald would not be coming back.

CHAPTER 8

The Other Siblings

Anita stepped out of her shoes as soon as she entered the front door of her townhouse and walked barefoot through to the kitchen. She poured water into the coffee maker, coarsely ground Brazilian coffee into the filter and switched it on. Dropping her handbag on a side table, she grabbed a pear from the fruit bowl on that same side table and went to open the balcony door. Sea air filled her lungs as she drew a deep breath. She finished her pear before she went back to the kitchen. She took a cigarette from the packet on the kitchen counter, lit it and drew deeply, poured herself a cup of coffee and sat down outside on the balcony sipping black, sugarless coffee, the cigarette close by.

The front door opened. Cathy bundled the two young children in through the door and send them to their rooms to change into play clothes. She went to the kitchen to start preparing supper. On the balcony Anita listened to the sounds in the kitchen, thankful that her path had crossed that of Cathy Morris. Without her help, life would have been a lot tougher. For Cathy too. Where would she have lived if not here?

Anita found Cathy at an au pair agency. Her parents were divorced and both lived overseas. Cathy was still studying, her grandmother, with whom she was living, had an accident and never fully recovered. Having become frail, she had to go into a home where she was taken care of. She gave up the house and walked out with two bags full of clothes and personal belongings. Most of her grandmother's belongings went to the hospice charity shop. Cathy would be homeless unless she could find a live-in nanny job.

Before the children started their homework, they ran to the patio to greet their mother. Anita hugged them both and smiling, asked:

"Are you all right, have a lot of homework?" Chanté replied first:

"No Mommy. I have a few sentences to write in Afrikaans, English spelling, but only a few words, and my favourite: History."

"That's good. Do it all as quickly as you can," Anita said unnecessarily.

"What about you, Donny?"

"I have a lot of homework. I'm not as lucky as she is. They always give us lots of homework. I never get time to play," complained Donny.

"Well, Darling, then you better get going. If you finish quickly, there will be enough time to play, or watch TV." Anita knows the mention of TV was a motivator for Donny. She kissed him on the cheek and sent him off. Chanté didn't need motivation. The eagerness with which she tackled her studies, and in fact everything she needed to do, was inspiring. Donny on the other hand always needed coaxing, pushing, even threatening and often the ultimate: depriving him of his privileges. His laziness was an issue and a cause of concern for Anita. The boy reminded her too much of his father.

Anita spoke to Cathy who informed her time and again that Donny was stubborn. It was hard to get him to study, and when he did, he never did it properly. He would spend a few minutes, writing one or two sentences; then his thoughts started to wander. She coaxed him to go on and he would respond by whining and complaining. It usually took threats of all kinds to get him to finish his homework. By the time he was done, Cathy was exhausted and in no mood to entertain him, which made him sulk and complain all over again.

Chanté had her father's looks. Very attractive, nutty brown eyes, dark blond hair and a small, pointed nose, but her personality came from her grandparents. She was as driven and purpose orientated as her maternal grandfather and had the quiet confidence of her maternal grandmother, a very pleasant person to be with. Her favourite pastime was playing all kinds of games; monopoly at the top of the list.

Strangely, it seemed at the time, she also enjoyed playing with her dolls house, making changes often, like rearranging furniture and also changing the inside decor. Anita thought she was getting too big for doll house playing, but never said anything, believing she would grow out of it at her own pace.

Anita walked past Donny's room to see if he was busy with homework or not. Of course he was not. His mother's promise of TV watching forgotten, he let his thoughts wander. And wander they did, right into his toy box where he kept his little green soldiers. Anita caught him in the middle of a fierce battle right next to his unopened book case. The result was a battle of another kind and one young boy was banned from the TV room for the rest of the week.

****

During the first visit to her aunt Francine's in Johannesburg, (that's me,) Chanté showed particular interest in the house. She strolled from room to room observing everything.

"Mom, this house looks just like my dolls house," she told Anita.

"You are quite right. Look at the upper rooms. Just like your house."

"But down stairs too. Look, the kitchen is in the same place, next to the dining room and the living room that side." Anita and I both were amazed at the girl's ability at such accurate observation. I remembered the doll's house from a previous time I visited them in Cape Town. Chanté had just received the new toy house as a birthday gift from her father, whom she did not see often. It was an enjoyable weekend and passed too quickly.

During a school holiday Chanté and Donny spent a week with their grandmother Gwendolyn, who owned her own estate agency. Donny preferred to stay home with the hired child minder, while Chanté would on the other hand never let an opportunity go by to go to work with her grandmother.

"Grandma, please, please can I go with you? I want to see the house that lady talked about yesterday. You said you will take her today. Can I please go with you? Please, I want to see the house."

"Of course you can come with me. Why do you want to see the house so badly? Do you want to buy it?" Chanté giggled,

"No Granny, I don't have money. I just want to see what the house looks like inside." So off they went leaving Donny at home to be spoiled by the child minder, who gave him everything he asked for and never made any demands for him to play outside and get fresh air and exercise. Back home from their viewing trip, Chanté could hardly stop talking about the beautiful house and all the nice things in the house.

The holiday passed and it was back to school for the children. Gwendolyn took it easy during the week her grandchildren visited, but returned to work with full force the next week. She thoroughly enjoyed them while they were there. If only the other grandchildren were allowed to visit. Marie was a bit overprotective and would never send Delia and Justin for more than a day's visit. Not to mention the 'Brits'. Edwin and Enid could not send their children on a visit for any length of time even if they wanted to. When Francine or Terrence will produce grandbabies, goodness knows. Gwendolyn smiled at her own thoughts, then returned to the paperwork on her table.

****

Donny, medium brown hair, brown eyes, used to be a little winy and lazy like his father, trying to charm his way through life. Until one day. Anita frowned when she saw Donny's school report card. She grabbed the boy by the ear and made him sit down at the kitchen table.

"Would you like to tell me what this is?" Donny just stared at her with quivering lower lip.

"I asked you a question, Donny, and I want an answer. Explain this to me." "I don't know, Mommy. I studied so hard. I don't know why the teacher gave me Es and Fs."

"Now listen, young man, I am going to show you something that might motivate you to start working. I told you last term I want better results on your report card. Es and Fs are not better than the Ds and Es you had on your previous report unless you work your way through the alphabet backwards. Put on your shoes. You and I are going for a drive."

Anita drove to a homeless shelter telling him that was where he would end up if he did not start acting up. Knowing his mother, he believed she would drop him in such a place without hesitation. That was the end of his laziness. He shot out of the blocks like a champion sprinter and made straight A's all through the rest of his school years matriculating sixth in his class in spite of playing first team hockey. No one knew or even suspected the little bit of cheating that occasionally got him his high grades.

****

Andrew and Marie settled in a comfortable routine, contentedly raising their two children and getting on in life and Dad's estimation. Andrew played the big businessman, while secretly longing for the freedom to do something else. He caught himself more than once staring into the blue yonder whenever an aeroplane passed overhead. Where did this interest in aeroplanes come from? Where might it lead? Did he just desire to get away from it all, or was there more? Was there some kind of interest in those sleek shapely tons of shiny metal that were able to defy gravity and 'float' high up in the sky? He stopped building model aeroplanes when his father left them. No more time for child's play. Yet lately he found himself more often dreaming of piloting his own aeroplane. Surely he was not too old to be trained? I wonder what Marie would say about this, he thought.

Marie hurried home from the committee meeting. The meeting took longer than expected. She did not like to get home later than the children. When they got home from school, she wanted to be there. She quickly parked her shiny Mercedes Benz in the driveway of the stately double story house in Newlands and climbed the stairs that lead to the front door.

"Mommy," the two youngsters called when they heard her entering. They stormed down the stairs to hug her.

"Easy now. Calm down. No running in the house. Mommy is here now, everything is fine. Hello my darlings, let's go see what's in the kitchen to eat." The two small children followed their mother to the kitchen, knowing she would have something special for them like always when she came home later than usual. They are so young and vulnerable, she thought, they need to be protected against disappointment. After giving them their favourite spaghetti lunch, prepared by the cook as arranged earlier, she scooped a generous helping of ice cream in for them and added a little wafer to each bowl. Only when they fell silent, stuffing their faces with the treat, did she take time to make herself a cup of coffee.

As soon as Marie got the children busy in the play room, she took out some papers from her attaché case and started on some work she had to do for the next meeting of the next committee she was involved in. The following day there was nothing on her busy schedule, but the rest of the week would be occupied by meetings and gatherings for three other organisations that needed her input. She is a hard worker and though not creative and original in her thinking, she is reliable and always available if something needed to be done in a hurry.

Marie always put the needs of her family first, therefore she made sure to cram her committee work in during the morning hours. Afternoon was family time, except for the short periods of time when the children could entertain themselves. Those times she used to prepare for future meetings, finishing paperwork or making phone calls. The burden of keeping house was placed on the shoulders of a fulltime house keeper.

A fulltime cook was employed when Delia was born with the idea to let her go as soon as the youngest child, (she was certain there would be at least one more child), reached schooling age. As time passed, they all became so used to the luxury of just sitting down for dinner without the worry of how the food got on the table, and the cleaning up afterward, that the cook was kept employed even now that Justin, the youngest, is already halfway through his second year at school. Convenience and comfort were trustworthy employers. It provided free time for Marie to follow worthy causes and satisfy herself with work that made her feel useful.

Marie busied herself overprotecting her children, doing voluntary work for organizations following worthy causes, serving on numerous committees and attending prominent social events. At the same time, she made sure nothing and no-one poor or unworthy touched her, as if it might rub off on her and taint her reputation.

Delia and Justin were carefully guarded not to come into contact with anything that might hint there was another side to life than the one Marie made them grow up in. But they never understood why they hardly ever visited their Uncle Terrence, why they were discouraged when asking about visiting Aunt Francine in Johannesburg; and why they were only vaguely aware of the existence of things like slums, public schools and welfare organizations as if those were merely part of bad fiction films. On top of that, she believed everyone who suffered in any way were guilty of some kind of sin and should confess and repent to get things on track again.

Marie went to Delia's room to see if she needed help with homework. No, she did not; she was almost done and it was easy. No problems. Marie smiled at her, touched her daughter's brown hair and went to see Justin. She found him playing 'wild rock music' on his school ruler.

"What are you doing? Is your homework finished?"

"Ages ago, Mom. Look, I'm playing guitar like Uncle Terrence. I wish I could play like him. He is so cool. Do you think he will teach me?"

"I don't think he has time to teach music. And I don't think he's had any formal training. I think you should go and wash up. It is almost dinner time."

After dinner that evening, Marie indicated to Andrew that she had something urgent to discuss with him. She waited until the children were in bed and they were sitting down comfortably in the family room before she stated her problem.

"I'm worried about Justin."

"Why? What's he done?"

"You know how impressionable he is. Ever since New Year's Eve when Terrence led us all in song and entertained us with his music at your father's house Justin showed some interest in music. Actually, he shows more than normal interest in the kind of music Terrence plays."

"Why is that a problem?"

"Don't you see, he is so fascinated with Terrence, he might want to go into that kind of music. He even asked me if your brother will teach him. Just imagine the house reverberating with the sound of rock music. I don't mind if he takes music lessons, in fact I think we should find him a reputable teacher in classical music. We have the piano, why not let the children use it. They both should take lessons, provided it is classical music that they study. What do you think?"

"What if they're not interested? Have you spoken to them?"

"No, Andrew, I wanted to speak to you first."

"Well, Dear, ask them if they are interested and we'll see. In the mean time you can start looking out for a good music school and get all the details. Doesn't the school have a music department?" Andrew was not sure he was ready to come home to the 'ting, tong tang' of practicing children, but anything to keep Marie happy. Besides, musical training is educational, socially appreciated and a good subject to talk about among the women, if just for a minute at a time.

"But what have you got against Terrence's music? Rock is a very small part of his repertoire. He plays a large variety, all kinds of music, you know. I rather like his music. He has a unique style. And I do like his Christian music, the gospel songs are rather absorbing, don't you think?"

"Perhaps, but even so. I would not like our son to follow the same life style which is associated with that kind of music. Apart from the gospel music of course. That kind of life style always causes trouble and our son should be spared." What she actually meant was: 'that kind of music' does not fit in with our social standing.

So it happened that both Delia and Justin started learning classical music. Both made good progress, but Justin's heart was not in it. He did it because his teacher convinced him that this training will provide a solid foundation for whichever line of music he might chose later on. He promised to do his best for at least two years so that he can then go on to train on the guitar. It might not be easy to convince his mother to buy a guitar for him, unless he was willing once more to study the classical kind.

Delia also showed some promise, but would prefer to sing. After two years of diligently studying music, Terrence gave Justin a guitar and encouraged him to do what his mother expected of him. The boy was thrilled and went on to classical guitar, dropping the piano lessons. Delia started singing lessons, but continued on the piano. Uncle Terrence was very proud of his niece and nephew for following him in music.

Justin became Terrence's biggest fan after he heard him playing that previous New Year's Eve at the family get-together. He loved to attend concerts when Tim's band was playing. He loved the rare visits to Terrence, forever asking questions and bugging him about music, the band and when and where the next concert will be. One time when his parents would not take him, he simply slipped out, took as many buses as necessary and visited his uncle. For a young boy it was an adventure, a big challenge, but it also meant big trouble. Yet, after his punishment was over he told Andrew it was worth it and nagged until Andrew gave in and convinced the boy's mother to let him attend concerts when the band was playing. He was a very unhappy boy when his uncle left the band and went back to Johannesburg.

Delia's life took a few turns that none could predict, but rebellion is often expected when a child's reins are drawn in too tightly. In her teens, she was influenced by friends at school, the children of supposedly respectable people. These friends pretty much did whatever pleased them while the parents paid huge sums of money to keep the trouble away. Delia followed their act, or at least tried to. Lucky for her, Marie saw trouble coming and put a stop to those friendships.

****

In England, life for Edwin and Enid were different. Enid's health was not always perfect. After exploratory surgery, a diagnosis was made which necessitated corrective surgery. Total correction, however did not take place and some more surgery was needed. Enid was never physically strong. She needed longer periods to recuperate than most people would need.

All the while, Edwin, very concerned about his wife, but not knowing how to show it, drowned himself in his work. The children were taken care of mostly by a full time live-in nanny. Fortunately, Enid selected this person very carefully, before appointing her. Janet Imri could just as well have been their mother. She took care of Howie and his sisters, Debra-Ann and later Tamsin, born five years after her elder sister, with as much loving care, balanced by good discipline, as could be expected.

Howie developed an interest in science, like his father, at an early age and would probably follow a career in the same direction. Debra-Ann was the compassionate one bringing home every sick or injured bird she could find. To become a veterinarian was her greatest desire. Tamsin turned out to be the wild one. She loved all kinds of sport, like her father and tended to turn to violence when things did not go her way. This caused a lot of concern for Enid, but fortunately, it never reached the level of explosiveness that was so typical of Edwin's behaviour in his younger years.

A year before her father-in-law passed away, Enid had her last operation, which proved to be successful at last. Enid was getting better to such an extent that she could resume her career as an accountant.

"Are you sure you want to work again, Love?"

"Oh yes. I've been sitting in this house doing nothing but being ill for long enough. I feel wonderful and I can't wait to get going again."

"You shouldn't have trouble getting a job. There are always room for a good accountant."

"Well, I've already asked around. There are possibilities, but nothing definite yet. I wanted to talk to you first before I start making appointments for interviews. But now that I have your blessing, I will seriously take action the week after next. First I want to send Janet home for a few days. Once I start working, she won't have much opportunity to take a break."

"Now that's a good idea. Perhaps we should also go somewhere. Spend some time with the children since it is school holiday. Where would you like to go?" "You choose. It is your idea. And an excellent idea I might add. Do you have a place in mind?"

"Actually I have. The Lake District has always fascinated me, but I've never really made and effort to see it. I think we should tour the whole area, if time permits."

"Let's go packing."

CHAPTER 9

Terrence Again

Terrence, ever the charmer, impressed a wealthy woman enough to marry him. The band he played with, used a number of songs written by him. He became well known among music lovers for his contribution to the music world. There was even talk of a contract with a recording company, including two or three of his songs in the first album. Things were going well for him for quite a while.

Then my youngest brother met this woman at an event organized by the company she worked for, her father being one of the founding members. The band was hired to play their music and entertain the hundred or so very important guests. Judy Dempsey was instantly charmed by Terrence, fell in love a week later at the first date and married him after six months.

Pressure from her family to get her husband in a more prestigious line of work, caused the first bit of friction between them. On top of that, Judy did not like the idea of Terrence spending nights away from home whenever he had to play outside of Cape Town. Her position in the company was so important and kept her so occupied, that it was unimaginable for her to accompany him. She could just never be excused.

The ringing of the telephone woke Terrence from a deep sleep. At first he slapped the alarm clock, thinking that was where the sound came from. But the ringing persisted and woke him thoroughly.

"Yes, what can I do for you." He said it as a statement, not a question.

"Sweets, it's me. Did I wake you?"

"No, yes actually you did, but it's okay. I suppose it's time to get up. What time is it?"

"It is twenty to eleven."

"Good grief. Suppose last night was more tiring than usual. Or maybe I'm getting old."

"You are in your best years. But perhaps life is passing you by. Working till the small hours would take its toll even at your age."

"Honey, don't start that again. You know it can't be helped. It's my life, it's what I do."

"Yes, I know. Listen, could you meet me for lunch? There is something I would like to discuss with you."

"Sure. When and where?"

"Mike's Kitchen. Let's make it early. Is twelve thirty all right with you?"

"Sure. What do you want to discuss?"

"Let's talk at lunch."

****

Terrence tip toed through the dark living room. He draped his coat over an easy chair, kicked out his shoes, pushed them under the coffee table and flopped down on the couch. With all ten fingers pushed through his hair, he sat, elbows on his knees, staring at the pilot light of the television set. The time on the video machine caught his eyes: 02h53. Judy is probably sleeping soundly. Not a good idea to disturb her. Not after what happened at lunch. It did not go well, especially after her old man turned up.

'Do they really expect me to give up everything that is important to me to dance to their tune?' he thought. He tried to remember everything that was said during the lunch that was supposed to be a special moment between him and his wife. He is convinced Judy had set him up. Her father did not walk in coincidently. A deep sigh escaped his chest. Leaning backward he let his head rest on the soft cushion. He put his feet on the couch and closed his eyes.

After what felt like five minutes a racket broke out in the kitchen. Burglars, was his first thought, but the smell of fresh coffee proofed otherwise. Judy was busy in the kitchen and had no regard for his need to sleep. On the contrary, she did her best to make enough noise to wake even the neighbours. The time on the wall clock said 07h04. With great effort he put the blanket aside, pushed himself up onto his feet and stumbled into the kitchen.

"Good morning. Did you sleep well?" Pretending nothing was different he smiled at her, which infuriated her even more than what she already was. He poured two cups of coffee, added sugar and a little extra milk for her the way she liked it and handed her cup over to her, still smiling. Judy wanted to ignore him and throw things against the wall, but fell for his charm instead, as always. She smiled back and sipped the coffee.

"Sorry about last night, but thanks for covering me with a blanket. I just could not make it to the bedroom. And I didn't want to disturb you. I know Melkbos is not far, I should have been here earlier. The guys had some trouble loading the sound equipment and everyone else was gone. Just thought I should give them a hand so they could also get going. Judy, don't be angry. Please when you married me, you knew what it would be like. I love you, Honey."

"I love you too, Terrence, that is why I want a better life for you. Do you really think it is for my sake that I want you to take Dad up on his offer? You'll never get such a generous offer again. Please, won't you just consider it?"

"Judy Darling, listen to me. I love what I do. I don't want to do anything else. I don't want to sit in an office pushing papers around all day long."

"Is that what you think I do? Pushing papers around?"

"No, Honey. I didn't mean that. You have a career and you love what you do. I won't expect you to do anything else. Why can't you allow me the same freedom, to do what I enjoy doing?" He put his arms around her and held her close. In response she hugged him, then, pushed him back. Smiling, she said:

"All right. Have it your way. I'll try to adapt, but it is very difficult for me. You must understand. We don't have enough time together. You come in late and I go out early. Most weekends I'm free, you never are. We have to find a way in between that suits us both. I just can't see how."

"We'll think of something. We can take a weekend off and go someplace to catch up. I'll talk to Tim and see if I can make it this coming weekend. There is nothing big booked and I'm sure they can spare me."

"Good. I'll see what I can arrange at my end and I'll let you know. But Sweets, look at the time. I must be off." Judy pulled his head down and kissed him on the cheek.

"See you early tonight. Love you." He winked at her, she smiled, grabbed her bag and left for the office. The sun is about to appear in the east.

Judy left Terrence alone for a month, didn't mention her father's offer of a job in his company even once. It was lovey-dovey all the time and Terrence got the impression she was beginning to accept his working circumstances. They spent a wonderfully romantic weekend in a mountain resort near Franschoek. All was good and seemingly getting better. What he didn't know, was that Judy's parents started putting more pressure on her than ever, to convince Terrence to get a better job.

She was nervous because they made each other such pretty promises about respecting each other's space and now she had to go back on her word to please her family. If his working hours didn't irritate her so much, she could learn to live with it. Being a musician was not so bad in itself. Especially when fame was becoming a factor. But to sit at home weekend after weekend while he was with his band is not much of a marriage. Judy did not make a cognitive decision to side with her parents. It just stemmed from her own dissatisfaction.

"Don't tell me you are going to spend the whole weekend away from home. Isn't it enough that you come home in the middle of the night? Now you plan to sleep away from home, again?"

"I told you this event in Hermanus is coming up. Don't you remember? I told you about it last week. And you know it is too far to drive out and come back home for a few hours' sleep."

"I remember you informed me. But I was hoping I could go with you. Now you tell me you will be leaving early on Friday."

"I don't see the problem. Why can't you take the day off and come with me?"

"You know I can't do that. We have meetings end to end. I won't be free before three-thirty."

"Come on! Do you really have to attend every meeting?"

"Yes, I have. Daddy will never let me go. The meetings are all about labour saving issues in my own division. How could I not be present?"

"Why can't you postpone till next week? What is so urgent about saving labour?"

"Postpone? Are you off your rocker?"

"And I suppose you couldn't possibly leave directly after the meeting." Terrence asked with just a trace of irritation in his tone.

"No, I can NOT! There will be at least one more meeting with Daddy and two of my managers to make decisions about the discussions in the first meeting. Why can't YOU say no for a change?"

"Sure. The band will be playing without a guitarist and only two singers. Jerry has not recovered from his laryngitis and Marty and Joanna are on their honeymoon. That leaves me to do both jobs. Sure they can get by without me too. Perhaps we could let everyone stay home and send a tape cassette to Hermanus. Oh, sorry we'll have to send a CD, only we haven't acquired the technology to burn CD's yet."

"I don't need your sarcasm, Terrence. I'm really fed-up with your job. Why can't you get a real job and live a normal life like everybody else?"

"Oh, I see. Now it's that old story again. I thought we sorted things out. I thought we were going to respect each other."

"Well I'm sorry. I just cannot live like this for the rest of my life. You better make some choices." The threat in her voice and in her eyes was unmistakable. Terrence just stared at her not knowing what to say.

"We can talk about this when I come back from Hermanus."

And talk they did. Or at least she talked and Terrence listened. She gave him an ultimatum: you leave the band or I leave you.

****

As soon as his contract expired, he left the band and took the job Judy had organized for him. It was a high-ranking job and the Hammond family too, was proud of him once more. With dark suit, starched collar and conservative blue and red striped tie; clean shaven, and tidy haircut he appeared in his new office on his first working day. It was also the first day of his slide.

If only Judy would leave him alone to at least attend his church where he was happy and taken care of, things might not have turned out so badly. At 'His People' he had not only found a spiritual home, but was a member of the worship team. Judy however, insisted he joined the cold and impersonal, traditionalistic church she grew up in, where people sat passively, listening to the preacher – or pretending to listen while taking a nap instead - saying many grandiloquent words and everyone left the service as empty as before.

He soon became depressed. It did not take long for Terrence to seek solace in alcohol. His work performance was soon affected negatively. Less than a year had passed when Mr. Dempsey, the father-in-law and C.E.O. of the company called him to his office early one morning. Before Mr. Dempsey could open his mouth, Terrence put his letter of resignation on the desk and walked out through the front door, into the sunshine.

****

The band was not keen on taking Terrence back. They had offered him another two-year contract and he had turned them down. He did honour the contract for their exclusive use of his songs for their next CD for which they had finally acquired the technology. But for old time's sake, and because he was so popular - people still inquired about him - they took him in on a six month probation provided he stayed away from the bottle, which he did not.

Terrence had an income, but he was miserable because of the way things had turned out. His wife was furious. She threatened him with all the horrors she could think of. When he would no longer dance to her tune and would not stop drinking, she kicked him out. Divorced, unemployed - Tim did not extend the six month contract because of Terrence's drinking - with unsure future, depressed and too ashamed to go back to his church, he once more turned to me.

He arrived in Johannesburg late in the afternoon of a sunny, windless autumn day in a well-used Toyota. The BMW Judy made him buy was given back to the bank. I was happy to have my brother once more under my roof, though sad about the circumstances that had brought him back. I was so hoping things would keep on going better for him, that he would reach the top and that he would fulfil God's plan for his life using his talent for music to the glory of the Lord.

I slowly got him to go back to church with me. He never got completely drunk, but it took time before he stopped drinking altogether. By the mercy of God he did not go back to smoking pot, otherwise it might not have been that easy. It was a matter of months before the depression lifted and he became his old, adorable, charming self. He recommitted his life to the Lord. He intensely studied the Word on a regular basis where before he did so whenever he felt like it. Soon he was part of the worship team. Before the year was out, he was selected to do internship and be trained as home-cell leader.

For income, he went back to entertaining my customers. He also found a club in a not so bad part of town that on and off needed a guitarist. It proved to be fairly secure and an opportunity for Terrence to earn a little something extra, and to witness. Before long, the lead singer of the band, who happened to be the club owner's daughter, started to go to church with him. She was a pretty girl, long, curly, light brown hair and big blue eyes, divorced from an abusive, junkie band member who was at that time in prison for drug trafficking and assault. She was not well educated, never finished school, but had enough common sense for both her and Terrence.

Some months later, she committed her life to the Lord. She was baptized one Sunday after church and the following Saturday Terrence married her. Her father, sister and husband, a cousin with husband, the only family Stacy had, attended the wedding. Mom and Andrew were the only family members on our side who bothered to come. Dad would if he could, but was out of the country. The news did not reach him in time. It was a small, cosy wedding, the reception was held under the bare branches of the jacarandas in my garden.

The couple promised to find a place of their own as soon as the honeymoon week was over. Andrew flew back the next day after a pleasant Sunday meal with Mom and me. Mom stayed a week to welcome the honeymooners back. She was happy for them.

Not much of a talker, more a listener, but witty and capable of maintaining a good conversation about any subject, Mom was exceptionally quiet. We did the usual things we always did when she visited, drove around, went for long walks round Zoo Lake, went shopping, relaxed in my garden, but always it was I who did the talking. Not being a talker myself, it became a burden. By Thursday, we just enjoyed each other's presence without saying a word for hours.

   When we said goodbye at the airport, Mom hugged each of us tightly for what seemed like minutes. When she released me, her smile seemed to be forced; her eyes seemed to focus on something in the distance. Terrence and Stacy did not notice, probably because they had eyes only for one another. On our way back home, I could not help wondering if something was the matter.

CHAPTER 10

Mother

I had to wait two weeks to find out. Mom called me early one morning asking me to pray for her. She was being admitted to hospital. She was having an operation. Her doctor discovered a huge lump in her left breast, it was confirmed by a mammogram and surgery was scheduled immediately.

When I put the phone down, I felt my insides tying painfully into a knot. The feeling spread from my stomach outward. No! Not my mother! Lord, God of Heaven, not my mother! I cried, prayed, cried and prayed, pleading with the Lord to keep her safe, to heal her, to comfort her.

She lay white as death on the white hospital bed when I entered the I.C.-unit. Slowly her eyes opened when I touched her free hand. She tried to smile, whispered: "Glad you could come..." she fell asleep again. I watched her for a few minutes before I was asked to leave, as it was midday and time for the patients to rest. I was welcome to come back after two pm. Then I could stay until supper, I was told.

I drove home slowly in the rented car. Katrina and Simon crowded me as soon as I brought the car to a standstill wanting to know how their *Merrim* was: "*Ag dankie Jirre!*" they exclaimed when I told them she was fine as far as I could tell.

I left my bags where Simon had put them and fell on the bed, exhausted by emotional strain during a sleepless night. I drank the tea Katrina brought me, lay down again and stared at the ceiling, wondering how she really was, praying she will get better.

I must have dozed, because an hour later I became aware of a change in the light in my room; it was early afternoon sunlight, not noonday sunlight anymore. I went to my bathroom, refreshed quickly, ran downstairs and scattered gravel as I sped away toward the hospital. At the I.C.-unit, I was asked to wait outside in the waiting room as the doctor was with my mother. In the waiting room, the Hammond family was gathered.

I first saw Andrew, who was facing the entrance, talking to a man with his back to me. I recognized the man as my father. I intended to slip away unnoticed, but Andrew saw me and waved me over. I had to face my father. They both hugged me; their bodies tense and fear and concern darkening their eyes. My father nevertheless smiled slightly at me showing sincere pleasure to see me. It has been a while since we've seen each other, even longer since we've talked.

The doctor came out and we all bundled together to get through the door to the I.C.U., but were stopped by a stern-looking person in white:

"Two at a time, please." My father motioned to me to go through. Then he followed me. Mom was awake, smiling ever so slightly:

"Did I dream, or did I see you earlier?" She asked me, her voice hardly more than a whisper. I took her hand again.

"You did not dream. I was here. I came directly from the airport. I was told you were supposed to rest, so they allowed me just a minute with you, just to say 'hello'". She smiled again, closed her eyes for a few seconds; and said weakly:

"My goodness, I've been resting … since yesterday when they put me … under, to cut me up". It was meant to be funny, to make light of her situation. She had never been one to enjoy pity. Still I had to blink several times to keep the moisture that was building up, from overflowing my eyelids.

Outside in the waiting room, while Andrew and Anita was inside with Mom, my father sat down next to me. I did not want to talk to him, but this was no time to let old grudges flare. He told me the operation was successful, as the tumour was removed. It seemed they got everything, including of course her whole breast as well as the underarm glands. The oncologist insisted on immediate follow-up with radiation therapy, he told me.

By the end of that week, when my mother was settled in a private room, the Hammond-clan came to see her during every visiting hour. The initial shock was over, so my father was slowly pushed out and even ignored by some. I remained polite, greeting him, but avoided conversation whenever possible without offending

****

I had to fly back to Johannesburg to see to my affairs and to make arrangements for my prolonged absence. After two days everything was settled. My assistant would take over. Anneke was quite competent and reliable. I trusted her to run the business in my absence and encouraged her to hire more help if she needed it. I left for Cape Town long before sunup on the day before my mom was to be released from hospital. This time I drove down, as I did not know how long I would stay. I was not willing to hire a car for an indefinite time. Besides, there was no hurry.

With my mother home the house became a beehive. Everyone wanted to visit, bring gifts and flowers and encourage. People were in and out all day for the first three days. Of course, they all meant well, but it would be too tiring if Mom had to see all of them. Many were thanked at the front door and asked to come back another day. Some were received in the living room where they left their presents. Few were allowed upstairs to actually see Mom. Many returned days later when she could see them, some phoned often and some were not seen or heard of again.

By the end of the second week, we all settled into some sort of routine. The fulltime nurse that was hired by my father became a part-time nurse. Mom received visitors in the family room during the mid-morning hours and again in the late afternoon after she had had some rest. At first only relatives and close friends were allowed to visit, as she was still very weak. As she became stronger, no one was showed away without at least saying 'hello' to her. There was still a steady stream of people wanting to show their concern, but thinning out.

Andrew came over at least four times a week sometimes bringing his family with him, sometimes alone. Anita was there, every evening during the first ten days. She seemed horrified at the thought of Mom being so sick and frail. Edwin and his whole family flew down from England the second weekend after Mom came home. It was like a big family reunion. Terrence had to be there too, so I paid their airfare, knowing they would not be able to come down otherwise. He accepted gratefully; never too proud to receive help.

Mom recovered slowly. She was violently ill after every follow-up treatment. Her strength built slowly; then fell back again. We were all worried, but life had to go on. Terrence could not fit his visit in over a weekend consequently he almost missed Edwin, who stayed only for a weekend, grateful that he could make it at all. Edwin was packed and ready to leave for the airport when Terrence and Stacy arrived from the airport in a rented car that Edwin would deliver back at the airport. Under these circumstances, Edwin was happy to see our baby brother, even friendly towards Stacy, whom he had never met. They said 'hello' and 'goodbye' in the foyer, Terrence coming and Edwin going.

After three more weeks, Mom did show signs of recovering steadily. It was time for me to go home. It was one of the most difficult things I had ever done, leaving her to go back to my life and see to my affairs. I phoned every day, flew down once a month on a Monday, which was slow business days and back early on Wednesdays. Edwin came for her birthday in October and again, with family, for Christmas. Both times, we had family reunions as I insisted Terrence and Stacy accompany me on both occasions.

All the while Dad was at her side constantly. He took her for treatments, drove around the shoreline on good weather days, helped her with shopping whenever she was up to it and wanted to get out of the house a bit. He also took control of the household like many years ago when he still was the head of the house. Only now, he played Mom's roll as well. All the while, he was just short of being ignored by all of us.

Early in the new-year, Mom phoned me telling me she was all right, but needed someone to take care of things. She had asked Dad to move back in and he had agreed. They would not share a bedroom, but she wanted him close by. She expressed her sincere hope that we, children would accept it and asked me to inform the others.

Mom died seven months later, a few days after Terrence and Stacy's first anniversary and less than a year after her first operation. She simply did not respond favourably to the treatments, became weaker and weaker until Dad late one afternoon phoned us to tell us if we wanted to see her, we would have to hurry. That was how Terrence, Stacy and I drove through the night to reach Cape Town just after peak hour the next morning, relieving each other every two hours. We were in time to share with Mom her last conscious moments. She had fallen into a coma by lunchtime and left her body before midnight. That beautiful woman with the thick, dark brown hair, deep brown eyes and sincere smile was gone. Before us on the white bed lay the emaciated body of Chantal Gwendolyn Hammond, pale yellow in colour, sunken eyes in a hairless head; the remains of my mother.

Anita and I took care of Mom's personal things after the funeral. We left it until everyone had gone back to his own life. Like Dad's sister and her husband, Aunt Emma and Uncle William, Terrence and Stacy had no desire to linger with the Hammond's. I put my brother and his wife on a plane back to Johannesburg on the same day Edwin left for England. Andrew resumed his regular routine. His wife Marie, I knew, was burning to help us sort out Mom's stuff hoping to be given something of value, just as a 'souvenir'. I would probably have given in and let her join us, but Anita was adamant: no in-laws.

Together we went through her jewellery. Together we decided what to give to each sis-in-law 'just as a souvenir' and divided the rest, which was quite a collection, between the two of us as it was stipulated in Mom's will. Mom knew we would not quarrel and she knew Anita would walk away with the best pieces. The same applied for the clothes.

Mom was slender while I had broader hips. Anita was one size smaller than mom, and shorter. I could use Mom's tops. The few pants and skirts that I fancied would have to be taken out at the seams. Anita would have to shorten everything and have the alterations made at the seams in the opposite direction on everything she took. Marie, Stacy and Enid were one size or more too big for mom's clothes, so no scoring for them there. We gave them each some accessories like handbags; purses; scarves, things that did not need to fit. We kept the things meant for Enid in a separate drawer until they could be sent over.

Mom had many friends who would like to have something to remember her by. Anita and I had no trouble setting apart an item or two for her closest friends. Her only sister, Francis, lived in Pretoria and suffered from multiple sclerosis. She could not even attend the funeral. Aunt Francis phoned almost every day. Her children were scattered all over the world, except for my cousin Steph who lived with her and took care of her. We agreed that I would take her a few items when I went back.

Mom's brother, Roger, two years younger than her, lived in Austria and we had little contact with him. He attended the funeral accompanied by his Austrian wife and youngest of three sons, Udo and only daughter Lisa, but stayed overnight and flew back the very next day. We agreed that it was not necessary to give them anything.

Then it was time for the make-up. It was awkward to look at the stuff she played around with to create a different look to go with every outfit. My skin was a shade darker than mom's, while Anita was a perfect match. Here, again, Anita collected most for herself. I took a few eye shadows and lipsticks. Over the perfumes, we almost had a fist fight. 'Worth' was our favourite and there was only one bottle. I saw it first, grabbed it and held tight. Anita tried to take it from me. She only let go when I agreed to let her have both the 'Meadow Breeze' and 'Midnight Flower'. We leaned backwards, laughing out loudly at our own childishness.

The rest of Mom's stuff did not interest Anita. She trusted it all to me and was now in a hurry to get back to her place to plan what she was going to do with the money Mom had left her. It would be available in a few months. She had to be ready.

There was not much left to be sorted out. Mom was tidy and disliked clutter. What was not used had to go, mostly to Katrina who took everything she did not need herself, to her church to be distributed among the poor. She did not need much. Her church had a big welfare department that was always appreciative of anything that could help the needy.

I systematically went through Mom's cupboards and drawers sorting what would go to Aunt Emma, to friends who would like to have something as a memory, and to Katrina and her family and to Simon's wife and daughters. As I pulled the last drawer inside a corner cabinet, it was stuck. I pulled harder and it came loose, but with difficulty, making a scraping sound as if something was sticking underneath. I took out the whole drawer, placed the contents on the floor next to me and turned it up-side down. There was a brown envelope stuck with masking tape to the bottom of the drawer.

Instinctively I glanced through the room to see if anyone was watching. Of course no one was. Was I becoming paranoid? I pulled the tape from the bottom of the drawer, turned the envelope over to see to whom it was addressed. There was nothing written on the envelope. I sat down on the bed and opened it. My insides started to turn upside down, as I emptied the envelope in my lap.

From the envelope, I took several postcards and one letter. The postcards all had pictures of some place in France. Scenes from various different cities, country sides; and my heart almost stopped. The village near Avignon. Several postcards with scenes from that same village that Mom and I visited a few years ago. Strangely, none of the postcards had anything written on them, not even a name.

I opened the letter and started reading.

'My Dearest,

I am so sorry about what happened. I should have listened to you not sending postcards to your home address. You told me expressly it was over, yet I kept on, hoping. Now I have ruined your marriage. Allow me one more time to plead with you to come to France, to me. I will be the happiest man and I know I will make you happy. Or would you like me to come back to South Africa?

Now that Howard knows and has moved out, what is keeping us apart? I know you love me as much as I love you, or almost. Please don't ignore me. If it is really over, write me and say so. Do not keep quiet or I will be watching the road every day expecting you to arrive at sunset like the first time.

Love you always,
F.'

For long minutes I did not move. How can this be possible? My mother had an affair! Did she really love him? How did she get herself to cheat on Dad? Or how did she get to fall out of love with Dad? Why did she take me to Avignon and show me the village? Did she ever take any of the other children to Avignon? How did she meet this man? This F, whatever F stands for. Who is he, where is he now? A million questions raced thought my head scrambling my mind. I read the letter over, and over until I could recite the words.

I took the postcards up again and looked at them, checking the dates; some were not so clear, others I could barely make out. They were all dated many years ago, some even from before I was born. Did Dad see the postcards? Did he confront Mom, made her confess? There were more questions that I could keep up with, that I could not find answers for, only speculate on.

Then something terrible struck me. Dad. We always blamed him for the separation. We hated him for leaving us. How selfish we were; how unfair. How much he must have been hurting. The tears started falling so suddenly that I could not prevent them from dropping on the postcards. I wiped them and put them together with the letter back into the envelope.

CHAPTER 11

More Deaths

Early one morning some time later, Dad called me. Aunt Emma's husband was dead. His car had a blow out on the right front tyre. He lost control on the high way, was flung in front of an oncoming truck and was dragged meters away before the truck managed to stop. An untimely flu kept Aunt Emma at home and saved her life. The funeral would be in three days if I would like to attend.

It was a small funeral. Uncle William had an elder sister and a brother who attended. Their children were scattered over the country, some overseas. Aunt Emma's children, my cousins, Erin, Annabelle - who was my age - Billy and Susan attended the funeral with their spouses and their children. It was good to see my cousins. We hardly ever saw each other since growing up. We swapped cell phone numbers and promised to keep in touch.

My cousins were all concerned about their mother. Aunt Emma had not worked after she got married. They all knew their father was not able to leave her more than just a small policy that would pay out goodness knew when. Erin suggested her mother move in with her. She could have the spare room. Her furniture; however would have to be sold. There was no room for that. Aunt Emma did not want to live with children. Erin's house in Tamboers Kloof was big, but not big enough.

That was where Dad stepped in. He offered his sister a place to stay. She would not have to give up any of her stuff. His house - my house - was big enough to accommodate all her possessions with space to spare. Her children agreed without much resistance. They knew their uncle well enough not to argue. His offer was more like a command. Besides, they lived busy lives and could not give her the attention, the emotional comfort she needed, while he could do with her companionship. That settled it.

Aunt Emma's stuff was transported before the end of that week. She moved in and being the good natured person she was, she was accepted and soon loved by the staff allowing her to take up the position of the lady of the house. Dad asked me later if it was all right with me. It was after all my house:

"Thanks for eventually asking me, Dad. Yes, of course it's more than all right. I cannot think of a better arrangement. She needs taken care of and you are no longer alone. Perfect."

"Glad you feel that way."

****

The phone rang in the middle of the night. I looked at my clock, two thirty-two. Who on earth ... it had to be bad news. I picked up. It was Terrence. Stacy's father had been shot. They were at the hospital. He was in theatre and it did not look good.

I dragged myself out of bed, washed my face, slipped into a sweat suit and drove to the hospital. Arriving there, Stacy fell into my arms, sobbing. They had just learned that her father had passed away. Terrence joined us in a group hug and we wept together.

Stacy's only sister and her cousin Deidre attended the funeral. Her sister, Amelia lived in Natal and was married to a policeman. They did not see each other often. At the gravesite they clung to each other and sobbed silently. Terrence put his arms around both women and held them close. It was a sad day for that small family. The windy, dusty weather contributed to the bleak atmosphere of the day.

Cups of tea in our hands, chewing on a pastry Stacy called her sister, sister-in-law, that's me, and cousin aside, faintly smiling:

"I have a tiny bit of good news. I am pregnant. Five weeks, I think."
Tears welled up in her eyes again:

"Daddy would have been so thrilled. I was going to invite him over
for a *braai* this weekend and give him the good news then. Now he
is gone without knowing he was about to become a granddad again."
Amelia hugged her sister, I did the same as soon as Amelia released her
and we both congratulated her sincerely.

"I am so glad for you, Stacy. But maybe Daddy knows, wherever he
is. Maybe he can hear and see us. He knew you loved him."

"No, I don't think it works that way. At least he saw your kids. I
know he loved them and it was hard for him that you live so far away.
He would have liked to see them more often." Now it was Amelia's
turn to have tears fill her eyes.

"Yes. I so wish we could come back to live here. Arnold has put in a
request for a transfer more than once, but without luck."

"Let him keep on trying. It will be nice to have you close by. Then
the cousins can get to know each other and grow up together." Amelia
nodded, smiled and finished her tea as Terrence, Arnold and Deidre's
husband approached our little circle. It was encouraging to have a little
bit of good news amid all this sadness.

****

Later they learned that Stacy's father was cashing up and finishing his
admin for the day when he was confronted by robbers, shot and left for
dead. All the cash was taken, nobody was arrested so far. Stacy, being in
charge now, closed the club for an indefinite time. She was capable of
running the club; her father had taught her well, trained her in every
aspect of the business. No one blamed her for not having the heart
to do it, considering the circumstances that placed her in command.

Five months later, she sold the business at a not too bad price and
gave half the money to her sister, as her father would expect her to
do. Having been a nervous kind of person, she became jittery. They
had moved into a complex with excellent security even before she
realised she was pregnant. Now they were grateful to have had the
fore-sight and never, if they could help it, stayed out after eight o'clock
at night. They even found another church nearby, but did not attend
evening services.

They also stopped visiting me, as things were changing in Yeoville. Shebeens, drug lords and pimps became part of the scene bringing crime and violence with them as North-West Africans moved in. Old residents started to move out. I lost a number of my students and later many customers and friends. New kinds of customers came visiting driving out the old ones. My friends from Berea, Eileen, Maggie, Greta and Shri hardly ever called. Eileen was mugged in the street, Maggie had more than one break-in at her flat. Each time her clothes iron was stolen. Laughingly she kept telling people the burglars probably wanted to start a 'steal-and-iron' business. We all know it was an old joke out of the 'Reader's Digest Magazine,' but we laughed along, knowing she tried to make light of a scary situation. I saw them only when I visited them.

Yeoville increasingly started to look like Hillbrow. All the interesting little shops were vacated and the pavement stalls disappeared, replaced by unruly groups of teenagers and pavement gamblers. The ambiance that the old Yeoville had was gone. Streets became dirty and cluttered with trash of all kinds. That was why I was so surprised when Terrence and Stacy stopped by out of the blue, at about mid-morning one sunny spring day. I could tell they had something they wanted to tell me, so I took them upstairs to my private quarters.

"We're going to move," announced Terrence carefully observing my reaction.

"Oh, where to?"

"Cape Town. Stacy always wanted to live by the sea. Our rental contract expires end of this month. We'll be moving in eleven days from today".

"Where will you stay? Do you plan to move into the house, ... with Dad?"

"No. We went down two months ago and found a nice place in Belville".

"That's nice. Have you also found a means of earning an income?" Having had no income for a year and a half and living on the money Terrence inherited from our mother, finding a way to earn a living might not be such a bad idea. The very small fortune cannot by any means last forever.

"We want to settle first. Then we'll check things out. Maybe start a new club or restaurant, maybe a guesthouse or something. We'll see".

"Good. I wish you well," I said, hoping they know what they were doing. They had obviously been planning this thing for some time now.

"Why haven't you told me earlier?"

"We wanted to, but we did not want to hurt your feelings. You were so good to us, and now you might think we're deserting you".

"Well, you can relax. I'm not hurt and I fully understand why you want to leave and go to Cee Tee".

"We also thought you might want to talk us out of it. Now all our arrangements are finalized. We cannot change our plans now".

"I would not want to. I'm really happy for you. Go and have my blessings. You surely deserve a break. I'll come and visit as soon as the little Hammond sees the first light," I said, looking at Stacy's bulging belly. She was just under eight months pregnant at that time.

****

Anita walked straight from the kitchen to open the patio door but the door was already open and Chanté was reclining comfortably in a chair.

"Hi Mom, how was your day?" Chanté asked. "Would you like some coffee?" she asked her mother while getting up out of the patio chair.

"Tea please. I already put the kettle on." Anita sat down and took another bite from the pear she had taken from the fruit bowl.

"Rooibos or green tea?"

"Just plain old circle bag. And bring my cigarettes please." Chanté returned with two cups of tea and handed one to Anita.

"You look tired, Mom. I hope you didn't bring work home again."

"No. No working at home tonight. Have you finished you homework?"

"Almost. Just taking a break then I'll go and finish science. I'll study for the English test after supper."

"Is the test tomorrow?"

"No. We write on Friday, but I want to be prepared".

"Friday is still far away. Why don't you relax and study tomorrow?"

"I don't like to cram everything in at the last minute. It's nerve wrecking and I don't have nerves strong enough for that."

"Excellent. I'm proud of you."

"Mom can I do something about this drab living room? I saw some things in a magazine and I have fabulous ideas how to cheer up the place."

"Just as long as it does not cost a fortune. I'm not a millionaire, you know. I wish I were. I would give you a free hand to redecorate the whole house. Where is Donny?"

"Hockey practice."

"Oh, yes, it's Wednesday. Hope he has enough time to finish his homework".

"Don't worry, Mom. I'm sure he will finish before he goes to bed."

"About redecorating the house, Chanté. I think I have to reconsider. We might move soon and your effort would be wasted."

"Move? Where to? And why? We're happy here, aren't we?"

"We are not unhappy, I suppose. But if we can have a better place, why shouldn't we have it? This place is kind of small for all of us. I don't want to let Cathy go. She is valuable to us and we all get along. So I think we should look out for a bigger place. I don't like being cramped."

"Mom, we've been living here for years and you have not complained … much. Why now all of a sudden?"

"Because I knew I could not afford a better place. Soon perhaps I will."

"Did you get promotion; a salary raise?"

"I got promotion last year. But that was not enough to enable me to get a better place, only to get you children a few things you needed. No, I got a letter from Grandma's lawyer. The estate is almost settled and the inheritances will be paid out soon."

"Oh, Mom, that's good news. May I decorate the new place?" Anita smiled at her daughter. She is so young, so idealistic.

"Of course Dear. I will leave the entire job of decorating the new place to you." A sudden brightness appeared in Chantés eyes. Moist was building up and her voice quivered when she spoke:

"Mom, a new place will be nice, but I miss Gran so much. I'd much rather have her back than some fancy new house or something." The door burst open and Donny trampled in: "What's this about a new house or something?" Cathy entered behind him and went directly to the kitchen to prepare supper.

"Mom's going to get a bigger place for us and I have permission to decorate it."

"Great! I can do with a bigger room. And Mom, please get us one with a view. We can see the sea through a small corridor between those buildings and a glimpse of the mountain from our little cross-street place. I'd like a one eighty view. Then I can tell those braggarts at school a thing or too."

"You mean you'll become a braggart too." Chanté chipped in against her better judgement.

"Shut up, silly face." Anita held up a hand, frowning at her children:

"That's enough. Both of you. Go finish your homework. There's little time before supper."

****

Anita, like my other siblings had received their inheritance from my mother's estate with great enthusiasm. For only the second time since I left Cape Town she made an effort to visit me in Johannesburg. She looked well, obviously having had a proper make-over. New clothes; new hair style; new way of applying make-up. All very stylish.

"Well, Sis, I must be honest. I am surprised at your place. It is really nice. I didn't expect such a grand place and I didn't think you'd be living such a good life up here." I look incredulously at her. She spoke the exact same words when she was here the first time.

"I'm glad that I brought my children along. If Cathy didn't need a break, I would have left them with her."

"It's a pity you couldn't bring her along. She might have enjoyed the trip."

"She would have. But her grandmother is ill. She wanted to visit the old lady while she still can. She's the only family Cathy has. Her mother is in Canada, her father remarried and lives somewhere in the Middle-East. Without my household to take care of, she can rest and see the grandmother every day."

"Her gran still holding up? She surely has a will to live."

"Yes, but she gets weaker now. I'd be surprised if she makes it to the end of the year. Cathy works hard at her studies hoping to take care of her again as soon as she qualifies and gets a good position."

"It almost sounds as if you overwork the girl. I hope you give her time off once in a while."

"Of course I do. Besides, she only works half-day so to speak. Cathy works when the children are at home. Her mornings are free to do whatever she likes. She can even take a second job - mornings-only - for all I care. As long as she is available to drive the children home from school and just be there for them until I get home I'm happy. She only works one weekend a month so that I can have a break. Besides, the children are big enough to take care of themselves. Cathy needn't be so involved anymore. She just needs to drive them around, to be there and to supervise, so to speak."

"Excellent! But don't get excited, I'm only teasing. Is she really still studying?"

"She takes it slowly, but hopefully she will graduate next year. Cathy will be heartbroken if the granny dies before she can take her in."

"Poor Cathy. Tell me about the new place you bought."

"Oh you must see it. It's lovely and has a hundred and eighty degree view of the ocean. I can see the mountain and the harbour in the distance on the left side right through to Blouberg on the right. From the back windows we have a glimpse of the Rietvlei Nature Area.

"Table Mountain?"

"No girl, Tyger Mountain. Of course Table Mountain. Tyger Mountain is behind us, about south-east. The house is a bit bigger too. Cathy has her own room to herself and she has her own en-suit bathroom. No more sharing with Chanté."

"I'll most certainly come and see your place when I go down to Cee Tee again. Anita, it's really good to have you here. I thought you'd never come after the first visit. Actually, you should have come earlier. This area was a lot better a few years ago. You would have liked all the tiny shops where you could find anything imaginable on sale. That first weekend you were here was just too short. Things are changing and I don't know how it will be in a few years. I might have to start looking for a place somewhere else."

"When I said I like your place, I meant the house. I'd rather not comment on the environment. More than ever I'm convinced Jo'burg is a dump, but I'd rather keep it to myself. But now that you've mentioned it…"

"Tell you what: Tomorrow morning we start off early and I'll take you to all the good places, show you why I fell in love with this city."

"Sure. If you think you can convince me, I'd like to be convinced."

So the next day we set out on a tour around Johannesburg, Randburg, Sandton, Bryanston, Bedfortview and back to Yeoville. We stopped in many places, visited art galleries, had coffee at Lemon Rose Farm, lunch in Hyde Park, ice cream at Gilooly's Farm and afternoon tea at Eastgate. When we headed back home, Anita asked me if that was all Johannesburg had to offer.

"Isn't it enough for one day? If you want to see more, we could take a day for each wind direction. The children will especially enjoy Little Falls, the botanical gardens in Roodepoort, Zoo Lake, Emmerentia Dam, Gold Reef City, The Wilds, Wemmerpan and you will probably enjoy all the shopping malls."

"Have you been to all the places you've mentioned?"

"No, actually I haven't. I've learned from the locals that some of the best places, like The Wilds and Wemmerpan are no longer safe. Even if you go in a group, you have to be careful and watch out for muggers and robbers all the time. Who can enjoy such a trip?"

Before showing them the rest of Johannesburg we paid a visit to Aunt Francis in Pretoria. Anita was still a teenager, about Chanté's age, when she last saw our mother's sister. Aunt Francis was in the early stages of her illness when she visited us in the Cape. We both remembered how she sometimes lost her balance and had to grab onto something to prevent her from falling. Now she could hardly walk with a walking-aid, and spent most of her time in a wheelchair.

Aunt Francis was happy to see her nieces after so many years and amazed at how grown up and good looking Anita's children were. How time flies, she said more than once. Cousin Stephaney remembered Anita as a skinny teenager the last time they saw each other. They were about the same age and Steph used to envy Anita her body because Steph had a battle against overweight from early puberty. It was obvious that she still had that same battle going on with only partial success.

That following weekend Anita and her children waved good-bye at the airport, wishing they could stay longer, promising they would come again. They saw a lot of Johannesburg, but they wanted to see all. Anita was not convinced Johannesburg was any better than her own, personal opinion of the place, but her children were thrilled. They enjoyed most of the places we visited. Chanté enjoyed Gold Reef City the most, asking questions about the history of the place more than we had answers. Donny was a bit sulky there, because it bored him; he wanted to go on the rides constantly.

Back home Chanté was very excited about decorating their new townhouse. She was highly impressed with her aunt's place in Johannesburg remembering how much it resembled her old doll's house. Looking forward to a visit from me, she used the rest of the school holiday to change the look of their place. She bought house and home themed magazines and collected as many ideas as possible to work with. Since money was no consideration anymore, Anita gave her a free hand. The girl proved to have a knack for this kind of thing because the end result was quite spectacular. Chanté used many of the tips and ideas that she collected to incorporate them into something that expressed her own unique personality.

"Chanté, my girl, I think you should make this your career," Anita spoke her amazement.

"You know what, Mom, this was just what I was thinking. I enjoyed doing this so much I want to keep on doing it for the rest of my life."

****

That was exactly what she did. After matric Chanté chose a good college and entered a course in home décor. She finished the course first in her class and found employment at a prestigious home fashion house. Her three months of probation passed and she was soon promoted. Soon after that she met her future husband. The client, a partner in an auditors firm was so pleased with her work in his house that he invited her to the party to celebrate his moving in to his newly decorated house. Samuel was another one of the partners in the firm and attended the party. Before the evening was over, Samuel asked Chanté to decorate his new house. She agreed and asked: "Where is your house?"

"I haven't bought it yet. You will have to help me with that."

"I can decorate your house, but how can I help you buy a house if I don't know what kind of house you are looking for?"

"You will have to choose the house, because you might be living there." Chanté looked at him as if he had just landed from Mars, which made him laugh. Chanté had never seen a man more attractive when he laughed. Careful not to betray her thoughts, because she knew he might be a very nice wolf in sheep's clothing, she replied:

"I have no idea what you are talking about."

"If you want to decorate it, you will have to buy it first. If you want to buy it, you will have to live in it. And if you want to live in my house, you will have to marry me. What do you say? Do you want to decorate my house?" Shocked and confused, Chanté excused herself and drove home, but not before she stopped at the promenade and walked a mile or two not hearing the waves breaking forcefully on the rocks below her. That following Tuesday Samuel phoned her. She brushed him off. Two days later he phoned again. She brushed him off again, but less forcefully. With the next call, he convinced her to have coffee with him. He wooed her with gentleness and sincerity. Three months later he put a ring with an enormous yellow diamond on her finger and took her to view the first house she might be interested in.

CHAPTER 12

Making Changes

With my brother and his wife gone, my business spiralling downward, I started thinking of making a change also. Every Monday I drove through the suburbs north, east and west of town. I was not sure what I was looking for. Was I going to duplicate what I had in Yeoville? Was I going to do the same thing in another area? I stopped for coffee at a coffee shop in Linden. I took a newspaper, sat down and ordered coffee and a sandwich. As the waitress moved away, my eyes caught a sign that said 'for sale'. What? Is this shop, for sale?

The owner of the business moved around among the patrons, chatting here a few words, enquiring there about someone's wellbeing. It is obvious that she knew most of her customers. They probably visit the place regularly and small wonder, it is a stone's throw from the school. Excellent location! When she stopped by my table I asked her about the 'for sale' sign.

"We've had the place on the market for a while now. There are enquiries from time to time, but no serious buyers yet".

"Well, I might be a serious buyer. Please tell me all I need to know, like business hours, rights, overheads, turnover, net income, so on". She sat down and we had a friendly chat. My order came and she had to go and attend to something in the kitchen, but only after we exchanged business cards and a promise from her to let her agent give me a call soon.

I turned to my food and my newspaper, reading while I ate. On the third page was a report about a famous artist, Francois Verduyn, who had "come home". After decades overseas, he decided to settle back in his fatherland. He was going to put up an art school in Johannesburg.

"Hmm, interesting", I thought. Perhaps I should join him. Then I would not have to start my own thing all over again. Or perhaps he'd like to buy my place in Yeoville. I turned the page and forgot about Francois Verduyn.

I drove around Linden some more after lunch checking every 'for sale' sign in front of every house that I passed. Not as many as I have seen in other suburbs. This must be a nice place to stay. People hang on to what they have. Nonetheless, it seems the property market is still booming.

That evening my dad called. Expecting bad news, because he hardly ever called me, and never after eight o'clock, my legs went jelly. I sat down:

"What is it, Dad?"

"I have to go to Johannesburg ... on business ..." he cleared his throat like he always did when he was unwilling to tell the whole truth and nothing but the truth.

"That's nice. Will I see you?" I cannot remember him having any kind of business in Johannesburg before.

"I was hoping we could see each other. In fact, I was hoping to stay with you while I'm there. Only for a few days". The tone of his voice betrayed uncertainty, as if I might refuse him.

"Of course, Dad, you're welcome". I hardly sounded convincing to my own ears.

"Thank you. I won't get in the way".

"It's okay Dad," I said, "you're welcome. I'd like that. We can chat and ..." and what? Shall I tell him I know about Mom? Shall I apologize for treating him with disdain all these years? Or shall I just ignore it and let it pass?

"Fine, my dear. Then I shall see you day after tomorrow". We said goodbye. I could not help wondering what that was all about. Perhaps it would be good to have him here. I was not planning to start a close relationship all of a sudden. It would be a bit awkward to have a real daughter-father-relationship after all these years. Maybe he did not even want that. But we could talk about business. I could show him the coffee shop in Linden if time allowed. Perhaps he could advise me.

He arrived by meter-taxi in the early afternoon. I had only one class during which he settled himself in the spare room. After that, I went to him to offer coffee. We sat down in my private living room with coffee and something nice from the kitchen below.

"So, Dad, what business do you have in Jo'burg?"

"Err, well, I have to meet an ... err ... old friend, you see".

"What old friend? You've never known anyone here?"

"Darling, it's just someone ... err ... from the past. Someone who happens to be in town right now".

"And I don't know him, do I? Or is it a her?"

"It's a man and, well, no, you don't know him. Perhaps you will meet him someday".

"Someday? Why not now?"

"There are things you don't understand. But you will. Later".

"That sounds a lot like John 13:7".

"What?"

"The Bible".

"Oh. Of course. Well it's true. But let's talk about something else. Tell me about yourself, your life up here". So we talked for a little while about me. Then I took him down, showed him through my place. We sat down again, this time outside under the budding branches of the Jacarandas in the garden. I ordered more coffee. I mentioned the coffee shop in Linden, explaining to him the changes here in Yeoville and my decision to look out for something someplace else.

"I could never imagine such tranquillity in the heart of Johannesburg. It all seems so peaceful".

"It still is, in a way, but crime is starting to take over and my business is not doing as well as before".

"In that case, it would be wise to move as soon as possible. If it is not just a season that might pass, then I think you are doing well to leave before something happens that you might regret; something that might hurt us all. Why don't you simply come home?" I was touched by his words.

"I don't know. I still feel I should be here. It just feels right for me to live here, at least for now. Someday I might pack up and go, but not now. Not yet. I'm just not ready to leave Johannesburg". He nodded, telling me he respected that, but it would have been pleasant to have me back.

"So, when are you meeting this friend-from-the-past?"

"Tomorrow, at three".

"Where?"

"Somewhere in Rosebank, I think. I still have to confirm the address".

"Well, if you are free in the morning, why don't we drive out to Linden and I can show you the coffee shop I told you about? Then you can tell me what you think".

"I would like that. Show me a little bit of your city".

"Fine. Afterwards I can drop you off where you need to be. Then you won't have to take a taxi".

"Sounds just right to me".

The next day I drove by some of the best places Johannesburg had to offer. Being Capetonians and used to the most beautiful scenes in the world, I could tell that he (like my mother and Anita when they were here,) was not impressed. We had lunch at the coffee shop. The bad news, when I enquired why the agent had not phoned me yet, was that they had found a buyer and the contract had already been signed. I was disappointed, but not shattered. There would be other opportunities. At two o'clock we left the coffee shop. I drove through Randburg, just to see what was there that's interesting. I found a road that lead to Rosebank, dropped Dad off and went home. He promised to find his way back to my place.

My father came back just in time to have a cup of hot chocolate with me before I went to bed. He seemed tired and not in a mood to talk, so I did not ask too many questions. The next day he showed some interest in my business, how I ran it; checked on some investments I had made from profits and savings and went over future prospects with me to see if my predictions were realistic. Eventually he sat back smiling.

"What are you smiling at, Dad? Do you find my little venture amusing? I mean, a big time businessman like you could in no way be impressed, right?" I asked apprehensively.

"On the contrary, I am greatly impressed. It's a rare combination".

"What is?"

"Being an artist and having such a skilful business head on your shoulders. Those two don't usually go together".

"It just shows you never to label a person. I must have inherited the business skills from you. I am your daughter, not so?" I said that, not having a need for his approval, but feeling quite happy to receive it.

"That's right, that's right", he said, not looking me in the eyes.

"But your mother was a skilful business woman too you know. She made good money selling property and invested so well that her assets turned into a nice little fortune. Now, may I have another piece of that gorgeous chocolate cake?"

Dad's first visit was the beginning of a pleasant and fruitful relationship between us. It all happened spontaneously. We connected on many levels and found comfort in this new friendship. We became more than daughter and dad, we were friends. We called each other on the phone at least once a week and talked for an hour.

After that first visit, he came back every three or four months just for the sake of fellowshipping with me. We became close and shared precious moments replacing old and bad memories with pleasant new ones. I was the Lord most thankful for providing the opportunity for Dad and me to restore what we both believed had been lost. Would it happen if I did not obey the Lord to come to Johannesburg?

CHAPTER 13

Time to be Creative

I handed each student a certificate at the end of the year, helped my staff find new employment and sold the business and the house in Yeoville. It was very fortunate to get a decent price, especially in that area, I was told. The property market was wobbling and showing downward trends. The decline in quality of life in Yeoville was helping the proses along. Nevertheless, I received more than seven times the amount I paid for the house. The property market was at its peak. I did not know how prices could go any higher, not surprised it was wobbling.

My new house was in a quiet, tree lined street in Linden. It was a big house on an enormous stand halfway up the hill and close to the shops and library. The rooms were light and airy and the kitchen and bathrooms were modern with low-maintenance finishing. Spacious living areas with built-in fireplaces completed the picture in a place where traffic was not heard, only birds chirping and the occasional barking of the neighbour's dogs.

Settled in my new house, I was not sure what I was going to do. It was a lovely December and I just enjoyed having no obligations for a while. It was almost like being on holiday. Early in the mornings I worked in the garden, have a light lunch, and then worked in the house, followed by a dip in the pool. I was relaxed and took life easy. Missing my old home-cell, some evenings I had friends, new and old, over for dinner. Other times I would go out, eat somewhere, see a movie with friends or alone or go to bed early with a good book.

I had not found a new church yet. It was far to drive to Joubertpark twice on a Sunday and it was becoming dangerous to attend the evening service. I never pretended to be a brave person. Since our church grew too big and multiplied into four or five new churches, things were different, though I still found it to be a good spiritual home. It would break my heart to leave the church, but I knew it had to happen sooner, or later. It would have to happen by God's guidance. I was not willing to go out and deliberately look for a new church.

I was just in time to find a new home cell, though. My first attendance was on the same evening the home cells closed for the holiday. It was good to get to know other people and make new friends. There were Martin, Gloria, Selwyn, Mona and Priya, James and the Joubert family. They told me their old home cell had just multiplied and they missed their friends from the old home cell. Astrid and Penny were among the friends they became very close to, but they had to stay with Fred April, their previous cell leader.

The Joubert family were also in my new home cell, Anton, Lindie and their children, Frankie, Heidie and Lara. These people intrigued me for some reason. There was something almost mysterious about them, especially Anton. I liked them from the first moment I met them, but as I got to know them I still could not put my finger to that something that made them different from everyone else I knew. That was, if I could get close enough to get to know them at all.

It was much later that I learned Anton was involved in some covert kind of work for the government or some other sort of organization years earlier. The family just could not shake off the cloud of secrecy that had been hanging over them for so long. I learned this from Lara after several informal art lessons, (and also posing for portraits,) at my house. Although it was clear that the child did not know much, she was never the less uneasy to talk about her home life. They did not talk much about themselves, but Lara had the desire to talk to someone and felt she could trust me. Just like the Hammonds, I thought. They do not talk either.

Once a week I picked up my friends in Berea, except Maggie, on a Saturday, find a place for them to sleep and take them home on my way to church on a Sunday, unless they wanted to attend with me in which case I would drop them off at home after the service. Maggie could never spend the night, because her husband would miss her too much. Besides, she had to take care of Eileen's cats whenever Eileen was not at home. Sometimes Maggie and her husband Peter would take them home from church. Occasionally Peter and Maggie visited me on a Saturday, but always left shortly after lunch, never wanting to return to Berea after four in the afternoon after the smash-and-grab incident they had a few weeks before.

On the twenty-third of December I activated my alarm system, locked the doors and the gate behind me as the taxi arrived to take me to the airport to fly home for Christmas. Maggie told me two days earlier when we talked on the phone that her son who had moved to Cape Town the year before, was coming home. I could hear she was quite emotional about it. She obviously missed him. It was a great comfort to her to have her three beautiful daughters still close by.

It was good to be home, as I have not been for a while. With my mom's sickness and death I went there so often that after she had passed away I did not want to see the place too often. All the memories, the empty house, it was all just too depressing. Now that Dad and I had patched up our relationship, it was different. The house did not seem so empty with him there. I was so glad that I had asked him to stay on. I was happy that he obliged.

The holiday was the best time the Hammond family had had since Mother's death. We all got together, brothers, sisters and all the grandchildren. We enjoyed each other until New Year, made many happy new memories. Edwin and his family went back to England on the second of January. Andrew and Anita returned to their workplaces the same day. Terrence and Stacy returned to whatever they were doing. On the third day of the next year, I flew back home knowing that I would soon have to start planning my future. Oh how I disliked the month of January.

The art supply shop in Eastgate was the only one that I really liked. There probably were lots of shops that stock everything anyone could ever need and more, but I would always go back to Eastgate. Two days after my return from Cape Town, I put the nose of my car in an easterly direction. It was far from my home and I did not like the roads that led to the east. Therefore, I had to make it worthwhile. It was time to stock up properly.

With thousands of Rand's worth of materials; canvas - I bought two full rolls - five big tubes of the colours that I used most, eight 200 ml tubes of white, and several other pre-mixed colours, varnishes, oil, white spirits, handfuls of good quality brushes of every shape and size, rollers, roller covers, pallet and paint knives and bags full of anything that I might need, all locked safely in my car, I headed back inside from the parking garage.

Since I was having a ball, I might as well go all the way. Clothes, jewellery, cosmetics and make-up, one or two good perfumes; none of these were on my shopping list. I was just enjoying myself. I did not do this kind of thing often. When I did it, I did it well and enjoyed it. Impulsive buying was one of my many weaknesses. Therefore, I restrained myself from it as far as possible. But once-in-a-while I just let go. After another trip to my car, that was by now chock a block full to the top, tired and hungry, I went back once more in search for a place where I could relax and replenish my energy.

Fillet mignon, baked potato with cream cheese and salad and a tall glass of passion fruit at Mantovani's; just what I needed. I ate slowly savouring every bite. The last good meal I had, had been in the Cape. Since I had come home, I had eaten sparingly, exercising vigorously to prevent the kilos from sticking themselves to my body, but that day, I spoiled myself, knowing it would not happen for a while. When I ate alone, I often neglected myself, grabbed, a fruit or a cracker, or anything that was handy at the time. That day I lingered over a rich chocolate desert before I asked for coffee and the bill.

Thoroughly satisfied with my day's spending spree - and that for a person without a job, 'very unwise,' I could hear my mother's words - I headed home. I carried everything that belonged in my bedroom to my bedroom, the rest I put in a spare room that I had not furnished. This room was spacious, had a good view of the garden and was light and airy; perfect for a studio. I neatly packed all the painting materials in the built in cupboards, stood the rolls of canvas in a corner, opened a window and closed the door behind me. The rest of the afternoon I spent dosing in a luxurious foam bath.

All the years that I taught art and ran a bookstore and coffee shop, I did not have much time to paint. There was so much inside me that I had to put on canvas. Now was the time to do just that. It was just as well that I did not buy the coffee shop near the school. It would have interfered with my plans to paint.

It was me and my own work and nothing apart from that, would fill my days. Those days became weeks, the weeks became months before I put my brushes down and stood back, empty and with nothing more to give. There were landscapes, seascapes, cityscapes, deserts, rivers, bushes, trees, flowers, wildlife, birds, whatever nature provided, I had put on canvas. As many nature paintings I had made, just as many portraits and still life pictures came into being, paying some of my former waitresses and friends, including Lara, to model for me. What had been in me, was now on canvas. I was empty and totally satisfied.

I looked through the window and observed a green haze among the bare branches. What was that? Spring? Have I painted through autumn and winter not even noticing summer was gone? Small wonder. I worked six days a week, sixteen hours a day. I slept through most Sundays only waking up in time for late afternoon coffee and rusks, if there were rusks. I did not do a lot of shopping that winter. Mostly instant frozen food from Woolworths or prepared meals from the hot meal counter and salad bar every supermarket offered lately. Although I ate little, I did not lose much weight because I was inactive. The only exercise I got was rolling myself on my wheeled stool from one easel to the next.

Being completely exhausted, I contemplated my next move. Shall I go to the Cape, or to Durban for a warm holiday? A shopping spree like in January? No, that did not appeal to me at all. I sat down on the back patio still in my pyjamas although it was mid-morning, with a cup of strong coffee and a bowlful of assorted biscuits. I'd better stop eating starches and get going on the treadmill, I thought. My body reacted to movement the same way a bowl of jelly did: wobble, wobble, wobble.

I half emptied the bowl of biscuits; poured more coffee and mentally made a list of things I would like to do. Having been in semi-solitude for so long, I probably needed to be among people. Running a coffee shop was different from entertaining people. Therefore, I would rather visit than invite. I had not seen my Berea friends more than twice since

December. Once we had coffee together in Killarney Mall, and they dropped in on me one Saturday in May. They probably noticed that I was distracted and not wishing for company. They did not stay long neither did they come again. We checked up on each other by phone only. I had better pay them a visit soon. New local friends and what was left of the old Yeoville crowd had to be contacted as well and soon.

But, first things first. The sparse provisions in my food cupboards had to be replenished. My fridge had to be stocked. I made a mental list of foodstuffs that I needed to buy: fresh fruit, vegetables, meat, fish, olive oil and balsamic or lemons, yoghurt and two or three kinds of pure juices. That was it. No pasta, very few potatoes, perhaps wild rice, kippers or eggs for breakfast and then, off to the gym. I sat back, chewed another biscuit, closed my eyes and gave a sigh of satisfaction. 'I'll start tomorrow,' I told myself and dozed off.

Two weeks later, I packed a bag or two, locked my house and drove away to the mountains. I desperately needed a change of scenery. Why I chose the mountains, I did not know. Not many visitors this time of year, it just meant solitude all over again. Did I really enjoy being alone? When I was working, yes, I answered my own question, but otherwise, no. Before the end of the week, after I had photographed every magnificent mountain from every angle three different times of the day, attended the Drakensberg Boys Choir concert, listened to every song every bird sang, rode ponies till my body ached, I checked out and turned my car in a south-easterly direction. Durban would after all not be such a bad idea.

Not many tourists there either - wrong time of year - but I made friends with many locals, spoke to everyone I met. I enjoyed in general being among the crowds in the inner city or the Indian market. Whenever the throngs of people became too much for me, I went to the botanic gardens or to the beach. I did not stay long before I craved the hustle and bustle of the crowds. After ten blissful days, I decided it was time to go back home to my life again.

****

Fit, toned, bronzed and thoroughly rested I unpacked my car and went straight to my paint room. I sorted the paintings, those to be framed and put up for sale, those to be exhibited right here in my living room. Shortly after midnight, I turned out the light, only halfway through the task.

Some time ago, I found a gallery that was interested in my work. They had heard about me and called to find out if I would like them to arrange an exhibition for me. Of course I would. I packed as many paintings in my car as I could fit in and drove in the direction of Rosebank. They were greatly impressed and told me these pictures would not be enough, could I please bring more.

The exhibition was a great success. I sold thirteen paintings to new, admiring fans. "Lord, how was I to handle fame?" This was all new to me and I was not prepared. I would have to find a way to deal with this side of being part of the art world. I would not allow fame, however flattering people's admiration was, to go to my head. "Help me, Lord to remember there is nothing good in me that You did not put there, as we are reminded in Second Corinthians three, verse five."

Another exhibition was held with pretty much the same results. My work was widely appreciated and I began to make big money. My home gallery was also becoming well known and visited often. People talked about me and newspapers reported on my work. I tried to fly low, but it was impossible to remain out of the picture when my work was becoming so well known.

Word about my work spread outside of Johannesburg. A gallery in Pretoria contacted me and offered to show my paintings there. Again, it was greatly successful. It was at this exhibition that I noticed a face that I was convinced I had seen in Rosebank. I saw him talking to the owner of the gallery. As I turned to ask someone who he was, he had disappeared. Ah, well he must be an art lover and coincidently attended on both occasions.

A month later Anita called me. Have I seen 'Arts and Sculptures Monthly'? I said no I had not. She bought it once-in-a-while, like this month's issue.

"Let me read it to you."

"Read what?"

"The article written by that Verduyn person. He is an art critic and gives regular appraisal in this magazine on all kinds of art. He also reviews on one artist every month. Guess whom did he wrote about this month? My little sister is becoming famous, it seems. Why did you not tell me your work is so popular?"

"What are you talking about?"

"Come on, don't play dumb," she scowled impatiently, "I am talking about your art. Verduyn sings your praises as if you were to be S-As own Rembrandt".

"What, is that in the magazine?"

"Shall I read it to you or would you rather run to your nearest bookstore, get it and read the article yourself?"

"Yes, I'll do that. I did not know my work was being appraised or reviewed or whatever, by anyone". The name Verduyn rang a bell, but I could not place it right away. I knew journalists were writing about me, but only one paragraph at a time on the back page of local newspapers.

"Thanks for letting me know." We talked some more, enquiring about everyone's well-being and said goodbye.

I went my merry way and forgot about this magazine article until I was reminded of it by a friend, Gloria, while visiting her. She told me about the article and asked what I thought about it.

"I haven't read it yet," I told her. She showed it to me. I was surprised to see my name in print in such a classy glossy magazine. I was even more surprised to read what was being said about my work. Quite emotional I thanked the Lord for giving me this talent to bless people.

I went straight home and stood in the middle of my living room. I looked at each painting, trying to be impartial, trying to see what others saw in them, which was quite impossible. No one can see in them what I saw; they were like my children. In no manner could I see what others saw. Everyone should have his own feeling, put his own interpretation to what he experienced while looking at them.

I went on painting but slowly, unhurriedly whenever I felt like it, or had the time. I made a point of getting my social life on track again. The galleries kept on showing my paintings and the local newspapers kept on publishing a paragraph or two at a time on back pages about me and my work. Well, not so much about me as my work; the way I preferred it to be. Until one sunny day five months later.

The phone rang. It was Mary Mullin from 'Art and Sculptures Monthly'. She talked about the review they had published six months earlier and asked if I would be interested to talk to her and tell my story. They wanted to do an article on me, take some pictures of my work; let the world know about me. I did not really want to, but the Lord urged me to say yes. It was an opportunity to witness for Him.

Perhaps this was worth more than anything I had ever done, telling what the Lord meant in my life.

The interview went well. I answered all her questions with as little detail about myself as possible. She took many photographs and was quite excited about what she saw. To the question why I did not open an art school like I had in Yeoville, I told her to drive around the area and see how many offers of art classes were being advertised. I did not want to compete. For now, I just wanted to paint and give all I had.

I asked her about that Verduyn guy who had assessed my work. She told me he was more famous in Europe than in South Africa. He lectured at a French University. Then at some point some time earlier he decided to come back to live in the country where he was born. I asked her if he was a political outcast who had fled the country when so many people had to flee. Surprised, she smiled and shook her head. No, she did not believe that was the case. I asked her how could he appraise my work and write about me without even interviewing me. She looked surprised, but then just shrugged.

Mary Mullin was a backslidden Christian. She was touched by all I said about how the Lord had come through for me, made my path straight, helping me out of difficulties and blessed me with all that I have acquired through His grace. My life had been an easy one. Not all people went that smoothly through life and I was Abba my Father extremely grateful for that, thinking about Anita and Terrence, - even Andrew and Edwin had had their ups-and-downs - but not mentioning any of them.

We talked a little about personal matters. I invited her to come visit our church, as she did not live a hundred miles away. She promised to do so and left me hoping she would. I trusted God had begun a work in her that would not die out as soon as she drives round the next corner. She promised to write her article as accurately as she could, according to the information I had given her.

The article was published in the next month's issue. There was not a lot of the Lord in my life mentioned in this article. I was rather disappointed. She was probably ashamed to write all of it. It was after all a secular magazine and her bread and butter. Mary had to do what was expected. "Lord, how many people lose their faith through compromise?"

Mary Mullin was clearing her desk. She had just resigned her job moments before she was being sacked. The editor refused to publish her article about me the way she had written it. Red strokes all over the thing leaving out the most essential parts; those about the Lord and what I told her His role was in my life; how it was through His grace that I had accomplished what I had. After a hot argument, he allowed her to keep two sentences (the ones that got Terrence thinking many months later). Mary was so depressed that she resigned not knowing what was next for her.

While she was still saying goodbye to friends and colleagues, her phone rang. It was an editor of the Christian magazine called 'Salt and Light'. Rosetta read Mary's article in 'Arts and Sculptures Monthly'. Would Mary be interested in a job in Cape Town, because that was where their head office was located. No longer depressed, Mary left her former office hopping, skipping and jumping. At least that was what she told years later when she did her second article on a member of the Hammond-family.

CHAPTER 14

Enjoying Life

Andrew took his family overseas during the Christmas holidays; the second time that year. Dad told me they had 'lived it up' since Mom's estate paid out. To my question how his business was doing, Dad just shrugged. I wonder what on earth was going on in my brother's mind. Did he really think that money was going to last for ever? When it was finished while at the same time he neglected his business, what would he do then? Why not rather use the money to extend his business? It was certainly none of my business, but I was a little disappointed in my brother's judgment. Where did he lose his wisdom? Did he ever have any? Well, yes he did. When he was young and idealistic he made good healthy decisions, sensible choices. I can clearly remember such instances.

I learned from Dad that Edwin was also changed by his inheritance: quite in the opposite way. At mom's funeral, he said something offensive to Dad. Dad told him to watch out, he was treading on thin ice. Now he believed Dad was going to cut him out of his will. He was keeping Mom's money in the bank and never touched a penny. What he could not afford from his earnings, he refused to even consider buying.

Anita maintained some sort of balance. After paying all her debts, put down a deposit on a town- house - the one with the one-eighty view

- she invested twenty present, put away some to secure her children's future and enjoyed the rest. Problem was she did not enjoy it alone. Lately there was always some young man at her side. She met them at a singles bar or the casino where she spent most of her free time.

I asked Dad how he knew all that. Did they all volunteer the information, like I did? Not at all, he assured me. He had his own ways of getting what he wanted. I asked him whether he discussed everyone's affairs with everyone else. He assured me: "Absolutely not". I was relieved to hear that and wondered why he discussed it all with me.

"Come on, now, concentrate. I am going to beat you. One shot and you're done." I took my cue and aimed at the last three balls on the table.

"No I'm not," I replied and sunk them all. It was a lucky shot as I was not the world's best Poole player.

****

Anita was forever cleaning house. Like Mom, she hated clutter. She threw out everything not constantly in use. At one such occasion, she emptied her magazine racks at the same time Terrence and Stacy dropped in on her just to see how she was doing. It did not happen often, but Terrence felt it necessary to keep in contact with his siblings. Once in six months or so, he would pay a quick visit to all within reach, which of course, at that time, were Anita and Andrew. They never stayed long. His charm did not work on them as well as on strangers and he knew he was tolerated, but not extremely welcome. With Dad and Aunt Emma, he was welcome and visited there also from time to time, but with less enthusiasm.

While Anita was packing the magazines she wanted to throw out into a box, Stacy asked her if they could have them for the guesthouse. Their guests often wanted something to read, especially on bad weather days. Anita had no problem giving the whole stack to her.

At home, Terrence paged through some magazines to see if there was anything interesting that might appeal to their guests. He came upon 'Arts and Sculptures Monthly,' the issue about my work. He was surprised and very proud of his sister. He did not know she was becoming 'famous'. He read the whole article and started thinking. The article loosely mentioned a quote from me that said: "God put every bit of good in me that there was". That it was thanks to Him I had the life I had. It was the only mention of the Lord in the full two-page piece. But it was enough for Terrence. He came to acknowledge how far he had drifted from the Lord. Again. That brought him to a final turning point.

He knelt down and prayed, asking God to help him never to stray again.

"Lord, I don't know what is wrong with me. You have always been so good to me, yet time and time again I forget and go my own way, messing up, because that's all I can do: mess up." Half an hour later Stacy entered the living room, Stevie on her hip, finding Terrence still on his knees. Unsure what to do, she sat down with the baby on her lap and prayed softly. Terrence said amen and got up from his knees. He sat down next to Stacy and smiled at her.

"You know what, Poppet, I have a feeling life is going to become a whole lot better. I know I've said it before, but I don't want to lose focus again. I know I can depend on you to help me. I give you permission to slap me if I fall spiritually asleep again."

"I will do no such thing. I will help you, I will pray for you but I will never physically slap you. I might find a way to spiritually slap you though."

"Whatever you need to do to keep me on track, do it," he said, still smiling.

CHAPTER 15

Restless

I grew restless living the lifestyle I did. Having my paintings shown all over Gauteng and reading about myself in newspapers and glossy magazines was thrilling to a point. It was not challenging. Running an art school, bookshop and coffee shop at the same time was a huge challenge and one that I managed quite successfully. But I did not feel like going that way again.

Sleep did not always come easy. The restlessness that grew in me kept me awake many nights. To make it worse, I often heard neighbours' dogs barking, often followed by alarms going off. Sometimes it was car alarms, mostly house alarms. As I lay awake at night I could follow the path of the robbers being chased by police just by listening to the alarms as they start screaming one after the other. At dusk every evening I locked every door, closed every window, checked and rechecked my own alarm and electric fence. Crime was now moving into the peaceful suburb of Linden as well.

I painted, cleaned house, shopped, checked the stock market, jogged and still felt something was missing. I visited friends as often as I could and felt extremely alone when I returned to an empty home. Maybe going overseas again would help. I packed my bags and flew to Europe. After a few days I got bored and took a plane to Stockholm. I've never been to Scandinavia. This should be interesting. Like everyone who sees the place for the first time, I was taken in by the spectacular display of the northern lights. It satisfied my need for new things for a while.

After two weeks, I was back at home. Perhaps I should explore the whole world. Two months later, I packed my bags again and flew to New York. In less than two months, I saw all of America that I always wanted to see. Sky scrapers; the Grand Canyon; California beaches; Las Vegas the city; the Arizona desert; the Mississippi River, and from there all along the coast to Florida. I always wanted to see the Keys. Driving over the ocean along the Florida Keys right up to Key West was the most exciting experience I had had in a long time.

I felt a lot better having seen new places, experiencing new lifestyles, making new friends. Opening my front door at my return, the house seemed emptier that ever before. Perhaps I should get a dog.

I carried my bags into my bedroom. From there, I walked through the house opening windows as I went. In the kitchen, I checked my provisions. One carton of long life milk. That would do for the moment. I ran the tap for a few minutes, rinsed the coffee jug, poured water and coffee in the right places and switched on the coffee maker. While I waited, I went to check on my phone messages.

There were messages form a few friends who did not know I was overseas and a few who knew and checked to find out whether I was back. And there were several from Gerald Compton. He was back in Johannesburg and wanted to see me. My heart leapt, skipped, then almost stopped. No. I would not call him. We kept in touch for a while after he left, then he got himself a wife and we broke off all contact. What would he want with me now?

Dad also left a message. He wanted to visit me. I called him and he asked me if I could please meet him at the airport in three days. It was wonderful and I was looking forward to having his company.

I went back to the kitchen, refilled my coffee mug, added lots of sugar and long life milk and went to the patio. I sat down and watched the dragonflies hanging almost motionless; then darting swiftly here and there playing over the pool. The phone rang. At first, I wanted to ignore it, but changed my mind. It might be important. It was Anita's number that came up on the screen. I was a second too late. It rang again and I picked up, assuming it was Anita again.

"Hello Francine, at last. I thought I was never going to get hold of you. Have you been out of the country?" My legs turned jelly and I sat down.

"Yes. I just got in from Miami. How are you?" I tried to keep my voice low and as normal as possible.

"Wonderful place this time of year, Isn't it. Listen, Francine, I have something to discuss with you. And then you can tell me all about your trip to the States."

"I don't know, Gerald, I'm probably going to be very busy during the next few days."

"I can wait. I'm back in Jo'burg for good. Look, it's very important that I see you."

"Do you want to introduce me to your wife?"

"You haven't heard." He said it as a statement, not a question. "She left me over a year ago. Married an American lawyer, took my daughter with her. They live in Chicago."

"Sorry to hear."

"It was a mistake from the beginning anyway."

"Still. It is sad when a marriage ends. It's supposed to last forever. Even more so when there are children."

"True. But it takes two and the choice is sometimes taken out of one's hands."

"Do you still love her?"

"I'm not sure I ever did. In the beginning, I was fascinated. We were both pressurized because the union would be so convenient."

"Convenient?"

"Socially, and for business sake. Look, I need to see you. I will answer all your questions over coffee. Can we meet tomorrow, say twelve-thirty?"

"I might not have any more questions about your marriage, but you're welcome to tell me whatever you want to get off your chest. Tomorrow is fine," I said trying hard to keep my tone matter-of-factly.

"Where?" He mentioned a place in Sandton. We ended the call and I just remained sitting where I was, smiling, staring at nothing.

Twelve-thirty was not exactly coffee time. I wondered what Gerald really had in mind. After an almost sleepless night, jetlag and all, I did not look my best. That day of all days, my appearance was very important to me. It would be my first real date with a man. At such short notice I could not get an appointment at a salon. I had to do everything myself to be presentable. I started early as I had little else to do: washed and blow-dried my hair; did my nails and applied a homemade mask on my skin.

Then, very critically I selected what I was going to wear. I chose a green linen suit, short sleeved, a soft green, turquoise and blue sleeveless silk blouse, dark green shoes and bag. The colours in the blouse brought out colour in my grey-green eyes. It was also a good contrast to my coppery brown hair, which I fastened at the back of my head with a brown and golden clip. The make-up I applied very carefully and very subtly; nothing must be overdone. Add to all that a simple gold chain for my neck and an emerald-in-gold ring on my right hand ring finger. I looked at myself in the mirror. Not too bad.

It was a beautiful late summer day, sunny with just a light breeze. I saw him the moment I entered the restaurant. He must have been watching the door for he immediately got up and pulled a chair for me. He had chosen a table in a cosy, private corner. He kissed me lightly on the cheek and pushed the chair gently in under me just as my legs were about to cave in under me. He did not notice.

Gerald ordered wine. The million questions we both wanted to ask evaporated. He started telling me about his new position in the company and that he intended to stay in Johannesburg for good. Then he asked me about my life. He learned about my success in the art world and said how happy he was for me. I told him about my travels, told him I have not seen South-America yet, neither Australia nor the Far East. I just did not feel like travelling anymore. I did not tell him I did not feel like travelling alone anymore.

We ordered food, we ate, we talked, we had more wine and we talked some more. It was not before three-thirty that we said goodbye in the car park and only after he got a promise of another 'date' out of me. It was early in the week. We would see each other again on Saturday. I drove home on a fluffy, pink cloud; my heart fluttered like a sugarbird. This was going to be the most beautiful season I have ever had.

I met Dad at the airport two days later in the early afternoon. We got home just before the peak hour traffic started. Dad told me he had to see his friend-from-the-past again. Would I please drop him off the next day at the same place as the previous time. He seemed tired, so

I postponed introducing Gerald to him to the evening following the meeting with his friend.

The day after he met his friend Dad joined me for lunch and asked me to have a meeting with him in my private quarters. He had some serious business to discuss with me. At first he made small talk mostly about my future plans and life in general.

"Now to business." He gave me two envelopes, a white normal sized one and a big brown one:

"Read the letter first. Then go through the documents in the other envelope, sleep on the matter and let me know what you decide. It is of great importance to me." He pleaded with his eyes. He looked so different, not at all the dynamic, confident decision maker I knew. A strange feeling started growing on the inside of me. He excused himself, said he needed a nap before meeting my new friend, Gerald. With a smile and a wink, he left the room. I took the letter from the envelope and started reading.

'Dear Francine,

I am not well. The doctors predict nothing good. My plans need to be in order should something happen suddenly. I have watched you over a period of time. You make wise decisions. You know how to work with money. My other children, I am sad to say, don't. Very casually and subtly I trained you in handling my business.'

So that was what all the business talk in the games room was about. Whenever I visited home, he always steered the conversation in the direction of Hammond Holdings telling me ever so casually all that was going on there. I read on:

"I cannot trust anyone else. I cannot dissolve or sell the company. Too many loyal employees might get hurt in such a process. I want you to take over. You needn't leave your life, just stay in control and supervise. See that everything keeps running smoothly the way it has always been doing.

Hereby I also give you my part of ownership, which is ninety-two per cent of the business. It will keep you in control for as long as you hang on to it. I will call a meeting together as soon as I get back home and reveal the situation to the rest of the partners who don't already know about you. I have fully informed my trusted friend, Trevor Higgins and my lawyer, Daniel Denton. Please do that for me. That way you will be able to take care of your siblings, as I firmly believe they will squander their inheritance and end up penniless in a few years. The way they have been carrying on with Mom's money, there will be no inheritance for their children.

If you don't want to take over Hammond Holdings, sell your part to any or all of the partners willing and able to buy. Give preference to my trusted friend Trevor Higgins who currently owns three per cent. Should you decide to adhere to my wish, he will assist you with everything. Confer with him before you do anything. In the mean-time, I will train you as thoroughly as I can whenever you visit. I will keep you informed about all new developments by e-mail.

Think it over and let me know what you want to do as soon as possible. It is very important to keep this a secret until I am gone. I don't want to make trouble for you with the other children. If you decide to take over my company, please keep it to yourself until the time comes for you to take over officially. If you accept ownership, please sign also the letter giving me full mandate to act on your behalf so that I can go on running the business as before.

It is a big responsibility. Consider it carefully before you decide.

Thank you,

I love you,
Dad.

At six, Gerald arrived for dinner with Dad and me. The two men seemed to take to each other nicely. Gerald drove us to the airport the following Saturday to see Dad off after a meeting with Daniel Denton and Trevor Higgins - who had just arrived from the airport and would leave again on the same flight with Dad - where we both signed some documents. Gerald and Higgins signed as witnesses. He smiled as he waved goodbye, holding up his briefcase containing the signed documents in a gesture of acknowledgement. I felt awkward and extremely sad.

****

Gerald and I went out to dinner, went for long walks, we drove out into the country side having lunch in small-town cafe's, we saw many movies and live shows together, visited friends and we talked and talked and talked. We had picnics at the botanical gardens in Roodepoort on exhibition days when the cream of amateur artists assembled there to show their best works. Getting to know him was the most pleasant experience I had had until then. He was kind, considerate yet a swift decision maker. He was talented, sang in his church's worship team, often solo, and he was not only a great talker, but a good listener as well. He had that gentle confidence in who he was in Christ.

We were not young and naïve; we both had seen life and know what it was that we wanted and what we did not want. After he left to go back to Cape Town, he thought he'd never come back to Johannesburg. He was also certain I would never return to live there. So he allowed himself to 'forget' about me; be talked into finding a Capetonian girl and was soon introduced to Tonia. She was beautiful, intelligent, witty and pleasant to be with. He did not realize the attention of one man was never enough for her. He found that out shortly after the honeymoon was over.

This information I dragged out of Gerald over several dates. That was enough for me. I did not want to know more. Our feelings for each other grew stronger and that was all that mattered. As I mentioned, we knew what we wanted and recognized just that in each other. After ten or twelve dates, he asked me to marry him and after mock hesitation, I said yes.

He chose a beautiful one-carat diamond and four small ones, gave my own design to the jewel maker and told him to please finish the job as soon as possible. The day after he received the ring from the jeweller, he put it on my finger and we left for Cape Town. We did not need anybody's permission, but desired everybody's blessing. His family received me friendly; his mother welcomed me warmly. His only sister, Cara, six years younger than him, lived in Canada and could not make it, but promised she would not miss the wedding for the world.

My own family was very happy for us. Dad had a glow in his eyes that I recognized by now. It said he was very proud of me. Aunt Emma instructed Katrina to prepare a big dinner. She invited the whole family, including her own children, those who were available.

Anita was sceptical at first and I did not blame her. She had not had positive experiences where it came to marriage, but she quickly warmed to Gerald and was happy for me in the end. I was wondering if they all sighed in relief saying to themselves: "At last!" but it did not matter to me what they felt or said. Gerald and I were on top of the world and that was where we were going to stay. We both received with appreciation their good wishes.

****

Dad told me about Andrew, Anita and Edwin's affairs, and, also, what Terrence was doing with his inheritance from Mom's estate. Gerald and I went to see Terrence and Stacy before we left. They used half their money as a deposit on a guesthouse in Boston, Bellville; another fifteen per cent on renovating, furnishing, equipping and decorating the place. They were doing fairly well. I was happy for them. The place was clean and well organised. During peak season they were quite busy. They were popular among the lower income groups who cannot afford the five-star accommodation in the more exclusive areas.

Winter season it was different. Sometimes there were hardly any guests and they practically had to live on their savings. They were consuming capital that should have been invested to add profit to their earnings. Neither of them knew a lot about managing a place like that. They could not afford a fulltime manager and struggled along. It concerned me, but there was little I could do but to encourage him to ask Dad's advice. Terrence just shrugged:

"Yes, perhaps I should." I doubted he ever would go to Dad.

"Justin is a great help," he said, smiling: "He's here almost every weekend, you know. I'm thinking of employing him fulltime once he finishes school." I smiled back at him: "Ask Andrew's permission first. But seriously, talk to Dad, will you?"

I know I should have cleared Dad from the blame for the divorce. I should have told everybody about Mom's infidelity. But how in the world would I go about it? Terrence needed him, but would not ever go to him again for help. When he was younger, he would use Dad without conscience, not as a son to his father, but as someone who owed him. Now that he had grown up and grown a conscience, he could not bring himself to take advice from the man he believed left him in the lurch so long ago.

Andrew, Anita and Edwin also needed, deserved to know the truth. They worshiped Mom. How can I taint her image by telling them? I owed it to Dad to tell the truth. At some point, I decided reluctantly to call them all together and break the news. 'I'll do it the first time I go down to Cape Town again' I told myself. They must understand why Dad had turned into a bitter workaholic who neglected us all after the divorce. As soon as he became a Christian, he tried to compensate, but of course, it was far too late. No one was willing to give him a chance.

My decision to enlighten them came too late. This morning we buried him. No one will ever have the opportunity now to restore a relationship with him. I felt my heart was breaking. For him, as well as for them. And what good would it do now? What was unsaid must now remain unsaid. Secrets must be buried.

We made plans to get married in the early spring. The wedding would have to take place in the Cape as most of our family, relatives and many friends live there. Most arrangements were in place when Andrew's call came that awful evening less than a week ago, telling me my dad was dying. I phoned Gerald. He made the arrangements for me to catch an early flight. I phoned him once every day and he phoned me once a day until he arrived for the funeral. With our wedding seven weeks away, there will be a shadow of sadness over the day that is supposed to be my happiest.

CHAPTER 16

Francois Verduyn

Now we are back in Johannesburg, trying hard to go on with life as normal as possible. Gerald is affected by my dad's death only for my sake. He liked him, but never had a chance to get to know him well. I feel lost and disrupted. I am also restless, cannot get myself to focus on even the simplest task. Sitting on a breakfast stool, staring through the window is where the tune of the telephone finds me, bringing me to reality, if just for a moment. If I thought it would be for a moment, I was mistaken. I pick up the receiver:

"It's Francois Verduyn. May I please come and see you and talk to you for a moment?"

"I'm afraid it is not a good time. Can we arrange a meeting for some other time?"

"I wanted to come to your house, but thought it best to phone first. I know you are going through a bad patch. It is really important that I see you. I won't detain you long." Upset and getting more so, I have to apply self-control not to be rude:

"I am really not prepared to receive guests or anyone else. I don't have any paintings ready of exhibition and I have no interest in anything to do with art right now. Will you please leave it be and call in a week or t..."

"It's about your dad."

"What do you know about my dad?"

"Let me come and explain, please. I can be there in five minutes." Two minutes later the intercom buzzed, I press the button and the gates swing open. If he insists on seeing me, he'll have to excuse my appearance: sweat suit, slippers, childish ponytail and no make-up. What a sight I must be. But I don't care. And he shouldn't either. He is not invited. He parks in the driveway and knocks on the door. I open immediately, shake his hand and move aside allowing him to enter. I show him to the living room and offer a seat. I sit down across from him. That is when I realize I have seen him before. He is the face that appeared and disappeared so elusively at more than one of my exhibitions. The grey-green eyes and wavy, greying copper-brown hair was impossible to miss.

"All right. What do you know about my father and how," I demanded.

"Getting right down to the point, do you?" He smiled. "That's how I prefer it too. Your father and I have known each other since our student days. We shared a room in a student apartment and were friends ever since. I left Cape Town shortly after we graduated, your father in economics and business management, I in fine arts.

"Yes, I know that much about you. Please continue." Somehow, I feel all hostility towards this 'intruder' dissipate. It is starting to feel as if I know him.

"First of all, allow me to convey my condolences. I know I'm intruding, you are still mourning and I wish I could postpone this visit. I would have liked to get to know you under different circumstances."

"Exactly what I was thinking."

"Well, your father visited me a while ago. I had just arrived from France when he called me and told me we needed to meet. He flew here and I think he stayed with you. A short while ago, he came to see me again. He gave me something and made me promise that I would give it to you after his death."

"He told you he was going to have a heart attack?" I ask incredulously.

"I think he knew his end was near. He told me he'd been having health problems. He did not want to leave anything to chance. His affairs must be in order should something happen suddenly." I arch my eyebrows in amazement. Francois Verduyn shrugged: "That's exactly what he said to me."

"So what did he give you?" I ask hardly audible, not understanding why he would tell an almost stranger about his health problems, while his own family except I, remained clueless. Françoise Verduyn opens his briefcase, produces an envelope and hands it over to me.

"He wanted you to read this. It explains a lot of things." He closes his briefcase and gets up from his seat.

"Is that it, are you leaving? Can't I offer you a cup of coffee?" He looks strangely at me with a half-smile:

"No, thanks. Not today. You will need time to digest all this. Give me a call whenever … if ever you feel like it. We might have things to … discuss. I'll find my way out, if you will open the gate for me, please." He takes my hand and looking intently into my eyes says: "A pleasure to meet you, at last." He kissed my hand and left. The French habits he acquired will stay with him, I am thinking. The moment the gates close behind his car, I open the white envelope, pull out a letter written in my dad's handwriting:

'Dear Francine,

What I have to reveal to you today, might come as a shock to you, or perhaps you have certain suspicions already. The truth is, I am not your father, biologically anyway. I did not become a workaholic after I left your mother. I have always been that way. I neglected her, and the children. Mom used to get upset, and then right down rebellious. That still did not make me see the light. Eventually she withdrew and I sighed in relief, thinking she made peace with my fourteen hour a day working routine.

We used to travel a lot, but always I took work with me on holidays. The phone rang constantly whenever I did not make calls. Mom did not want any part of holidays of that kind any more. So I stopped going anywhere but to work, and she went either taking the children, Andrew, Edwin and Anita, or going all by herself. We grew further apart until that time she returned from France. She was nice to me, I mean, very nice. I thought she missed me and wanted to show me she still cared. Six weeks later she announced she was pregnant.

I considered it a new beginning and tried to make her happy. I even cut back on work, some. Of course, not much, but some. You were born a little earlier than expected, still you were not premature. You were a healthy, six pounder. You grew up looking different from the others, neither stocky nor tall and skinny, copper brown hair and grey-green eyes and facial features different from any ancestor I knew. You had a different temperament, unique talents not like anyone else in the family. Of course, I was suspicious, but did not want to pursue the matter. I did not want to upset the family, did not want to believe there was anything going on.

In spite of your mother growing cold towards me again - because I resumed my former working habits, Terrence was born and I settled into a comfort zone believing everything was fine. Then your mother went to America with a friend just for a short while. That is where everything changed. They attended a Jane Mulder conference and Mom became a Christian.

For weeks and months after her return, I watched her. She acted as if some heavy burden was on her shoulders. She would cry for no apparent reason and at other times, she would just sit and stare at nothing in particular. Then one evening she asked me to come home early. She could no longer live with this burden, she said. There was something she had to tell me.

Some years previously, when she went to France alone, she toured the countryside. She went by train from Nice westward. At Avignon she stepped off to explore that area. It seemed so peaceful; she just had to stay a few days. That was where she ran into Françoise Verduyn, freshly divorced – for the second time. She had known him from university days like I did. In fact, she had her eyes on him before she met me. I don't have a lot of detail but all I know is that they fell in love there in Avignon all over again.

She told me she had to pretend to be glad to see me, because she suspected that she might be pregnant, just not by me. She had to make it seem that way though. She cried and begged for my forgiveness. My ego bruised, my pride deeply scarred, I packed a bag and left the house.'

So it was not "F's" postcards that caused the trouble. What made him think it was? I put the letter down remembering something Mom said when we were in Avignon. She said: "It's the right time of year." That was three months after my birthday, or nine months before the next. She seemed so different then, so far away in thought. I wondered whether she longed for him, whether she regretted letting him go. I read on:

'It was not before I met Christ that I managed to forgive her betrayal. We managed to make contact with Francois and even renewed our friendship. Only then did he learn about you. After Mom died, he decided to come home. Still he hesitated and postponed to take action for years. He told me he left South-Africa because Mom married me. Now that she was gone, he felt it safe to come back, not wanting to disturb the peace between us. She had made it clear to him that what had been between them was over.

As you already know, I am not well. Doctors predict nothing good, so I decided to confide in him so that he can take care of you if something happened to me. Please, be understanding and accept him into your life. He is a good man. He never meant harm, like mom. I carry ninety per cent of the blame in the situation. I am not unhappy to have you, to have had you as a child. Please forgive me for not being there for you when you grew up. I was a real pig-head.

Thanks again for agreeing to take over my company. Set a meeting as soon as possible and get the ball rolling. If you still prefer to stay in Johannesburg, keep in contact with Trevor by e-mail and let him keep you up to date with all the goings-on down here. I know you have the courage and 'in-born skill' to do it. My dear daughter - I still consider you my child - if you read this, it means I am dead. But not to worry, I am with the Lord where I have longed to be for a while. Don't mourn too much and too long. Live your life to the fullest. Be good to my children.

I love you.
Your 'almost' dad.

This is all too much. Yes, I had some suspicions, but nothing like this. Francois Verduyn, my father? I feel like crying, but it's too big, it cannot escape my throat. My insides tie in a knot. My life has been simple just as I wanted it. Suddenly all kinds of complications are being heaped upon me. First Dad's company under my control; now this? Suddenly I'm in at the deep end of the ocean and I have no clue which way to swim, don't know if I can! Don't know which direction the nearest shore is where I can beach like a whale. No wait, beached whales die. I have no plan to do that. Dying is not on my agenda. Not for another fifty years. I wanted to laugh at the thought, but could not.

Francois Verduyn, my dad, my siblings, who are now half-siblings. Do they know? I doubt it. How will they react when they find out? Who is going to tell them? Certainly not I. I'll get the lawyer to inform them. Call me a coward. I don't care.

This man, my real father? He knew all along. He followed me around. Was it he who tipped off the galleries? He knew when he wrote about me in his article in 'Arts and Sculptures Monthly'. Is my 'fame' thanks to him?

A million questions, no answers. Somehow, sometime I'll find the answers. Now I first have to digest it all, process it all. Francois Verduyn. Francois Verduyn, my father. Steven Howard Hammond, not my father. Thoughts churn around in my mind, emotions in my heart until I feel like I am about to explode. I read and reread the letter until it was too dark in the living room to make out the words on the paper.

'Your almost dad.' My 'almost' dad. The dam brakes and the tears stream like rain in the days of Noah. After forty minutes, that feel like forty days, when my cheeks and tummy muscles are tight and sore, do I manage to stop the flow and control the convulsive sobbing. I'd better call Gerald, get him over here and inform him of the turn in my road.

****

Four days after I received the letter written by my dad informing me about my biological father, Gerald and I boarded a plane to Cape Town. I was scared to bits, but it was not the first time I had to do something I dreaded. Just do it afraid, they say. I kept thanking the Lord that Gerald was able to accompany me.

I had phoned ahead telling Andrew, Anita and Terrence I needed to see them. It was urgent. I also asked Andrew to set up an internet-conference with Edwin. He needed to be involved even if he could not be there physically. When we arrived, everyone was present as required and the conference was in place with Edwin. They gathered around the dining table, all eager and apprehensive to learn what this might be all about.

I take my place at the head of the dining table and open my briefcase, facing Edwin's image on Andrew's laptop screen:

"Dear brothers and Sis. I have news that might shock you, but please, be patient and hear me out before saying anything. You all remember the day Dad walked out on us..."

"That's forgiven and forgotten, isn't it?" asked Andrew.

"I certainly hope it is forgiven, by all of you. But now it is no longer forgotten. I want you to go back to that evening, because that is where my story begins. I always believed it was my fault that Dad left us."

"Did not we all feel that way, that it was our fault?" Andrew again.

"Perhaps. But only I was right."

"What? What do you mean?" Anita asks.

"I mean it was my fault, not directly. The reason that I exist, was what made Dad go. To all of you who suffered because of it, I am deeply sorry."

"Come on now, what is all this? How can you blame yourself? Dad walked because he wanted to. How can you..."

"Please, Edwin, I asked you all to give me a chance to explain. Afterwards you can discuss the matter all you like. Do I have your attention and co-operation now?" They all nodded.

"Fine. Thanks. Dad explained it all to me in a letter. Someone delivered the letter to my front door less than a week ago. Perhaps I shall just read the letter to you." I took out the letter and started reading. As I come to the place where my mother's infidelity is mentioned, there was fierce comment and even protest from all except Terrence. He just lowered his head and studied the table in front of him.

"All right guys, please let me finish. There's a lot more you need to know."

"But how can he say Mom cheated on him. Where is the proof? How do we know Mom confessed?" Andrew asked indignantly.

"Yes, we have only his word for it, and what is his word to us?"

"Edwin, I have the proof. Unfortunately it's true. Let me finish the letter and I will show you the rest." I resumed reading. As I ended Dad's letter, Anita spoke for the first time:

"You said you have proof of Mom's affair?"

"Yes." I took out the postcards I found under the drawer in her cupboard after she died. I read the letter signed 'F' and then showed Edwin the letter and the postcards. Then I sent them around the table for everyone to inspect.

"So is this 'F' your real father?" Anita asked without hostility.

"Yes. He is the one."

"Is it the same person who wrote about you in that magazine? This Francois Verduyn?"

"Yes,"

"Have you met him?"

"He was the one who delivered the letter to my house."

"And you never had a clue just like us?"

"No. There were things that did not always make sense, like why don't I have dark hair and brown eyes or fair hair and blue eyes, why am I the only one with a love of art, why was I so different from you all in so many other ways. Why did Mom come to my room the night when Dad left, why not to any of yours, and later, why did she take me to France, to Avignon, probably to show me where I was conceived but without telling me the reason why we were there. Small tell-tale things that became significant only now, with hindsight."

"Avignon? When did she take you to Avignon?"

"That time when we both visited you, Edwin, just after Debra-Ann's birth. Remember? She went with me for a day or two, then returned to spend more time with you and Enid."

"Yes. I recall Enid was quite curious about it, but Mom was a closed book. She never said a word about it. Always steered the conversation in a different direction whenever she was asked about it."

"So," Anita asked, "what is this Francois Verduyn like? Is he a good person like Dad said?"

"Well, I haven't spoken to him much. I suppose I'll have to get to know him better, later. I just thought you all had to know the truth first. When I go back I will decide whether I want to cultivate a relationship with him or not. And, oh yes, he has grey-green eyes and copper-brown hair. Have any of you seen that before?" They all smile at me.

"There is something else you need to know. Before Dad died, he gave me another letter and some documents." I did not read this letter in full.

Stunned silence followed as I read the relevant parts of the letter Dad gave at his last visit to me about my having to take over his company. The part where Dad expected me to take care of my brothers and sister when they have squandered their inheritance, I very cowardly left out. To myself, I thought: as for this request to 'take care of them, be good to them': absolutely fricken not! Not one of them has offered me as much as a sympathy card when they all thought I was disinherited. They are mature, grown up people. They have to bear the consequences of their own actions. Why should I?

"So you're the mysterious new owner of Dad's company. Why haven't you told us before?"

"Dad swore me to secrecy. He did not want to reveal this before his death and he did not want his company to be fought over, that's why he did not put it in his will."

Andrew asked: "What is your next step. Are you going to run Dad's company? Do you really think you can do it?" He sounds just a little bit condescending.

"There's a meeting tomorrow morning. We'll see what happens then."

"And you, Gerald, how will you fit into all of this?" Edwin asks, obviously testing my fiancé.

"As Francine says, we'll see tomorrow. In a little more than five weeks, we'll get married, and her future is mine. I'll support her in whichever way she wants me to. In the meantime she decides for herself what she wants to do and what she doesn't want to do. She is now and always will be in control of her own life." He smiles at me and my heart melts as always.

"I simply can't understand why Dad gave you his company. You should think he'd rather trust his own son with it. What do you know about business?" Andrew directs his question to me.

"I don't know whether I know enough. I'll find that out tomorrow also. What I don't know I can always learn. My future husband and my clever brother can teach me all there is to know." I smiled ever so sweetly in Andrew's direction.

"Would you like to teach me business, Brother?"

"If Marie and I did not have such a full schedule, I'd love to, you know, but..." He cleared his throat and I knew he was trying to find a way out. It is so obvious that he is quite relieved that he did not find himself in my shoes.

"Well, people, if the meeting is over, I'd like to go now. Things to do, you know. It's a bit awkward to think of you as a half-sister and not a full sister anymore. I suppose we'll have to get used to it. Congrats and good-luck with Dad's company, Sis. Go and make a killing. Bye, all of you." Edwin's face disappears from the screen.

The next day I announce myself at the meeting I have called with the partners. After consultation with the chief executive officer, Trevor Higgins in his office, I make my speech, show to all those present Dad's letter and express Dad's wish to keep everything the way it was. At first, there is fierce resistance from some. Following a heated debate, Trevor explains that Dad has trained me and placed him in charge of me until I have mastered all I still have to learn. At least until the next meeting, things will remain the same.

CHAPTER 17

My Great Day

The rainy season is not completely over in Cape Town. But spring is in the air and every living thing is bursting with fresh new life. Gerald and I drove down together. He dropped me off at my house and drove away. He was not allowed to see me during the next three days. What he would do to keep busy I do not know. Aunt Emma and my cousin, Annabelle is right now making sure I am pampered. I am not allowed to do anything more strenuous than brushing my own teeth.

They drive me to the 'pamper parlour' to prepare my body for the big event: mud masks, massages; special skin treatments of all kinds. They have trained Katrina on what I have to eat, keep away what I should not, and all but force two litres of water down my throat every day. Their loving kindness, however harsh, pays off. When the day dawns, I look good, to put it modestly.

Precisely at ten-thirty, slowly, stately, dressed like a princess in a champagne coloured silk and Chantilly creation, adorned with a thousand crystals form Swarovski, designed by 'Buckton and du Toit,' I walk down the aisle on the arm of my father, Francois Verduyn. I do not hear the gasps. I do not observe the sniffing of Anita and Aunt Emma. I do not notice the held breaths being let out. My own heart is filled with the awesome moment when I am handed over by Francois, my father, to Gerald, the man of my future. As he gently pulled the veil over my head, uncovering my face, he whispered in my ear:

"I never thought it was possible that any woman could be prettier than your mother, but today you are. My beautiful daughter; she would have been so proud of you." I look up into his face, smile and whisper back:

"I would have loved to have her here, but then you wouldn't be, and I'm glad you are," then turn to Gerald. For a moment time stall; then move forward in slow motion up to the moment we both say 'I do'.

****

We spend a week at Sedgefield and another week at Clarence in the Free State, the most tranquil place on earth. We have never enjoyed a holiday this much simply because we have never spent a holiday together before.

Gerald gave up his apartment in Hyde Park, I sold my house in Linden. Together we bought a house in Craighall Park and that is where we are driving now going through the mountains of Golden Gate.

CHAPTER 18

Big Spending Begins

Looking back at the years following Dad's death and considering all that happened until now, like a black thread, the line of increasing decadence becomes clear to see for anyone who cared to observe. Except for Terrence, who did not allow the money to make his head dizzy, the other three threw all sense and caution overboard. They started spending and losing money as if they owned the reserve bank. It was sad to watch them taking the downward spiral. It was hard to keep cool and stay quiet.

****

Anita turned into the driveway of her new place of residence on a cliff high above the rocky beach of Bantry Bay. She parked her yellow Lamborghini, next to the red Ferrari of her latest in-resident young lover, climbed the steep steps to the patio where the young man lounged on a deck chair by the pool. Life cannot get any better.

Anita trotted through to her bedroom and put the parcels down on her dressing table. She took a tiny box out of one of the shopping bags, opened it and admired the glittering gold and platinum chain holding a diamond and sapphire pendant. Looking in the mirror, she held it in front of her neck and smiled. Perfect! Carefully she put it back in its little case and put the case in the safe. She placed a tiny box on the nightstand on the other side of the bed. This little case came from the same jeweller as the one containing the chain she just put in the wall safe behind her dressing table. This boy liked jewellery.

One item at a time she unpacked the rest of her shopping. The sheer under-ware went into the laundry. Anita never wears anything that has not been rinsed after purchase. Everything packed away it was time to relax. She stepped out of her shoes, took the sunglasses from her forehead and put them where they belonged.

Dressed in a red and black bikini covered by a matching red and black silk wrap, she joined her young man on the patio. Having kissed him on the cheek, she fluttered down on a deckchair and closed her eyes.

"Mind mixing me a drink?" she asked. Reluctantly the young man lifted himself out of his comfortable position.

"Sure, anything for my favourite woman. What would you like?"

"Daiquiri please. But be light on the alcohol. It's too early to get drunk." He handed her a carefully mixed drink and flopped back onto his chair again.

"So what has my lady bought today?"

"Oh, a little something of this and a little something of that and a little something for you. It's on your nightstand." A smile of satisfaction spread over his lips. His eyes, though, betrayed none of his thoughts.

Although she was hardly wearing anything, Anita couldn't bear the stifling heat. Emptying her glass, she got up, dropped the wrap and dived into the pool. 'This feels great,' she told herself. 'Life really cannot get any better'. She swam a few lengths, slowly and relaxed, just enjoying the flow of the cool water round her body. She turned on her back and kicked lightly with her legs so as to just keep moving. The sky was a deep blue, soft fluffy clouds drifted lazily above.

The sound of a car stopping in the driveway plucked Anita out of her nothing-box.

"Mom!" Anita jumped out of the pool and quickly wrapped a towel round herself.

"Here, by the pool!" she yelled back. Chanté came jogging up the steps, kissed Anita on the cheek and ignored The Boy.

"Hi Mom. You asked me to bring you this." She handed Anita her mail that she picked up when visiting Donny. Some mail still went to her old address in spite of Anita letting everyone get her new address.

"Thanks Dear. Would you care for a drink? There is a variety of soft drinks." Chanté gave The Boy a dirty look.

"No, thanks. Some other time, perhaps. I have to run. Samuel is waiting for me."

"Still house hunting?"

"Yes. But he sounded really excited about the one he wants to show me tonight. Who knows? This might be the one."

"Alright, Dear, let me know as soon as you have chosen a house. I'd love to see it. Say hello for me."

"Bye, Mom. Will do." She turned and without looking back, skipped down the steps to her car and off she went.

****

The townhouse Anita bought in Table View years ago was now owned and occupied by her son Donny. Some of her mail was still sent there. In the garage of Anita's old townhouse is his silver Lancia. Next to the Lancia was the white, sporty Mercedes owned by the girl who was frequently seen in his presence, more so after the gift of the car; and often overnight. The car that Anita almost killed him over when she found out what the quarter of a million rand was for that he 'needed so urgently'. Donny and the girl had just finished their studies and the long, long holidays had begun. (Or rather Donny finished and the girl stepped out shortly before the exams. She was only a first year student, her second try.) 'Who cares about exam results; who cares about finding a job. Who cares about anything?' was their attitude.

The girl parked her car minutes after Chanté left to collect Anita's mail. She struggled two large suitcases out of the boot of the car and yelled:

"Donny, come help me, please. These cases are heavy." He appeared around the corner and hurried to help his girl. 'Be the rescuer'.

"Wow! What have you got in here? Gold bars?" He took both suitcases and started towards the house.

"Why don't you get those cases on wheels?"

"I have those. They are still in the boot of the car. If you can just get them out for me I can get them inside by myself." Donny put the cases down and got another two cases out of the car, took up the first two again to carry them inside.

147

Now this is life! Donny was very pleased that this little beauty queen had agreed to move in with him permanently. With her at his side, he will be the man of the moment at every party. And the next party will be right here in his own place where everyone can see his wealth. Chanté did an excellent job of redecorating the place with the best of everything. He poured himself a whiskey while 'Blondie' unpacked her stuff into his cupboards.

"Want something to drink, Darling?" he asked when she made her appearance from the main bedroom, refreshed and wearing very little.

"Yes please. Something bubbly. We should celebrate, don't you think?"

"Of course." He was on his second whisky, but poured it out in the sink because the Champagne was waiting. He handed her a glass filled with the sparkling liquid.

"Here. To us."

"To us." She smiled sweetly at him, convinced she was getting the better end of the bargain.

"So what's next? What are we going to do tomorrow?"

"How about a little shopping?"

"Shopping for what?"

"For a party. I think it's time for our friends to be entertained. We've attended parties at everyone's house. It's time to give a little back of the hospitality we've received." She smiled that sweet smile that showed perfect, white teeth, but never reached her eyes. And to herself she said 'give a little back, my foot. You just want to show off, Darling.'

"Great idea. We'll invite everyone that's not away on holiday."

"There are quite a few that are back, already interviewing for jobs."

"Good. A party is just what those poor souls need to keep their spirits up."

"Let's do it." Donny wrapped his arms around her slender body and kissed her intimately.

"Wow, Lover boy. Save it. Right now I'm starving. Shouldn't we have something to eat before the alcohol settles in our brains? I haven't had lunch. I want our first night together to be perfect, not clouded by undiluted drinks." She clearly misunderstood Donny, while Donny was thinking 'if you had brains to be affected by alcohol it might have made some difference'.

"Are you going to make supper?"

"What I have in mind is that cosy little street café two blocks down from here. The one where you can watch the sun setting over the bay. It's within walking distance."

"Sure. Let's go."

"And after dinner we can go to the casino?"

"Now there's a good idea. Lucky me to have you." Donny did not know a spider's web was waiting to take hold of him. That was the beginning of an addiction to gambling that would take him down all the way.

****

Back from a dream honeymoon in the Seychelles, Samuel picked his wife up out of the taxi and carried her over the threshold of their new house in Tokai. Chanté kissed him passionately before he set her gently down. The taxi driver entered and put their luggage down in the entrance hall. Checking that everything was there, he paid the driver, adding a generous tip, thanked him and closed the door. Their new life had begun.

Chanté took the cash she got from her mother and invested half of it; the other half went into a special savings account to be touched only in desperate circumstances. She and her husband, Samuel preferred to make their own living. They did, however give in when Anita insisted on giving them the wedding of the year.

Chanté's husband, an auditor bought them a good house in a good upper-middleclass suburb where he parked his three-year old BMW next to her five year old A-class in the double garage. This is one couple without greed and not taken in by sudden wealth. They did well for themselves and lived comfortably without help from out-side.

Chanté insisted that he take part in buying furniture for the new house, but did most of the decorating herself. They started their new life together, contented with what they earned themselves and planning to go on the way they have always lived. If they wanted something, they would work, save and then buy.

****

Andrew was a little grumpy about the new management of his father's company, but only for the show. Thirty-seven-and-a-half million Rand takes one a long way towards forgiveness. He sold his company after a while and retired early. Time to see the world. Of course Marie would not hear of leaving the children behind on their travels around the world in their own private jet. Therefore, the two private tutors had to travel along. Education would continue.

Andrew was as excited as a toddler in an ice-cream factory. He stormed up the stairs in search of his wife, finding her in her study where she always worked this time of the day.

"Guess what! It's coming. The plane will be delivered tomorrow. It still feels like a dream. But now it's a dream that has become reality. Can you believe it?" Marie smiled at her husband's childlike enthusiasm.

"It is hard to believe, isn't it?"

"Will you come with me to take possession?"

"What time do they expect you?"

"Mid-afternoon, round about three-thirty, four o'clock. And after that you and I can go celebrate."

"All right. I'll get the child minder. It seems to me we will not be home early."

"Good. I'll take the children to see the plane on Friday after school. Just think about it, Darling, our very own jet aeroplane. It's what I've always wanted."

"You should have pursued your dream when you were young. You should have become an airline pilot, then you wouldn't have to find pilots to fly your plane. Have you found suitable people yet?"

"No, but I have two coming in for an interview on Monday. I do hope they will be the right ones. Now that the plane will be here, they can demonstrate their skills to confirm what's in their CVs."

"Make sure you take someone from the flight school just in case." Andrew smiled at this.

"That might be a good idea. He can help me decide as well. He'll be able to tell whether those boys really know their job or not."

Friday afternoon Andrew collected his children at school and took them straight to the airport except for a quick detour through the nearest fast-food drive-through. He parked his car as close to the hangar as possible and lead the way to the sleek white and dark blue Lear jet awaiting inspection.

"Wow, Dad, this is cool." Justin was highly impressed and immediately started peppering Andrew with questions about the aeroplane. They climbed the steps to inspect the inside and Justin headed straight for the cockpit, sitting down in the left seat. Delia goes to the cabin testing every seat and inspecting everything else carefully.

"Dad, it's so small inside. How will we survive hours and hours in here without stretching our legs? I can hardly stand up straight," she asked.

"We'll make many stops for refuelling and sightseeing. We won't just fly all the time."

"And shopping?"

"And shopping. Of course." Delia smiled for the first time. She wouldn't admit it, but she was scared of flying, especially in such a small plane. The trips they took overseas after her grandmother died, was nerve wrecking for her. And those trips were in Jumbo jets, big and powerful. This little aeroplane looked so inadequate.

"Dad, when will you take us up a bit?" Justin could not conceal his eagerness.

"As soon as I have employed pilots. I wish I could do it myself, but I think I might be too old to train as a pilot."

"No, Dad, I don't think you're too old. It would just take too long." Andrew laughed out loud:

"For sure. It will take ages. And by the time I get my licence, you will be old enough to start training."

"How old must I be before I can start training? Eighteen, like for a car licence?"

"No, I don't think so. A bit older than you are now, I expect. Why, are you really interested?"

"Yes. I think I want to be a pilot."

"Alright, let's think about it. I'll get all the information for you. If you really still feel like it when the time comes, I'll see if we can make a plan. Come now. We better get home. Mom's waiting."

They left the airport with Justin talking incessantly while Delia made herself as small as possible in the back of the car, wondering how she will survive. At home she jumped out of the car and went up to her room without a word. Justin found his mother and told her everything he had experienced that afternoon. Marie asked what Delia's reaction was. Andrew just shrugged, telling her to ask Delia. He was not sure what the girl actually thought about it all.

****

"Mom, do you really expect us to give up our school and friends to go travelling with you and Dad?" Delia complained. She felt insecure away from home. "You're not giving up anything. Just think how much you're gaining. You will see new places, get to know other people, make lots of new friends. Doesn't that sound exciting?"

"Yes, no, I don't know. Mom, how long will we be away? Where will we stay? I don't know if I can stay cramped up in that small aeroplane for so many hours. Not with Justin around."

"You will be too busy studying. You will not even notice the time passing. And don't talk about your brother like that. He is supposed to be your best friend."

"Mom, come on. He is a boy, he is childish and he is forever preaching to me. Perhaps I will enjoy going with you if you leave him with Uncle Terrence."

"You can forget about that. We all go or we all stay. Once we get going you'll love it. You'll see. Just give it a chance. Come now let me help you to pack." Marie opened her daughter's wardrobe to inspect the things that should be packed.

"Mmm. I think your old clothes are not suitable. Let's go shopping."

"Yes! Now you're talking." Delia jumped up and down. Marie watched her with a smile knowing she had used the magic word: shopping. This always improved Delia's mood.

Marie and Delia thoroughly enjoyed themselves in the shops. Delia fitted item after item and Marie let her have everything she liked. The same happened at the shoe stores. She let her buy a pair of shoes to match every outfit. Besides that, Marie was a bit more relaxed about her daughter's choices. Delia enjoyed for the first time buying clothes that looked a bit more like the clothes of a teenager, outfits that might allow her to fit in with her peer group. This utterly overjoyed the girl.

"Thanks, Mom. This is so cool. Why didn't you allow me earlier to buy stuff like this? Oh, Mom, thanks." Back home she could hardly wait so show off her shopping to her dad and brother.

"Hey, Mom, what about me? Don't I get anything new to wear in Europe?" was Justin's response when he saw the heaps of new clothes on Delia's bed.

"I was thinking of taking you tomorrow, unless Dad wants to take you shopping." Marie looks at her husband.

"Son, I'd love to take you, but there are a few things I need to take care of before we leave. But you and I will have lots of fun together once we get going."

"Sure, Dad." Justin smiled at his dad. "I'm sure Mom will know what to get me. I'm not even sure I really need anything. Since it is spring there I can wear the stuff we bought six months ago. They still fit me."

"Nonsense! You go shopping with your mother."

"I agree." Marie said. "You simply have to get new things. How will it look if your sister is properly outfitted and you go around in old, worn out clothes?"

"It will look like I'm a regular boy and she a regular girl. Girls like to shop and dress up and boys don't." Andrew and Marie looked at each other, smiling. Where did we get a child with so much wisdom?

"Maybe, but I still think you should go with your mother. You will enjoy it as much as she does and afterward she just might treat you on something cold and sweet at your favourite coffee shop."

"Alright! Now you've convinced me." With this the boy ran outside to play while he still had the chance.

CHAPTER 19

Emigration

E dwin finally allowed himself to relax and take life a bit easier. He gave up his job: a professorship at the university, and started to make plans to travel. Enid was not willing to follow the example set by Andrew and Marie. Edwin himself was not keen on living out of suitcases too often and too long. Besides, they were both fed-up with cold weather. Their itinerary went one way and ended in Australia. They would spend Christmas with all of us in the Cape, and then go back to finalize their emigration plans.

Life in Australia was getting on nicely for the newest immigrants. It was a sad good bye when they greeted Janet Imri. She had been part of the household for many years. The children knew her from the day they were born and now they had to leave her behind in England. Time would come sooner or later, that the children did not need her anymore, but had they not left England, that time would have been somewhere in the future. Besides, a number of reasons could have been used as an excuse to postpone that day indefinitely. Now, suddenly, the time had come too soon, and the farewell was tearful.

They arrived in Brisbane on a bright sunny day in May. Enid at first felt lost. For the second time she had to give up everything and everyone she was fond of, to put down roots in a different place where she didn't even understand what people said. It took a while to get used to the accent. But she made it a purpose to adapt and help her children to do the same.

"Edwin, dear, I hope you don't mind, but I've invited the neighbours over for a *braai*."

"You mean a barby," he teased her.

"Ah, yes, of course. I forgot. A barby," she copied him with exaggerated stress on the flat 'a' sound."

"Now will you please find out what these people eat at their barbies."

"How must I find out? I thought you have everything under control."

"I have some ideas, but help me out. I don't know everything yet. I don't want to look like an ignorant fool."

"You won't. Just be yourself. Let's do it the South-African way and to the moon with those who don't like it. They know we are not from here. They won't expect us to do things the way they do. They might even find our way of doing things interesting."

"Perhaps, but I want to fit in. I don't want to feel like a stranger for the rest of my life."

"It will take time. Just take it easy, one step at a time. And the sooner you stop calling them 'these people,' the sooner you will feel like you're one of them."

"Yes. I suppose you're right. Well let's get on with it then. Let's have a South-African *braai*. Never a British one."

****

Enid transported the children everywhere they needed to go. She encouraged them to make new friends, but at the same time warned them to be careful and not trust anyone too quickly.

"Get to know them first. Invite them here so that we can get to know them before you accept an invitation," she said more than once.

"Mom, have you noticed how funny they speak? I don't always understand what they say. Why don't they speak English?" complained Tamsin.

"Yes, Mom. I don't understand them either. It's worse than the people in South-Africa. They speak a little different from us, but these children here sound totally different," added Howie. Debra-Ann nodded in agreement.

"Yes, I know. But this is our home now. We just have to get used to it. When I married your dad I had difficulty getting used to the way they speak in England. And I'm sure Dad, when he first went to England he also had to get used to it. But you know, you are young and will adapt nicely. I'm sure in a few years from now you will sound just like them and use the same strange words they use. You will learn quickly and soon you will forget the British English you grew up with."

"Not so, Mom," Howie said. "I like it here. People are relaxed, you know, not so stuck up. But I shall always be a Brit, I think."

"You may think so now, but let's talk again in a few years. You may be more Australian then, than the most Australians. Now, what about schoolwork? Is there anything you need me to help you with?" They answered in the negative and excused themselves, each going their own way.

It took some effort to get used to being Australians. It was a challenge each took seriously and each handled it in his own way. Enid got involved in community work. Edwin got involved in a neighbour's business venture just for fun and to satisfy his need to have a friend. The children of course, had their friends and activities at school where they learned the best ways to fit in.

For Enid it was harder than for the rest of the family. She had to put in some effort to make friends. But her persistence paid off. At a parent meeting she sat next to a woman who seemed to be shy or sad or both. After the meeting she found an excuse to speak to this woman.

"Excuse me, could you please help me out. My name is Enid Hammond, by the way. I'm new in the area and I need to find a place where I can…"

"No, I'm sorry. I have to go."

Tamsin had no problem at all making friends. She simply invited one or two children from school almost every day. Before long she was the centre of a large circle of friends. It so happened one day that Enid's new friend from the parent meeting turned up to fetch her daughter, who happened to be Tamsin's visitor of the day.

"I'm so glad to see you again. I'd like to apologise for the other day. I was a bit distracted. I didn't mean to be rude."

"Don't worry. We all have our moments. I'm sure you had a reason for not being your adorable self that day." The woman smiled at that.

"I don't know about adorable, but, yes, I was not myself."

"Would you like to come in? I just made fresh coffee."

"That would be lovely, thanks." She stepped inside and took a seat in the living room waiting for Enid who re-entered the room with coffee and biscuits. Forgive me but I forgot your name.

"Megan Toerien. And you are Enid Hammond, right?"

"Toerien? That sounds like a South- African name."

"That's right. I am from South-Africa."

"What do you know? I'm too, originally. Where did you live in S.A? And how long have you been living here?"

"I was born in Bloemfontein in the Free State. My husband was an engineer. His company sent him here on a two year contract. He renewed the contract last year. It's now just over three years that ..." Her lips quivered and she dabbed her eyes.

"I'm sorry. I, it's difficult for me. You see, there was an accident at his workplace. He and two other men were killed, several were injured."

"I'm so sorry. How long ago did that happen?"

"Three weeks, almost."

"I am really very sorry."

"No, I'm sorry for dumping all this on you. We hardly know each other. Maybe it's your accent that attracted me. You sound British."

"We lived in England for many years, but actually my husband and I were both born in Cape Town." Megan bit her quivering lips. As soon as she had composed herself, she said:

"My husband was also born in the Cape. In Villiersdorp. He was still a boy when his parents moved to Bloemfontein."

"I can't imagine what it must be like for you. Have you made any plans concerning your future?"

"I am waiting for the school break. Then I will go home. I don't have many friends here. At home there is a huge support group in the form of brothers, sisters and other family waiting for me."

"I'm sure that is the best thing for you to do."

Enid told Megan she went to the parent meeting to meet people, Australian people, whom she might befriend and the only one she met was a South-African who didn't plan to stay, so much for improving her social life. They had a good laugh and kept on exchanging stories about life here in their new country and how to fit in among strangers. It was quite late when Megan left with her little girl. They promised to stay in contact.

CHAPTER 20

Terrence and Stacy

Terrence was the one once more to surprise us all. He did not buy a mansion on a hill. He did not buy two fast Italian cars, jewellery or furs. He did not desire to travel the world. Instead, he stayed in the same guesthouse in Boston, Bellville where he had been for years. The changes he made, surprised us even more.

For the guesthouse, he hired a manager and a housekeeper as well as a cook and two extra cleaners. The upper level of the house remained the same, except that Stevie now will have his own room and bathroom. They didn't need the income from that room anymore and Stevie was growing up. He needed a room of his own. The three remaining bedrooms were separated from their own living quarters by a security gate, - just like his sister did in her house in Yeoville years ago. Terrence was considering installing a mini bathroom in the biggest one to make the place more attractive to prospective guests.

On the ground level, he had two rooms separated from the rest, to be made soundproof so that the guests of the guesthouse part of the place would not be disturbed. Down stairs there remain only two rooms for guests. Another room was converted into a place where a band can perform with stage, chairs and all the necessary sound equipment. Here in this room a band would be entertaining guests as well as anyone from outside who would be willing to pay a small amount to attend a concert.

All his years in the music-business finally paid off. Now the knowledge came in quite handy. In one of the soundproofed rooms he installed recording equipment. He made an effort to learn all there is to know about the recording side of the business.

His dream was to find as much talent as possible in the poorer areas of town and get the children off the streets by teaching them music and getting them involved in his own band. The second soundproofed room were used for music lessons. He had already found someone who can take the classes from beginners to advanced stages. These advanced students would eventually make out the members of the band.

Being involved in the worship team of his church once more, he had great contacts in the music world. People are excited about what he intended to do. More than one of the church band members offered their support in whatever area is necessary. Even people from Tim Tanner's band learned about what he was doing. They were all thrilled and wished him well.

Stacy took charge of redecorating the guesthouse. At first, she was scared to spend money, not used to unlimited cash. She went to the shops where she had always seen pretty things, not being able to buy anything. She would choose something nice, consider the price, then put it back and walk out. This went on for a while until Terrence one day asked her:

"Why haven't you started the changes you wanted to make to the house? You were so enthusiastic a few weeks ago. I thought by now the house would have looked a whole lot different."

"I, …, I don't know. I can't get what I want, not at a decent price."

"What's the price got to do with anything, Poppet? Don't tell me you're scared to spend money. If you are, you're the first woman in history."

"Well, I'm just not used to spending big amounts, you know. It feels so wasteful, so, so…"

"Extravagant?"

"Yes. That's the word. I just can't get myself to pay those high prices for things that just look nice without any other use than just looking nice."

"Come on. We are not going to waste the money. But we are allowed to enjoy it. Just a little bit. Besides, if you do up the house, it's not just for us, it's for the benefit of the guests too."

"You really think I should buy all the nice, good stuff I've always wanted to?"

"Sure. Go all out and enjoy it. Why don't you ask Chanté's help? That girl knows what she's doing. I don't mean you don't, but a little help can't hurt."

"Chanté does not work for nothing. I'll have to pay her."

"Then pay her."

"Are you sure? It will cost a fortune!"

"Sweetheart, listen, I really don't care what it costs. Just make the place as nice as you can and use whatever or whomever you have to."

"Oh, I don't know. But I promise I'll think it over. Then I'll see what I can do. I'm not going to waste your fortune. I refuse to go the way your brothers and sister are going. But it will be nice to have good things, quality things in the house."

"That's my girl. And remember: it is our fortune, not mine. You and I are one." Terrence smiled reassuringly at his wife knowing how uncertain she felt.

"I wouldn't mind if you start buying better quality clothes at more expensive shops either. I don't mean designer stuff to wear at home. But a few nice outfits to go out with, can't do any harm."

"Honey, don't tempt me. You've almost convinced me to spend on the house. Now let's take it one thing at a time."

"In that case, start with the clothes and leave the house for later. You worked so hard all your life. It's time you reap a little. Tomorrow you take the car and go to Canal Walk and treat yourself on something nice."

"What's wrong with Parow Centre? It's where we always do our business."

"Nothing. But it's just a shopping centre. Canal Walk is an experience. And after a proper spending spree you go sit in a fancy restaurant and have a nice lunch."

"No way. I'll have lunch at Wimpy. If you want me to eat out at a fancy place, you take me. We get a babysitter, dress up and go eat out at a nice place." Stacy's eyes sparkled as she tugged at Terrence's sleeve. "What do you say about that?"

"That's my girl. Now you're talking. Let's do it Friday." Stacy's mood had changed from hand-wringing nervousness to almost childlike excitement. A new life had begun for her. No more turning cents, no more worrying about next month's bills. It felt so good to relax and know God had provided like He always did. But old habits did not die easily. She tensed up at the mere thought of going on a shopping spree, unlimited funds or not.

Stacy parked the car in the carport, took several parcels from the boot and with a glow of satisfaction in her eyes, climbed the stairs to her bedroom. One by one she took the dresses out of the shopping bags, held it up in front of her, looking in the mirror, then set it down again on the bed in a neat pile. With every dress she whispered 'thank you, Yeshua'. Carefully she snipped the price tags off and took the dresses to the laundry where she gently pressed them down in soapy water, rinsed them once, a second time in fabric softener and hung them on hangers to drip dry.

Back in her room she pulled closer some more shopping bags and shook them out on the bed. Small pants and shirts fell in a heap on her bed. She smiled broadly at the thought of dressing her little boy in his new outfits. He was going to look so cute. But first they will have to get washed also. So, off to the laundry again. This job can be done by the washing machine and tumble dryer. As if programmed, she heard a screech and little footsteps on the staircase followed by heavier ones.

"Mommy, Mommy, Mommy."

"Hallooo. Stacy, are you up there?"

"In the laundry," she called back.

"Well? Did you enjoy your trip?" Terrence asked his wife, kissing her on the temple. She pointed to the hanging dresses while picking up the toddler and hugging him.

"What do you think? Aren't they pretty?" she asked, smiling, eyes sparkling.

"Hmm, yea, not bad."

"Don't you like them?" Her smile dropped, eyes big with disappointment.

"I think they are quite pretty. But on you they will look a whole lot better than on hangers. I can't wait to see them on you." Stacy slapped him playfully on his arm:

"Beast! I thought you didn't like them."

"Oh, I like them. But as I've said. On you they will look much better. Like everything you wear. You will look good in sack cloth."

"Flatterer!"

"No, Poppet. I mean it. You are beautiful just as you are. But I'm very glad you spent money on yourself. You deserve it. And this is not the last time, only the beginning. I want you to go once a week or so and get yourself something nice, make-up, jewellery or whatever you want. Pamper yourself a bit."

"Do you want me to look rich, just because we are?" she asked, big eyed and serious, wondering how she got herself to use the word 'rich' in context with herself.

"No. You have always been rich. Now you just have money. Enjoy it."

"Mommy I'm hungry."

"Come, let's go see what we can make for supper."

****

Stacy refused to go shopping every week like Terrence told her to do. It took her a month to work up the courage to go again. And this time she decided to be bold and do what Terrence suggested, she went to Canal Walk. So here she was in the big shopping centre walking from Foschini's, to Truworth's, to Edgars, to Milady's, to Jet, to Pep, to Ackerman's, to Woolworths, to Mr. Price and out of habit, watching out for price reduces. Just so that Terrence would not be upset with her, she bought a small item at almost every one of those shops.

Like the first time, she bought a bagful of the cutest items she could find for Stevie, which were not many. It amazed her that there was such a large variety of pretty clothes for girls, but for boys there was little variety and hardly anything really cute. Boy's clothes in all the shops are so dull and without imagination even at her favourite shops. And then you get clothes with all sorts of evil pictures, symbols and words printed on them. There was not a chance that she would ever dress her precious little boy in any of those.

For herself she found a few more pieces at Mr. Price and a few at Woolworths. 'Oh, goodness,' she said to herself, 'how can anyone spend so much money on clothes? Just look at these prices.' Thinking back she remembered a time when she bought clothes at many of those shops, but the prices have soared since then. Not that the prices of supermarket clothes did not go up. Some of those, too, have become just as expensive. These thoughts spun around in her mind as she went from shop to shop. The experience was so overwhelming that she turned on her heels to run out to her car and go home. But as she turned, she almost knocked over a woman coming from the other direction.

"Anita! I'm so sorry."

"Hello Stacy. Nice to see you," Anita said with a tiny smile. "I see you're on a shopping spree. Good. Enjoy it. Say, I haven't seen you and Terrence in a while. How about having coffee with me."

"Actually I'm finished. I was just on my way … "

"Come on. Relax. You look so tense. Who's looking after Stevie?"

"He's at home with Terrence."

"Excellent! Then you have nothing to worry about. Come join me. I was supposed to meet a friend but she cancelled. You and I can just as well do some catching up." Anita seemed so friendly and convincing that Stacy could not think of a polite way to excuse herself. 'Better tag along, then,' she told herself.

"Sure, why not."

"Let's just pop in at Stanford's first. I bought something yesterday, but it's coming loose at the seam. It's such a *schlep* to exchange. And I wouldn't have bothered if I didn't have to come anyway. So now that I'm here, I might as well get value for my money, don't you think?"

"Of course. Absolutely," is all Stacy could think of to say.

"Just don't think I always buy clothes here. I was with a friend and saw something cute. There is always the possibility that you might bump into someone wearing exactly the same outfit as you. I don't want to run that risk. I have two boutiques where I have been buying my clothes for quite some time. One even designs for me whenever I need something special. I found a third boutique with amazingly beautiful clothes. Very original. Of course they charge original prices, be assured. But what the heck, I have money that begs to be spent." Stacy just nodded and moved along.

After the exchange, Anita decided to browse a bit. She found something that she liked, found the right size and held it out to Stacy.

"I think you will look good in this. Come on, fit it on." Stacy did not know what to say and let herself be bullied into the fitting room.

"Give me your parcels. I'll keep them for you while you're in there. Come out and show me. And if you like it, keep it on. Don't even bother to change back into your old dress." Speechless, Stacy obeyed.

"Well, what do you think," she asked coming out of the fitting room.

"Great! You look great. Let me take the price tag off so they can scan it at the checkout."

"Actually, I would like to rinse it before I wear it."

"Of course. I usually do too. Just thought you look so good. You will take my brother's breath away when you walk in there wearing this. All right. Change back. I'm not in a hurry."

From Stanford's they went and found a place to sit down, have coffee and a chat and let their feet rest. It was one of those expensive looking places where Stacy would never dream of entering. They ordered coffee, Anita a salad and Stacy a sandwich. Anita took the lead and kept the conversation going, trying her best to make Stacy feel comfortable. Stacy tried her best to respond appropriately. She managed to relax hoping Anita did not notice how out of place she felt earlier. She even started to enjoy Anita's company. After a pleasant time together, they said goodbye and each went her own separate way.

At home, Stacy unpacked her shopping. At the sight of the price tag on the dress she bought at Stanford's, she nearly choked. She felt so intimidated that she did not even look at the price, not even at the checkout. Now it made her gasp for breath. The price was more than three times the price of the most expensive item she bought at Woolworths. How can this be? Isn't it a mistake? She wanted to check the till slip, but remembered that Anita paid.

Such extravagance is unheard of. She will not tolerate it. Tomorrow she will go back, return the dress and demand that they credit Anita's credit card. Will they do it if she did not present the invoice? She wondered. Anita might not care about such a rip-off, but she, Stacy Hammond will not have it! She was about to bundle the dress back into the shopping bag when Terrence entered the room. "Well now, aren't you going to show me what you got? What's that you have there? Show me," he demanded. Embarrassed beyond words she held the dress out towards him.

"Now this is pretty." He held the dress in front of her and looked her up and down.

"This dress is made for you. Put it on, let me see."

"Actually I eh, I was going to return it."

"Why? Is there something wrong with it?"

"No, well yes. There is. Look at the price tag." He looked. And he looked again. She expects him to throw the dress on the bed and tell her to return it right away. Instead he chuckled.

"I don't see anything wrong with the price tag. It looks legitimate to me."

"Sweetheart, it's too expensive. I simply cannot … "

"Yes you can. And you will. You can afford this. So wear it. Monday you and I are going to see a movie and have an early dinner somewhere. You are going to wear that dress. But tomorrow you are going to go back to the shop where you bought it and get the right accessories if you don't have anything appropriate to go with it." He handed her the dress, smiling.

"Take off the price tag and throw it in the bin. By the way, where did you buy it and why, if you didn't like the price?" She told him all about her meeting Anita by accident and what followed. All the while he listened intently, smiling.

"I think I should thank Anita. It's not like her to do something like that, but then again, nothing is really unlike her. She often surprises me by acting out of character."

To her own surprise, Stacy felt excitement rise up in her as she sniped the price tag off. She held the dress up in front of her and looked in the mirror. A smile began to reshape her face. Teeth started to break through the parting lips, eyes brightening, a chuckle escaped and she began to dance. First just a gentle swaying in front of the mirror, then turning and skipping gracefully all around the room, laughing out loudly. Terrence grabbed her round the waist and together they danced and laughed.

Breathless at last, he pulled her in and held her close. The laughing changed into sobbing. Stacy wept against his chest until his shirt was wet. All the while he held her, stroking her hair kissing her on the temple whispering that it was alright. As the sobbing subsided, he felt how her body relaxed, her back straightened and the tenseness in her shoulders soften.

"It's okay, Sweetheart. I understand. It's all too much to absorb at once. No more worrying about bills and food and fuel … and price tags," he reassured her. She smiled through her tears:

"Or what your family will think about us, what we wear or how we live. We can now shop at the same shops as they and wear the same clothes as they." She pulled back and looked him in the eyes.

"We might never be good enough for them, but at least we can look as good as they do."

"That's right. Now put away the dress and I'll help you make supper."

"No need for that. With two guests downstairs we can eat from the guest house kitchen. So, let's go."

The very next day Stacy was back in Canal Walk. She skipped all the shops that she had visited the previous day and headed straight towards Stanford's. Relaxed and light hearted she fitted one garment after another. Then shoes; a handbag or two; belts; stockings and underwear; even a few pieces of costume jewellery. She looked longingly at real gold and diamond jewellery, but she and Terrence had agreed to leave those for gifts on special occasions. It is too easy to become blasé about everything, take it for granted never to appreciate special things anymore.

Now for the sleep wear. There she also spent quite an amount, not even looking at the price tags. Every time her throat began to constrict or hyperventilation tried to set in, she deliberately levelled her shoulders, lifted her chin and took a deep breath.

Looking in the mirror in the fitting room, she was amazed at what she saw, yet something was missing. Something was not right. Something did not fit the whole. In passing a mirror at the cosmetic counter she caught a brief glimpse of her image. That's it! She needed more than just clothes. She needed a complete makeover: Hair, facial, make-up, manicure and pedicure, the works.

She pulled the ridiculous looking elastic from her hair and shook it loose. This felt like freedom. The elastic went into the first trash bin on her way. Never will she bind her hair in a stupid, childish pony tail again. At least, not outside the house. As soon as she got home, she will scour the yellow pages for beauty salons and make an appointment. On her way to the parking garage, she rounded a corner and there in front of her it was. A fabulous beauty salon waiting just for her to enter.

With all the parcels in her hands, she could hardly free a hand to push open the door. Inside she motions to her overload and asked for a business card. The receptionist handed her a card, which she dropped in one of the bags. With a promise to call for an appointment, she struggled out through the door and walked straight to where her car was parked. With everything safely in the boot, Stacy now had to go back to pay for parking. It was just too much of a hassle with all the parcels to search through her handbag for the ticket and cash to pay it. That done, she finally got in the car and drove home, smiling and singing a cheerful praise song: "God is so good to me."

CHAPTER 21

Some More Spending

Less than a year after Andrew showed his jet to his son Justin, the boy started taking flying lessons. He acquired his PPL in record time. When he prompted Andrew to buy him his own aeroplane, Marie put her foot down. He is too young to have his own plane. She imagined him to neglect schoolwork and music lessons and spent all his time in the air. She was partially right. With his own aeroplane he would not find it hard to get someone to drive him to the airfield to go flying.

On the other hand, Justin would spend at least half his time with Terrence. His love of music would draw him to Terrence's place at least half the time, the other half of course in the air. Andrew took him once a week, hired an aeroplane, a Cessna like the one he trained in, and let him do solo flights for an hour at a time. Once or twice Andrew went up with him and Justin felt very proud to show off his skill in the air.

"Dad, when do you think I can start training for a CPL?"

"Slow down, Kid, you just got this one. You need a lot more experience for that. And there is probably an age restriction. Get your matric, and I mean a good matric, not Ds and Es, then we can take it from there. Why do you want a CPL?"

"So I can make a living someday. I have to do something with my life."

"That's good thinking, my boy. But first get your matric not forgetting there is a drivers licence that has to be fitted in somewhere"

"Alright, Dad, I promise if you promise. About matric, I mean. And I'll get all the information and let you know. I mean, about the CPL and stuff. I also want to know about a license for a gyro-copter. Now that's something that interests me."

"Good grief, you plan far ahead, don't you? Before I'll let you go for a gyro license you'll have to acquire at least one tertiary qualification."

"No problem, Dad, I'll do it."

"Just like that, hey?"

"Sure. Piece o' cake." They both laughed out loud and Andrew put his arm around his young son's shoulders as together they walked back to the car.

"Our son is quite a pilot, Marie, I went up with him today. He does everything by the book, doesn't take chances, no short cuts. He's so diligent in keeping the routine and making sure to follow all the right procedures. I'm very proud of him."

"That's good to know. And I'm proud of you too."

"For what?"

"For having the courage to go up with him. Not that I don't trust him, I just don't think I'm brave enough, yet."

"I assure you it is perfectly safe. He will take care of his Momma and he will love to take you."

"Right. Perhaps in a year or two. In the meantime I have already a few excuses ready, should he invite me. But don't you dare tell him."

"Don't worry, it hasn't occurred to him that he can provide entertainment to the family by flying them around. He just took me up to show off a bit. I think he enjoys going all by himself. Makes him feel independent."

"Good. Let's keep sleeping dogs lying then."

"Besides, he has other things on his mind."

"Like what?"

"Like going for the next step."

"Which is?"

"He wants to train for a Commercial Pilot License. Tells me he wants to fly commercial as a career. Isn't that something?"

"We have a very special boy. If only Delia could find direction."

"Yes. Sometimes she worries me. She does not seem to focus on anything, just goes with the flow. And I don't trust those friends of her. They are all a bunch of spoilt brats and their parents are too busy to pay attention. But they have their wallets ready to keep trouble away. We'll have to keep our eyes open."

"Or better yet. Keep her away from them."

"Right. And the best way to do it, is take a trip overseas again. The plane has been sitting in the hangar for too long."

****

Enid adapted to life in Australia fast because of the effort she put in. For Edwin it came naturally. He was a people's person, jovial and at ease in any environment. How popular he was, might be a different matter. He was opinionated and critical, but most people liked him as long as he did not come too close. It was easy to get along with him keeping him at a distance. Among all the newly acquired friendships, only a few showed sincere interest without trying to get to the money.

Most people, however, befriended them for what they could get out of them. With Enid it did not work so well. She saw through the schemes. Edwin, though, wanted popularity and one way of getting it, was to treat, to entertain, to party and to dish out gifts and money. The children followed his lead. When Howie was not on the boat with his friends, Enid had to put up with parties at the house. Tamsin was a real party girl and had her way since her early teens. Daddy made sure of that.

"I already told you there will not be any of your friends this weekend; not in this house."

"Sorry, Mom, but Daddy said yes and so I've already invited seven girls and some boys. We'll just be having snacks, cool drinks and watch DVD's. It's not a major party."

Enid was furious. She stormed out of the kitchen to find Edwin and give him a piece of her mind.

"If I told you once, I told you a hundred times to check with me before giving the children permission to do certain things. Having friends over for whatever reason, is one of those things."

"Calm down, Enid. I presume you talk about Tamsin's little get together on Saturday."

"Yes, Edwin, that is what I am talking about. I told you I was planning a family outing for us. Just you, me and the children. We hardly see each other lately. Every weekend there's a party, either here or at some questionable friend's house. More often than not we split up and attend different parties, one child here another there and you and me some place else. Do you enjoy living like this? Do you enjoy having no family life at all?"

"Stop being melodramatic. Your whining about your silly rules and regulations is getting on my nerves. The children are growing up. Do you want them tied to your skirts forever? I certainly don't want them around till they are grandparents. You have to let go and live a little." Enid was speechless. She managed to control her emotions until she was out of earshot before she let go of the tears burning her eyes. She fell down on her bed and cried. God, what is happening to our family?

Edwin followed her when he realised he had hurt her feelings. He found her in the bathroom washing her face.

"Enid, I'm sorry for the things I've said. I didn't mean to hurt you. Please, forgive me." He put his hands on her shoulders and turned her to face him.

"I'm really sorry."

"Yes, Edwin, I'm sorry too. I'm sorry for what's happening to our family. We're not a family anymore, and it is all because of the stinking money."

"No, Sweetheart. We've struggled to get by. Now we have money to burn, so let's just enjoy it. Just relax. Things will work out, you'll see."

"We've never struggled. We lived modestly, but comfortably according to western standards. We had everything we needed with some to spare. Upper middleclass in fact. With the life we lived, we never struggled. We were a close family, loving and respecting each other. But not anymore. What happened to the respect? The caring about one another? No Edwin. I'm not happy about what is happening to us. And with you against me, I don't know what I can do to reverse the proses."

"Okay. If it will make you feel better, I will try to do differently. We can have this weekend for the family. We'll take the children out on the boat, or do you have something else in mind.

"No, an outing on the boat is fine. I did have a picnic by the river in mind, but the boat is good." She gave a little smile, saying: "at least the kids won't be able to slip away."

"That's settled then. I will inform them."

"Tamsin will be furious."

"She'll have to get over it. I'll handle her since I was the one telling her she can have her party." Edwin turned on his heels to inform the children of the change in plans.

****

Stacy spent a small fortune on clothes for herself and quite an amount on clothes and toys for Stevie. She had her makeover: new hairstyle, cut in a trendy fashion with highlights that covered the mousy look and put a glow in her hair. She learned about the right make-up and the best way to apply it. Then followed the nail-do. She came out looking like a picture in a fashion magazine. Even her sisters-in-law were amazed, raining compliments down on her.

Next it was Terrence's turn. She took him to the shops and made sure he bought a few good suits with matching shirts and ties. If he were allowed to have his way, he would have come home with a dozen jeans, T-shirts, sweatshirts and tekkies, maybe even a pair of crocks or two. Stacy helped him choose a number of chino's, slacks, cotton buttoned shirts, blazers and a pair of leather shoes to match every colour scheme.

It surprised Terrence how much he enjoyed shopping for clothes. She suggested, he fitted, she approved, he paid and together they had a lot of fun, laughing, teasing each other like two teenagers in love. Together they agreed to make this a bi-annual event. Shopping for summer clothes and again in autumn when the winter clothes come in. They ended their shopping trip with waffles and ice-cream at the nearest coffee shop.

****

After all the personal stuff was taken care of, it was now time to fix the house. Stacy did not have the heart to ask Chanté's help. She had a good sense of what goes with what, balance, colour and she knew what she liked and did not like. She got brochures and catalogues, bought home deco magazines and studied them carefully, making notes as she went, planning every room before she made any decisions.

When every room was laid out on paper exactly the way she wanted them, she stood back from her notes and sketches to observe the picture as a whole. Wherever things did not connect to retain the whole or created a breech in unity, she made the necessary adjustments. She wanted the whole house to have one specific look to create a specific atmosphere. Yet every room had to have its own character and still fit into the flow of the rest of the house. Satisfied that her planning was perfect, she started off to the shops to see what she could find.

This was the best part of the adventure; shopping for what she needed to make her house as attractive as she could. It took quite a while, but Stacy was not in a hurry. She knew it would take time and enjoyed every minute of roaming the shopping centres, browsing here and there and never bought anything that she was not completely convinced it was what she wanted.

"What did you think of this?" She always asked Terrence every time she brought something home.

"Beautiful," "great," or "stunning" was his response most of the time. Sometimes he would comment giving more detail of what he really thought. But mostly his comments were positive. Hardly ever did he tell her he didn't like an item. He was very impressed with his wife's skill, imagination and natural talent at that game.

When the guest house part of the project was done, she tackled Terrence's part of the house where he would do his music thing. She was scared because she didn't know what would be appropriate décor especially for the 'concert room' as they called the room where he would have his band perform in front of an audience. The rooms where music training would take place, was easy. She kept it simple and practical. Eventually she gathered the courage to phone Chanté about the concert room. Chanté came over, had a look at the place and made some useful recommendations without charging a cent.

Over a cup of coffee in the sitting room of the guesthouse, Chanté asked:

"Who did the décor of this room?" Oh, no, here it's coming, thought Stacy. Critique has arrived.

"I did. I know it might not look professional, but it was a lot of fun," she replied uncertain of herself and trying to make it off as a triviality.

"I might have done it a little differently, but I think you did a good job. It looks professional enough to me. I didn't know you were so talented, Aunt Stacy. Let me know if you want a job. I might have something for you," she said smiling.

"Why, thanks for the compliment. But for now I just want to stay at home, take care of Stevie, although he is attending playgroup four times a week. In the meantime the guesthouse keeps me just busy enough to stay out of mischief."

"Well, just keep on doing what you are doing and have fun." Stacy did not take Chanté's compliments too seriously, but felt good inside nevertheless. Chanté was not known to be a flatterer; but she usually said things that would make people feel good about themselves.

****

Andrew had just sold his business at a fraction of its real value, but he smiled broadly as he left his office for the last time. It was all over. The battle to achieve, to impress. Freedom was waiting. He drove slowly, unhurriedly through mid-afternoon traffic in his new metallic grey Mercedes convertible. A sea-fresh breeze ruffled his hair. The sky was blue, the trees were greener than ever for this time of the year. Everybody just seemed friendly and happy.

Instead of taking the M3 home from the city, he went onto Western Boulevard, round Signal Hill and onto Beach road. With one eye on the road and the other on the waves breaking violently on the rocks below, he almost missed the turn-off to Anita's new townhouse in Bantry Bay. On impulse he decided to pay his sister a visit. He was free to do that. No more excuses about work waiting to be done and schedules to be obeyed.

"Hey, this is a surprise. What brings my big brother to my doorstep this day?"

"Do I need a reason to visit my sister?"

"No you don't, but you never visit without one."

"Let's just say I am free and I intend to enjoy my freedom. I've just exited the world of labour and entered life."

"Meaning?"

"Meaning I sold my company. Handed the thing over half an hour ago and I am a free man. Coming from there now."

"This is great. But what took you so long?"

"Well, I did have some responsibilities. I wanted to make sure none of my staff gets retrenched. I just hate job losses in the event of a take-over. It took some persuasion, but eventually the new people saw the light and signed the contract that binds them to that effect for the next two years."

"I'm proud of you caring for your employees."

"It caused me to bring the price down to an absolute minimum, but that's alright. I don't need the money. The people need their jobs."

"True. When did you get this new baby in the driveway?"

"About a week ago. Ain't she nice?"

"Very. Of course she does not compare to mine, but she's nice enough since you are going to be flying more than driving. Have you tested the plane already?"

"The day I interviewed the pilots. Taking me up was part of the interview. Since then we've done about ten thousand miles. What a thrill."

"When will I have the privilege?"

"State the time and date. I'll be ready and my pilots will be at your service."

"Right! Let's surprise Francine this weekend."

"Will they be able to accommodate us all? And what about your boy? Where is he, by the way?"

"He's out shopping. And he is not going with. I don't want to stay the night. We just fly in early and back late afternoon."

"Sounds good to me. You phone her and I'll check with Marie. I'll confirm tonight."

"Super. Another drink?"

"No thanks. I best be going. Marie is probably waiting. Call you later."

"Sure. Thanks for dropping in."

Andrew drove home and parked his car in the garage next to Marie's big black Lexus. Her 'ancient' four year old burgundy BMW was replaced a week earlier. He found her in the living room where she was making sure the table was prepared correctly for dinner, tugging here at a flower in a vase, straightening a knife there or fixing a linen napkin at another place setting. Satisfied that everything was correctly in place she went upstairs with Andrew to wash up and fix her hair and make-up. The housekeeper rang a small silver bell and they all went down the stairs gracefully to have dinner together as a family the way they do every evening.

Halfway through the main course Andrew remembered Anita's request to visit Francine over the weekend.

"Is anyone busy this weekend?"

"Why? What do you have in mind?"

"I just came from Anita's. She suggested we all go visit Francine and Gerald on Saturday. How would you like that?"

"Will she be alone?" Marie asks, making her eyes big to motion to Andrew not to mention Anita's young companion in front of the children.

"Yes, absolutely. Chanté has her own life and Donny his. No, for sure she will be alone."

"Then I suppose it will be alright. In fact, I think it's quite a good idea. I've seen Francine's place only twice in all the years since she left. It should be fine to spend a little time with them. Gerald is after all our best brother-in-law. Good family tree and so on."

"Fine. That's settled then."

"Just one thing. You have your plane now; I would like a new house. We have discussed it, remember?"

"Right. We'll start looking out next week. Are you sure you don't want to fix this one up?"

"I have considered it, Andrew, but it's such a mess and it will take ages to have everything done. I know exactly what I want and it will be a lot easier to find the most suitable house, than to fix this one to meet our needs."

"No problem, Darling. You can check the market and see what is available and next week we'll seriously go house-hunting."

****

Anita's return to her own home Saturday afternoon just before sunset caused quite a stir. Her boy, for some reason did not expect her back before Sunday. Anita walked in on a wild, topless pool party, half of the partygoers already half drunk, the rest more than half-drunk. The boy himself was in her shower when Anita entered her room. He was not alone.

That evening the boy had just become homeless, carless but with most of his clothes and jewellery. He left the townhouse in Bantry

Bay with one big suitcase and he left it with his shower companion. Together with the keys to the property, the keys to the red Ferrari was handed back to Anita with great sadness. He had grown attached to that red horsepower.

"Don't be discouraged, Honey, we'll get ourselves another mama," the shower companion said in his deep, melodious baritone. "Next time you must be more attentive about details, alright?"

"Sure. I'm sorry," the boy said and lay down his head on the man's shoulder as they turned into the street. Lucky for them, the BMW they were driving was already paid in full from the generous gifts of cash from Anita. She never found out what the boy did with the money she dished out to him.

Later, in the darkness, Anita folded her small body into a deep easy chair, her knees inches from her chin, and clutched a warm mug of Milo in her hands. 'God, what a mess am I making of my life! To get involved with trash like him!' Crying did not come easily for Anita. Only tears trickled down her face. 'God, what a miserable mess. What must I do now? Please tell me.'

The night was long and mostly sleepless. She tried to sleep in a spare room and used a spare bathroom. Her bedroom will have to be fumigated, she told herself. She would phone Chanté and tell her to redecorate the room, better even, the whole house! How else can she use it again without being reminded? Sunday morning dawned. Without paying much attention, she dressed, applied the minimum make-up and drove to the nearest church. Perhaps she might get answers there.

She did not. So after church she called Terrence and asked if she may come over for a bit. Surprised, he told her it will be good to have her over and that she should stay for lunch. Since there were guests, the cook was on duty and a wonderful meal was awaiting them.

"Just don't come with the Lamborghini. It might attract the wrong kind of people's attention." She arrived in Donny's old car, a twelve year old Honda she bought for him when he started university. She planned to sell it, but had not got around to it yet.

"I wish you would get yourself a place in a decent area. I don't particularly enjoy driving this *skedonk*."

"Want to show off your Lamborghini?"

"No, I just like to drive it. That's why I bought it."

"Too bad, Sis, I'm not moving. You'd better not sell this Honda. Better keep it for days like these when you feel the need to visit your poor, backward little brother."

"Just remember, you used the word 'backward,' not I. I never said you were backward."

"Did you ever think that?"

"No, honestly, I didn't. And I didn't come here today to join your pity-party either."

"Sorry. I didn't realise I was sounding pathetic. Well, what brings you here then?"

"*Ag*, I just felt like visiting you. We don't see enough of each other." Sure, and you expect me to believe you missed me, Terrence thought, but let it go.

"It's nice to have you. We should do it more often. Where is that young guy I saw at your place? Do you still see him?"

"No, he moved out."

"You mean he lived with you?" Terrence should not have been surprised, but he was. He didn't think his sister would go that far. He knew she often had a young man at her side, but living together is different. His heart ached for his sister. How did she wander so far off the track?

"Yes, Terrence he did. But don't you dare judge me. Your past is not so innocent."

"I'm not judging you. Everyone makes mistakes. Though I'm far from perfect, I try not to make mistakes anymore. With practice and by the grace of God it becomes easier. But living with a man is a big mistake, Sis. One that might cost you dearly. I don't want so see you get hurt."

"Well, then you better look away, because I am hurting. The stupid twerp brought his lover, a male lover, into my house while I was away." Anita dabbed her eyes as she spilled the beans so unexpectedly. For several minutes, Terrence did not know what to say. When she had composed herself, he said:

"I'm really sorry."

"I went to church before I phoned you. Unfortunately it didn't make me feel better. What do you get out of going to church that I don't?"

"It's not the church, it's Yeshua. Church can't do anything for you. You have to get to know Yeshua. Only He can give you freedom. And you have to get to know what the will of GOD is for your life. HE has a purpose for you and you must find out what it is. You cannot do His will if you don't know what it is."

She scowled at him telling him Francine is also forever talking about God's will. "If He is such a loving Father as everyone makes Him out to be, He would want His children to be happy. I want to do whatever makes me happy. So, if I am happy then He is happy, not so? And that means if I do what makes me happy, then I am doing His will, not so? Isn't that what freedom is all about?"

Terrence was speechless again. He was not an evangelist and did not know how to answer her. How do you argue with such a distorted view of life, he asked himself.

"I don't have answers for you. All I can say is that God is faithful to forgive our sins if we confess and repent. The Bible says He will remove our sins as far as the east is from the west; He will throw them in the sea and so on."

"Throw them in the sea? Well, my sins are so many, I guess, they probably heaped up so high from the ocean floor that they have already formed a small island in the middle of the Pacific." Terrence was still trying to find something else to say when Stacy entered

"Hallo, Anita. I'm very glad you are here. Sorry I couldn't join you earlier. But now, let's have coffee. Lunch is almost ready. Suzy will let us know as soon as she has everything together."

CHAPTER 22

Time to Go Home

It was now a number of years later. Gerald had reached the top in this division of his own company with nowhere higher to go. I offered him a higher position and he declined. He would rather go back to his head office and see what he can accomplish there. One of the top dogs in the company died and Gerald was offered his position. I had also had a nagging in me about packing up and go "home". Jo'burg did not feel like home anymore with the increasing crime; my car stolen with five paintings in the boot, muggings and burglaries going on.

I went to Berea to say good bye to my friends there. They told me life was becoming difficult. New owners took over the building and in spite of extremely strict security, undesirable elements were moving in one after the other.

Eileen had just returned from Canada where she visited her brother. On her way there she was on the aeroplane with her mother, waiting to taxi out to the runway when the announcement came about the Trade Centre in New York being destroyed and that there would be no flights out to Canada for an indefinite time.

They had a choice: either stay on the plane and await further news in Frankfurt where they would stop over awaiting their connection to Toronto, or go home and wait for the notification of a new flight scheduled to Canada. They went home and after a week, the airline called to book them on a flight that would depart in two days. Her mother was old. She was so shocked about all that had happened, she almost cancelled her trip to see her only son. The delay caused them to miss the nephew's bar mitzvah.

Eileen also informed me that she was going to move back to live with her mother who was slowly becoming frail. Maggie and her husband were moving out. Shri already found a new place to stay; she was moving in with her sister and Greta is looking for a better place in a better area.

****

With so much to do in Dad's company - having accomplished everything in art that I had - which is more than I ever dreamt of - it was time to make some decisions. My favourite art supply shop was driven out of Eastgate by greed; strange changes in the church (it grew so big, it was more like a company than a church, with CEO and armed guards at the front gate) and some other happenings, left us with little reason to stay. Except my father. We grew quite close. Dad was right. Francois is a good man. It was a privilege to get to know him. We were going to miss him, but from both sides there were promises to visit often.

We were in a hurry now to get going. I wanted the first little Crompton to be born in the city where his parents originated. That gave us four-and-half months to get settled in the big house in Pinegrove, Constantia. My father promised to be there to welcome his grandson - he firmly believed it was a boy - into the world.

I was still unpacking and organizing the Crompton baby room when the phone rang. It was Terrence:

"Guess what. You'll never believe what happened."

"No, I probably won't. So tell me."

"Yesterday I had a call from someone who wanted to do an interview with me about my music school and the band for the poor children and so on. She just left and she is going to do a two page article on my work for her magazine."

"What magazine?"

"'Salt and Light'. She took lots of photo's".

"But that's just wonderful. Will it be in next month's issue?"

"Yes. But guess who the journalist is."

"Sorry, I've no idea."

"The same one that wrote about you that time, remember?"

"Mary Mullin? But how? Isn't she with 'A and S M' anymore?"

"No, they fired her. Well she quit actually. She told me the whole story how she resigned minutes before they sacked her, and all because of that article about you. They refused to publish it the way she wrote it. She kicked up a fuss, threatened thunder and hale. The editor started yelling back at her. Told her it was not a religious magazine. Told her to behave or else. Then she did the 'or else' part herself. While she was still clearing her desk, the editor of 'Salt and Light' phoned and offered her a job. She is also here in Cape Town now."

"Can you absolutely believe it? I was wondering about that article. Wondered whether they cut out all the good stuff about Yeshua, or whether she did not have the heart to write it."

"No, she was disappointed when her editor figuratively cut the thing to pieces with his red pen. But I had some consolation for her. Told her, those two sentences they had left in were the ones that brought me to my final U-turn to fully commit to the Lord. Then she asked me if I knew you; weather we might perhaps be related, since we have the same surname and all. She almost went flipped when I told her you were my sister. I did not mention the half-sister-thing. Did not think it was relevant."

"No, I don't think it is. But I'm so happy for you. And for her. This is just great news. Things are really working out perfectly. About this half-sister-thing as you call it, remember the day I informed you all about it? You reacted strangely, as if you already knew something."

"I was cross with you one day, can't remember what about. I think I was about ten years old. I threw a clot of soil at you, yelling: 'Dad loves me, I wish he was here to take care of you.' Mom heard me, grabbed me by the arm and said: 'Dad loves all of you. He loves Francine just as much, even though she's not ... ' Here she checked herself, but for some reason those words stuck in my mind. For many years I wondered what she meant, what would come out if she completed her sentence."

****

During the past years, I have learnt more about business than all the things put together during the first forty years of my life. I was running my dad's company. Things do not always go smoothly and I could not have done it without the help from Trevor Higgins. In the beginning after my 'taking over,' he ran the company while I observed, taking everything in like a dry sponge. I often felt like a little dog following her master wherever he went.

After what seemed like a lifetime and umpteen times of wanting to give up, things slowly started to make sense. Slowly, very slowly I began to actively do my part, relieving Higgins of this burden of teaching me in addition to actually running the business. Gerald also, was supportive often taking care of the household and the two little Cromptons, Robert and Gwen we managed to produce in spite of busy lives.

****

I watched my brothers and sister. As the years went by, their money disappeared like water in the sand. Except Terrance who found a reliable broker recommended by Gerald, and invested his money wisely. Anita threw all restraint overboard. She swiped her handfuls of credit cards up to smoking point buying everything she laid her eyes on. Andrew no longer watched the sky for passing aeroplanes. He bought his own, employed two pilots and off they went. They were more in the air than on the ground at home. Every 'civilized' city with a decent airport became a possible destination, shopping an obligation. Jet fuel and airport tax gobbled up his millions.

Eventually Andrew and Marie had to take a break from travelling. Delia sought out old friendships, Justin either flew a rented aeroplane or spent time with his favourite Uncle Terrence. Marie organised dinner parties at their new house in Bishops Court, which she furnished with stinkwood and yellowwood antiques. In the entrance hall, the size of a small ballroom, she strategically place a huge display cabinet which she filled with dozens of Ming vases and Chinese crafted ivory figurines and artefacts, while Andrew occupied his time looking for ways to invest his money.

These attempts often ended in losing more money than investing. He came home one day from an appointment with some agent of sorts, excitedly telling Marie of his latest venture:

"How would you like to own a villa on an island?"

"That sounds romantic. Where is this island?"

"In the Mozambique Cannel. Many of those islands off the coast of Mozambique have property in the market. And guess what: you are looking at the newest owner of one of those properties."

"Did you already buy a place? Without talking to me about it first?"

"Darling, what is there to talk about? I wanted to surprise you. Would it have been a surprise if I discussed it with you first?"

"No, but we agreed to…"

"I know, I know, perhaps I should have spoken to you first. But you see, it all came so suddenly, I had to make a decision fast or lose the opportunity. Those places are becoming popular and will soon be sold out."

"Alright, don't worry, I'm not upset with you. Just tell me more." He took some brochures from his pocket.

"Come, let's sit down and I'll show you." They sat down at the kitchen table and he shoved the brochures over to her.

"The one encircled in red is the one. It now belongs to yours truly."

"You mean the sale is done and sealed?"

"You can put it that way, yes."

"Without seeing it?"

"The agent assured me it looks exactly like in the photographs. He goes there all the time."

"Oh my dear, it looks marvellous. Look at that garden! It looks like a small forest tidied up and manicured. How big exactly is the place?"

"The whole property is about two-and-a-half acres. Imagine, two-and-a-half acres of tropical paradise just for us."

"When can we go and see it?"

"In three more weeks all the paper work will be done. The children can take a break from their studies and we can go for as long as you want."

"I'd love to live there, but I think for now a week should be enough. I don't want to upset the children too much. They might forget about school work and that won't be good."

"Well, let's not tell them now. Let's wait, say two weeks or till I get the papers. Then we tell them to pack for our little adventure."

"Sounds just right to me. How about some tea?"

****

Her children grown up and independent, Anita started living more freely, doing things she found too much of a hassle before. Like travelling. She visited her only sister in Johannesburg only twice. Most of their holidays they used to spent in a guesthouse somewhere in the mountains or visits to the beach. Shopping malls provided lots more fun. She took her children to visit Edwin and Enid during a July school holiday when they were still in school. That was the only time she ever crossed the border into another country. To her, it was an exhausting experience and refused to do it again.

But now, with no one else but herself to take care of and money to burn, she decided to try a little adventure. Passing a travel agency in a shopping mall, the bright pictures against the walls invited her in. White beaches, tall palm trees swaying in the wind, blue and turquoise water, lazy clouds drifting above the horizon. Friendly pleasure boats in a harbour. Her imagination was in motion.

"Tell me about the Caribbean cruises you offer," she asked the agent.

"Philip, baby, I hope your passport is valid," she said to her lover boy when she came home.

"It is, why do you ask?" She handed him a handful of brochures and watched his reaction.

"A cruse, hey? Have I ever told you that you are brilliant?"

"You don't have to."

"When are we leaving?"

"I think January would be a good time to go."

"Isn't it hot that time of the year?"

"Sweetpea, January is in the middle of their winter. It's in the northern hemisphere." To herself she thought 'if I were so brilliant I wouldn't put up with ignorant young idiots'.

"I know that," he replied indignantly. "But why do you want to go in January?"

"Because it is outside the hurricane season. You wouldn't want to cruise through a storm, would you? If January is a problem for you, I can go alone."

"Come on. I was only asking. January is fine. We'll go cruising in January. Can I pour you a drink?"

"Yes thank you. Bring it out to the patio." He mixed her a Martini and poured Vodka for himself. Outside he sat the drinks on a table and slumped down into a deckchair across from her. Sandy will just have to understand he cannot see her on her birthday on the nineteenth of January. What can he tell her: Sorry Honey, I can't come to your party because I'll be on a luxury cruise in the Caribbean? It will be the last of him and Sandy. He'll have to think of something convincing. Maybe some favourite aunt can be on her deathbed somewhere in Natal, or even better: New Zealand.

"Have you booked the trip already?"

"I'll do that tomorrow. If you're not going anywhere you can come with. Make sure you take your passport with you."

"Sure. Can't wait to get onto that boat."

****

Edwin and Enid came to visit over Christmas that year bringing Tamsin with, not leaving the two elder ones behind as they would have preferred. He bragged about his good life down under, how safe it was, how free and all the good friends they have. He also bragged about all the nice things he had as if he were the only one in the family to own millions.

"Say, Andrew, why don't you buy a boat? Then we can all go see that island paradise you bought. How about we all hop on your plane and fly there? Is there a big enough airport to land a jet?"

"Actually, I don't have an island paradise."

"Why not? Did it fall through?"

"You could say that."

"It's a pity. What happened? How did you lose the deal?"

"It was a scam," admitted Andrew for the first time in front of us all. "If you don't have Mozambiquen citizenship you are not allowed to own property there."

"That's a pity," said Edwin again, "you sounded so excited when you told me about it last time we skyped. The way you described it, it must be a beautiful place. At least you found out in time. You could have lost a bundle."

"I didn't find out in time. The agent disappeared with my 'bundle' as you call it. How is that factory of your New Zealand friend doing? The one you helped finance?"

"It went belly up. Didn't I tell you? I lost big on that one, but I've stumbled across some real, solid, deals lately and at least one of them will start making money soon. I'm sure of it."

"Hey, you guys, you talk too much. Is the fire ready yet? Can we bring the meat? Or shall we braai on the stove?"

"Coals are almost ready, Anita. You can bring the potatoes, but hang on to the meat another ten minutes or so." Anita took the potatoes wrapped in foil out, Terrence followed with a bowl filled with green *mielies* and the money talk continued.

"So, Anita, how's your latest toy-boy doing? How much money has he sucked out of you?" Edwin showed no tact; neither did he ever care about anyone's feelings. Just as well, because Anita was beyond being embarrassed.

"The drunken sod went over a cliff. In my car." Shocked faces all around.

"Don't worry, he's not dead. He'll walk again in a few months. But he'll never drive again. At least not a Ferrari. Certainly not my Ferrari, because my Ferrari is now a heap of scrap metal. He will not drive any one of my cars ever again. I'll pay his medical bills and therapy bills, but he will not come back to my house. He's out." The meat was now on the coals and an appetizing aroma was filling the braai area and also the rest of the spacious lapa.

"How's Debra-Ann and Howie doing? I would have liked to speak to them, but they keep hiding in the TV-room. Are they okay?" asked Anita, deflecting the attention from herself, not wanting anybody to know she had already replaced the 'drunken sod' with a dumb boy called Philip. Enid spoke for the first time saying:

"Howie lost his motorcycle in a bet, so Edwin bought him a bigger, better one. He didn't like the old one anymore anyway," she replied bitterly. I was surprised at the acrimony of her words. It was the complete opposite of the Enid that we knew. She continued in a softer tone, more like the Enid we were used to:

"Debs will hopefully graduate from high school next year."

"What are your kids up to, Andrew?" With this, Edwin tried to deflect the attention from his wife who had been walking around with a sulking attitude for months.

"Justin can answer for himself, Delia is fine, aren't you Sugardrop?. I would like you to hear her singing. Justin, get your guitar and play something."

"Okay, but after I've eaten. And you will join me, Uncle Terrence, won't you?"

"Sure. We can play a few of those new songs we've practiced with the band last week."

"How's it going with your flying, young man?"

"Very well, Uncle Edwin. I can take you up a bit if you like. Just say when." Andrew had to use this opportunity to make an announcement: "I've ordered him a gyrocopter. He is going to start training next year." Just then Marie and Stacy appeared with bowls of salad.

"Andrew, we've talked about this. Are you now telling everybody you are going to buy that machine after we've decided to wait a year?"

"Anyone want anything to drink?" Anita asked sensing some more unpleasantness coming. She called Stevie Gwen and Robert who were playing on the lawn to come and have ginger beer and stand with us for the prayer before we all start eating.

****

They landed on the twenty-sixth of January. The plane came in sideways onto the runway in a fierce South-Easterly wind. The relationship between Anita and young Philip was blown sideways while still on the boat. Reclining on a deckchair he did not notice Anita standing at the railing right behind him on the morning of the nineteenth of January. She could not miss a word he was saying on his cell phone:

"Good morning, Beautiful. Happy birthday. How are you doing?"

"Hi Philip. Thanks, I'm fine."

"You don't sound fine, Baby. What's wrong?"

"Gee, I don't know. Maybe I'm tired of waiting for your call. You say good morning, but it's almost half-past-one. Like you're in another time zone or something."

"Sorry Sandy Baby. I was so busy I didn't realise. Time flies, you know. But I'll make it up to you. I promise. As soon as I'm back home, I'll take you out to some nice place for a whole weekend. Just the two of us."

"That sounds great. I think I can forgive you now. I really thought you forgot my birthday."

"Never. I can never forget your birthday. You are the sweetest thing I know. I love you. Can't wait to get back to you. As soon as this business trip is over you will see me so much, you'll get tired of me."

"And what if your boss sends you again somewhere?"

"Then I'll tell the old girl what she can do with her job."

"You can't do that, Babes. How will you buy me nice things if you quit your job?"

"Only joking, only joking. But I will try my best to cut down on the travelling business trips."

"Why don't you take me with you?"

"You will distract me and I will not be able to do my job properly. Then I'll get fired and I won't be able to buy you nice things anymore." At this point Anita decided she had heard enough. She moved quietly away and flirted with the first male passenger she came across. She didn't feel jealous or rejected. She had been flirting, from the moment she set foot on the boat. Now she did it without a second thought of Philip.

They reached home in the early afternoon. Anita was tired and not in a mood for arguing. So she just calmly told the boy not to unpack his luggage. Instead, he should pack the rest of his stuff and go to his little Sandy's place.

"Tell her the trip was unsuccessful and that the 'old girl' fired you." He was stunned and could not believe she was serious. Only when she slammed the bedroom door in his face, did he realise she meant what she said.

"Can we talk about this?" He tried to reason with her through the closed door.

"We have. I told you to leave. So do as I tell you."

"Can you at least phone for a taxi?"

"Can't you do that yourself?"

"My airtime is finished." How pathetic can you be, she thought. She made the call, then said to him: "You have twenty minutes to get out of my house. The taxi is on its way. Now pack and go. I don't want to see your face again and I don't want to hear your voice again." A miserable ending to a pleasant holiday.

CHAPTER 23

A Losing Battle

B rother Edwin was expected to live in comfort for the rest of his life. Not so. Being a man that could not sit still, got himself a boat and learned how to sail. He also started several undertakings and ran them in the ground. One failure followed another. He often got involved in friends' affairs, friends who knew even less about the business world than he did. Enormous sums of money went down the drain that way.

Where there is money, there will be people. Edwin's yacht was more popular than its owner. Parties on the yacht every weekend, not always attended by him, more often by the friends of Howie and Tamsin. When they managed to sink the boat on a coral reef, Edwin simply bought another.

Enid tried to keep the money from spoiling her children, but Edwin gave them everything they asked for. As time passed, their requests involved bigger and bigger sums of money. The most demanding of the children was Tamsin. She had always been the apple of her dad's eye and got away with everything including truckloads of dollars. She did finish school, but never intended to work one day in her life.

Howie studied science at the University of Brisbane, but dropped out during his second year. Life at varsity was just too boring. There was some living to do and the money prompted him to do just that. He shacked up with one girl after the other, married once, divorced soon after and again jumped from one bed to the next. Tamsin followed the example, but never even bothered to marry.

Debra-Ann managed to finish her studies. She became a beautician, not a vet like everyone predicted. Later she opened her own practice, but left most of the work for her partner, while she spent her days with friends partying away. Yet, of the three she was the least irresponsible. Whenever she was not out enjoying life, she did keep an eye on her own little practice making sure things run smoothly.

Gerald and I were heartbroken when we visited them and saw the decadence of their lifestyles. I loved Howie to bits when he was a small boy. I admired Debra-Ann for her compassion and insistence always to be of help to anyone in need. Money smothered that compassion to a great extent.

Every time Edwin handed out undeserved gifts to the children, Enid got upset, tried to stop him and each episode ended in unpleasantness, if not fighting.

"Edwin, you are spoiling my children. If they end up worthless brats, it will be on your conscience. They are beginning to forget they have to earn a living."

"Calm down, Enid. I love my children. I want them to have the best of everything. They are young. Let them enjoy life a bit. They will work when they get older. Debra-Ann is doing well. Let Howie take a break. He can continue his studies next year. Let our children have a little fun, for goodness sake. All you think about is work, work, work!"

"Excuse me. When the children were small and I needed you, you were the one who could never stop working. If it weren't for Janet I would never have coped."

"That was why I employed her. You were always sick and I had to earn a living. Now we can all relax and have a little fun, but no. Mama says the children must earn a living. Lighten up, Enid. Try to enjoy life a bit. It's passing you by."

"Edwin, please I don't want to fight, but really. You give and you give and they are already forgetting that life is more than holding out their hands to receive what's being dished out. I want their lives to have meaning, not spent in idleness, chasing one party after another. Tamsin is already becoming disrespectful towards me. Whenever I tell her no, she pulls faces at me and runs to you for approval, which she usually gets. I want them to grow up to be responsible, useful citizens."

"They will. I'm sure they will. Just give them a break. And give me a break too. Stop bickering about this. Tomorrow I'm going to chase them off the boat and you and I are going to sail away for a day or two. Just you and I. So instead of hassling me, go pack your bikinis. I'll get the supplies. We can only benefit from spending a little time on our own. How would you like that?" She wanted to protest, but thought better of it. Perhaps he is right. They fight too much and spend too little time together just enjoying each other's company like before the money.

"Good idea. Let's do that." She went to her room and packed a few pieces of clothing, enough for three days and called the regular child minder for Tamsin. To entrust her to the care of her elder sister and brother would end up in nothing but trouble. The presence of the child minder also might deter the two elder ones from getting out of hand.

Edwin and Enid sailed north for a day, admiring the scenery of clear blue and turquoise water, thousands of green islands, some framed by bright white sandy beaches, others rising steeply up from the water. The weather was perfect. A breeze blew just strong enough to fill the sails and keep them moving slowly, unhurriedly, allowing them time to relax and breathe fresh air. Enid hardly wore anything but a bathing suit. No bikinis. Edwin's mention of bikinis was just his personal figure of speech. He himself never bothered to put on a shirt. Round noon when it was hot, they stayed in the shade of the canopy or in the cabin, reading, chatting, watching TV or sleeping.

The second day they moved further from shore and closer to the reef and the islands. The lower the tide, the more islands emerged. During high tide they disappeared again. Enid liked to watch the many different species of fish playing among the coral. The water was so clear, one could see almost to the bottom in places. She took close to a thousand photographs and filled at least three memory cards. What a lovely time they had. No fighting, just relaxing. It was a pleasure to get away from home a bit. Together they decided to do it more often like in the beginning before the children grew up and claimed the boat.

By late afternoon Edwin made a routine check of the weather report. There was a warning of possible foul weather coming. Small boats were advised to watch out and stay close to shore. He turned the boat around and headed back to Brisbane. Before dawn the next morning, Enid woke up to the gentle pitching on a less than flat calm sea. Edwin was already on deck, tacking against a now fresh breeze of a few knots more than the previous day. He smiled at her as she handed him a mug of strong, hot coffee.

"Is there a storm coming?" she asked a little nervous.

"Yes, but it's still far away and heading northwest. We'll probably miss it."

"What if it changes course?"

"We can still outrun it. We'll be home before it hits, even if it comes straight at us, which it won't."

Reassured and satisfied with Edwin's predictions, she went back down to shower and dress in shorts and sweatshirt. The wind on deck is too chilly to have much unnecessary skin exposed. Even Edwin was wearing a long sleeve tee-shirt.

"Want some breakfast?" she asked as he was coming down into the cabin.

"Yes please. And more coffee." She poured him another cup and started preparing breakfast. They ate in silence. Enid did not feel like going home just yet, but the storm compelled them to head for Brisbane and do so without hesitation.

Edwin kept staring to his left to see if any storm clouds were coming crawling over the horizon towards them. By lunchtime white fluff on top of a long, dark-grey stroke of cloud appeared on the north-eastern horizon. The wind grew stronger by the hour and the sea choppier. The Great Barrier Reef took much hammering causing the sea to the west of it to be a little calmer. Yet it made little difference to the huge waves caused by the storm surge of a cyclone. What lies on the horizon might very easily become a full-blown cyclone.

Edwin is still confident that they will reach Brisbane before the storm hits. But just in case they don't, he contacted the closer harbours at Bundaberg and Maryborough to let them know they might have to dock in. Gladstone is already behind them. During the next few hours the storm just lay there. It did not come closer. According to the report on the radio, it was wobbling and predicted to turn north-north-west and make landfall at Cairns. It has just been declared a category one cyclone and named Gregory.

"So we'll make it, won't we?" Enid said with relief. She gets quite nervous when storm clouds start building up. A cyclone is something she has not yet experienced neither does she desire to. And most certainly not on a boat in the middle of the ocean.

"Yes. I reckon we're safe. We'll make it."

They sailed in less than calm; the breeze quite fresh; sky was now overcast. They reached Brisbane harbour in a light drizzle just before sunset. Howie fetched them at the quay and drove them home.

"Is everything alright?" Enid asked. Yes, Mom. Why wouldn't it be? I'm fine, Deb's fine and Tam is fine. She is a real little brat, but she's fine.

"Just asking. What have you three been doing these past few days?"

"Nothing much. The usual, I guess. How was your trip?"

"Very nice thank you. We've decided to do it more often, now that you children can take care of yourselves."

"Stiff competition for the boat, huh, Dad?"

"You bet. You and Debra-Ann can find some other form of entertainment. From now on I claim my boat back. Mom and I are going out on the boat at least once a month."

"Can I have it tomorrow? Some friends want to have a look at the reef directly east from here. Unbelievable scenery, they say. We'll do some snorkelling and so on."

"I don't think that's a good idea. I don't trust that storm. Rather wait a day or two."

"That's no fun. The guys want to go tomorrow. See what it's like in choppy waters."

"No. Typhoon waters are a lot more than choppy. None of you are experienced seamen. Even if you were, I wouldn't allow it."

"Come on, Dad, the storm is moving away from us and already losing steam. And it's a cyclone, not a typhoon."

"It's the Pacific Ocean, so it's called a typhoon. And you are wrong! It's wobbling and building in strength. But let's keep an eye on him. If it makes landfall by tomorrow night, and north of, say Cairns, then you can go the day after. But I'd much rather you wait another day. The water may still be rough and the swells too high for this little boat. Not to mention debris everywhere." Howie did not respond to this. They reached home in silence. Howie excused himself, mumbled something about going to see the mates and discuss some other activity to engage in, except boating. If the weather is good, perhaps they could go for a round of golf.

****

Howie did not play golf the next day. Instead, he found something much more adventurous to do. He fought for his life. After he had delivered his parents to their home, he drove to a friend's house, Tom, the one who wanted to go boating. There was a party going and everyone was in a bold and adventurous spirit.

"So, Howie what did your dad say about the boat? Can we go?"

"No, he's worried about the storm. Said we better wait a day or two. It might not be safe."

"The storm is passing, Mate. By morning the storm will be forgotten. No worries."

"What about debris floating all over?"

"That shouldn't be a problem. We're not going anywhere near where the storm has been. We're going south. So how about it?"

"He won't let us go. And you said due east. Now you want to go south suddenly."

"Who says he has to know?" Howie was stunned. He had never done anything behind his parents back. He shook his head.

"No. I can't do it without his permission. It's his boat. Taking it without asking him is stealing it. No. I won't do it." His friends started mocking him.

"You want your daddy to come along and hold your hand?"

"I thought we are all nice and grown up. But it seems some of us cannot make decisions without Mommy and Daddy's permission."

"Come now, Howie. He'll never know. We go out for a bit and return and what's the harm?"

"Yes, Howie. I need to get out on the sea. Let's do it."

"What's the rush? Why can't we wait a day or two? The ocean will still be there, and a lot safer."

"Oh, I see. It's not your dad. It's you. You're the one who is scared."

"I'm not scared, just careful."

"Don't worry, little boy. I'll hold your hand."

"Lay it off, guys. I'm not scared. What's wrong with being sensible?"

"Is that the new word for scared? Sensible?" They laughed, they mocked, they made Howie feel like an imbecile. For a fleeting moment he thought: 'who needs enemies?' But the next moment he caved in under the pressure.

"Alright, alright. That's enough. You guys have to promise me we'll be back tomorrow before dark. And every one helps clean up before leaving the boat."

"That's more like it. Our Howie is growing up fast. But I didn't plan on staying away that long. Just out and back for the day. You see, it already is tomorrow. So let's pack a few things and get going. Pack the beer first."

Day was breaking when they reached the marina. They loaded their provisions for the day on the boat, checked the diesel and when everything was right and ready, Howie started the motors. Thick low-lying clouds covered the sky form horizon to horizon. The swells were high, but the brave little boat managed easily. Howie checked the weather report. Gregory was still wobbling and slowly building. When he started moving, he simply could go anywhere.

The party on the boat was in full swing in spite of the howling wind and high seas. Howie became nervous thinking the weather should be improving while it was not. On the contrary, it felt as though it was getting worse. With the boat on auto, Howie did not hear the warning because he was not in the cockpit. He had joined the party in the cabin. Gregory was moving. He had reached a category two cyclone and was still building, but now moving slowly, steadily in a South-Western direction.

Waves began pounding the little boat, heavy rain splattered against the windows, lightning flashed in the distance. Visibility was only a couple of hundred meters. The girls started screaming and the brave boys looked nervous. Even Tom, the one whose idea it was, agreed when Howie announced that he was turning around. They'd better get back as soon as they can. They were making slow and difficult progress when a thunderous crash was heard. The boat shuddered and started taking water in.

Someone yelled 'get the life raft!' Another yelled something inaudible. In minutes the boat was sinking and doing so fast. Each managed to grab an inflatable safety vest, screaming and scrambling helter-skelter trying to reach the life raft. Almost all of them made it.

By nightfall Gregory changed course again, going north-north-west. When a rescue-team picked up a little life raft many hours later, Howie was not in it. No one knew where he was, where they had lost him. No one had seen him since they left the sinking boat. And no one could say for certain where the boat went under. No one seemed to care much, just glad to be saved.

Late the next afternoon Howie was spotted on a tiny island about five hundred meters south from where the boat sank. He was hungry, cold, exhausted and except for a few scrapes and bruises, he was alright. He had managed to grab an extra bag full of flares that he knew Edwin kept tied securely close to the helm. Just in case. By the time he had loosened the bag of flares and secured it under his vest, the lifeboat was already fifty meters away.

With the sinking boat under him, he had no choice but to jump and swim. He did not believe he would survive, but he was not willing to give up easily. He had swallowed an ocean full of water when he was thrown onto the rocky beach of a tiny island. There he had shivered through the night and watched the horizon from the moment the sky began to turn grey. Every time he saw movement, he fired a flare. The rescue-team saw his third flare and went for him.

At home he was first welcomed with tears and then sat down for a lecture.

"You don't know how lucky you are. That storm changed course and you went through the outer edge. If it went straight on its path, none of you would have survived. Of course we are thankful that it happened this way. It could have been so much worse. I don't even want to think about it. Now, you have to hear the rest of it. Your irresponsibility has cost me dearly. I'm going to make it cost you dearly," Edwin said, red in the face with anger. Enid kept close by in case Edwin lost his temper and became violent.

"Dad, I'm very sorry. The guys nagged and nagged until I gave in."

"You still could have let me know. What if I went to the marina, saw my boat was gone and reported it stolen? And now I have to lie to the insurance people; tell them you had permission to take the boat. In spite of the fact that you're not licenced, they might we willing to pay out, which I doubt. They will pay if I tell them you stole the boat, but then there will be criminal charges. Is that what you want?

"Tom is licenced. And he is the one who wanted to go out."

"Excellent! Then I can tell the authorities he stole the boat and get him arrested. How will you explain your presence if Tom stole the boat? No, my boy, things are complicated enough. Don't blame Tom. You are the one who made the decision and you will have to bare the consequences."

"What consequences?"

"I'll think of something, be sure of that. Apart from explaining to the insurance company why your friend, who is licenced, convinced you to go out in a typhoon, when he should have known better. I will look like an idiot, because I will have to tell them you had my permission. The chances of them paying out, is less than zero."

Anyway, I have decided you must learn a lesson. I was going to give you your own boat for your twenty-first birthday. But, I'm sorry to say, you have forfeited your gift. I'll think of something else. But a boat? Perhaps for your fortieth birthday. Mom is right. You children are not responsible. Lately we can rely on you for one thing, and that is messing up."

Howie celebrated his birthday five months later with a few new friends. The friendships from the boating episode fizzed out when he realized how little they cared. His friendship with Tom ended ugly when he learned that the purpose of the trip was to meet another boat and pick up a parcel that could not be delivered by regular mail. After all that had happened, Tom expected him to take part in a second try to retrieve the parcel. Howie did not live a moral life style, snorted once in a while with the mates, but dealing in drugs was where he drew the line.

****

Howie got his boat for his twenty-second birthday shortly after he became licenced. It was a beautiful white and bright blue two-hull catamaran with all the necessary safety trimmings and the newest navigational equipment. Howie was so glad, he promised to go back to university as soon as the new academic year opened. It was so good to be at the helm of his own boat. Since he sunk his dad's boat he was not allowed to go alone on the new one.

When the academic year started, Howie was somewhere on the ocean with friends avoiding registration at the university to continue his studies as he promised. The sky was blue; the sea bright in the sunshine and life was an adventure. Who can waste time studying when the outdoors is calling and with so many beautiful girls available?

Weekends Debra-Ann and Tamsin joined Howie and his friends on the boat. Tamsin was still at school and Deb a college student. The latter intended to finish her studies no matter how long it took. She had already failed one semester but felt compelled to go on. Their little sister had no intention of studying after school. To spend life partying with friends, especially Howie's friends was much more tantalising.

****

A month after Howie lost Edwin's boat to Gregory, Edwin bought himself a new boat. This one was better, bigger and equipped with all the household appliances Enid could dream of. Their boating experiences became much more enjoyable. They had more friends than ever and these friends never declined an invitation for a weekend on the water. All the expenses of the weekends with friends on the boat, was carried by Edwin. Except when Andrew and his family visited. A friendly squabble usually got them to share everything equally.

"So," Andrew asked him one day leaning on the railing, staring at the clear blue water that gently glided by underneath, "how is that business you talked about when I phoned you? Any profits yet?"

"That neighbour of mine is an idiot. He expected me to push money, unlimited and then do all the work too. I pulled out and now I can't get my money back. He's all talking and no action. Looks like I will have to write it off."

"Was it a big amount?"

"You don't want to know. But don't worry. I met a man with some good ideas. I'm thinking of going into business with him."

"Just watch out. Don't get involved if you're not sure history won't repeat itself."

"Sure. I'll make sure there is a contract next time."

"You didn't have a contract with the other guy?"

"No. He is my neighbour. I trusted him."

"You can't trust a soul anymore."

"I've learned my lesson. Hey, I'm hungry. Let's go see what the women are cooking."

"Good thinking."

"And as soon as we get home you take us up in your plane, right?"

"Where to?"

"I have a friend in New Zealand."

"Another friend? Another business proposition?" Edwin smiled, shrugged and disappeared down to the galley. Andrew shook his head in disbelief and followed him down the steps to the galley.

CHAPTER 24

Surprise

Most of his friends got cars for their eighteenth birthday. Justin received a tiny parcel, wrapped in pretty red and silver paper. When he came down stairs for breakfast, no one made a fuss. His father just congratulated him, seemingly absentminded and handed him this tiny package. His mother pecked him on the cheek and Delia wished him happy birthday without much enthusiasm. She gave him a packet and said she hopes it fits. It was just a sweater.

Justin thanked everyone, a bit disappointed. Eighteen is a big deal. His friends got big gifts, like cars, and parties. Not that Justin cared much about that, but he surely expected a bigger gift and a little excitement. Especially because he was such a good kid. He did well in school, respected his teachers, he never messed up, did not disobey his elders, did not mistreat his sister like most boys did. Now what was this? 'Don't they think he would have liked a little pat on the back on his big day? Just shows you what happens when pride steppes in. 'Lord, it is painful, but thank you for putting me back in my place,' he said in his mind as he helped himself to some bacon.

Andrew looked at Marie, Marie looked at Delia and Delia looked at Andrew.

"Sorry, Son, but that's all you're getting. We haven't had time for shopping. Just grabbed a little something passing by the tool shop yesterday. Hope you like it." Marie and Delia were both very interested in their food.

"Well, aren't you going to open it?" Andrew asked and took a bite. They all watched him, but pretended not to. Justin slowly, humbly opened the little parcel. It was a key ring with a Cessna logo on it.

"Gee, thanks. I'll surely find a use for it." If he were ten years younger, this would be a good moment to start crying.

"I'm sure you will. Like for these perhaps." Andrew took a set of keys from his pocket and handed it to Justin.

"What is this?"

"What does it look like?"

"Keys."

"Well, let's finish breakfast then I'll show you where they fit."

Andrew drove Justin to the airfield. Together they walked to a nearby hangar. Inside Andrew directed him to a tiny white and yellow aeroplane.

"I think you'll find that those keys might unlock the door. Go, see if they fit." Justin was stunned. For a few seconds he could not move. He looked at the little Cessna, then at Andrew and back at the Cessna. He looked again at Andrew and a smile broke through.

"Dad, I don't know what to say."

"A plain and simple 'thanks' will be in order. Well, what are you waiting for?" He motioned with his head towards the plane and Justin does not wait for another prompt. In a blink he had opened the door, jumped in and made himself at home in the left front seat.

****

Anita had no struggle to replace The Boy, and the next one, and the next. In a singles bar that she frequented, she met a man, not as young as the others, but seemingly more mature and not what can be described as pretty, like the others. Tony was handsome and treated her as if she were the queen. It did not take long before he moved in and took possession of the new red Ferrari. As with the others, Anita did not bother to get to know him before letting him into her home.

The lovers Anita had previously were of the obvious parasite types. They did not even try to hide their dependence on their wealthy women. This one, Tony however, was a businessman in his own right.

He had more than one fork in the hay and all his undertakings were doing well. There was just this one deal that had some hick-ups. Something was preventing it from coming down smoothly.

That little something – no surprise – was money. It needed a cash injection, but couldn't pinch it from any other source as his money was all tied up. Patience was all he needed, he told her. In time some assets will become liquid and then he will move. When she offered to help, he would not hear of it. The amount is too big. But after a few days, he felt that time was running out. He was about to lose the deal.

Anita made another offer and 'reluctantly' he accepted. It was after all only one-and-half-a-million. As he received the money from her, he solemnly promised to share the profits with her, not only give back the borrowed amount. That was the first of many transactions that needed cash injections from Anita following each other with shorter intervals every time. The dividends, however, never materialized.

After several attempts to make quick money in some vague scheme, every time telling her sorry it did not work out, she became irritated. He kept asking more money for some uncertain business plan or to help out a friend in dire need of a few hundred-thousand. She started refusing where upon he punished her by disappearing for a day or two. At his return, she usually gave in and wrote a cheque. The amounts grew bigger with promises of great profits which never materialised.

"Sorry, Tony, I just can't do this anymore," she told him one day. "I keep giving and I keep giving and all you can do, is keep on promising. You haven't returned one cent of all the money I've poured into your schemes."

"Just this one more time, Honey."

"No, really, I won't. I've given you close to four million in the eight months we've been together. Enough is enough. No more."

"We're almost there, Anita. You don't want me to back out just before payday, would you?"

"Tony, if there were a payday, it would have come long ago. There is no payday." What Anita saw in his eyes at that moment, made her skin crawl. She reached for her chequebook.

"Just this one more time. How much?"

"Three million." His eyes narrowed, his smile broadened, he held out his hand.

"Are you mad? I can't give you a cheque for such an amount. Let me rather EFT the money."

"Even better. Can you do it now?"

"Give me the banking details. I'll do it right away. If I hurry up, I can catch the bank open."

"Why don't you do it from your computer?"

"The thing is giving me trouble. I was planning to get a new one tomorrow, a laptop."

"Right, let's go then."

"Why do you want to come with me? I can do this on my own. I'm a big girl."

"I have nothing else to do and I'll miss you." Anita's heart beat a thousand beats per minute.

"Sure. Suit yourself." She grabbed her keys and trotted down to her car. He wanted to drive her, but her car was behind his and she was already in her car, starting it up when he emerged from the house. At least she can drive herself and not let him drive so that he might find a chance to stop on the way back home and push her down a cliff. She realised the thought is ridiculous, but you never know. About the deal there was no way out for her. No way to stall the transfer. 'Lord, what did I get myself into this time? I just don't learn, do I?'

The next day Tony got up early and told her he had some business to attend to. He dressed in a new Armani suit and left the house looking nervous. Anita dressed in something inconspicuous, no make-up except a pale lipstick, pulled a brush through her hair and left half an hour after him. She drove Donny's old Honda using the GPS on her cell phone to find her way. At an address in Woodstock she parked in a narrow street. Looking around, she stepped out of the car and pushed open the brown office door of Hein Hoffman, Private Detective.

****

Two weeks passed in relative peace. Although the atmosphere between Anita and Tony is a bit strained, they found a way to live around it as if things were the way they used to be. Not a word about the money was spoken. That episode just did not happen. Anita got the impression there is something bothering him. Something that had nothing to do with her but she shrugged it off and told herself it was her imagination. Until she received the next weekly report from the detective.

Hein Hoffman saw her coming and prepared to leave his table in the coffee shop. The moment she reached his table, he got up, pretended to offer her his seat and left, leaving a brown envelope on the floor under the table. Anita took the seat, picked up the envelope but did not open it until the waitress had taken her order.

She first read the letter, then, as soon as her coffee arrived, took out the photographs. There were three photos of Tony talking to three different people. In two of the photos was the same woman present. The first photo showed him with a Nigerian man. They looked angry as if in an argument. In the second photo, Tony looked agitated. The man with him was indistinct, of no particular race or nation that could easily be determined. He could be anything from Coloured to Mexican to Arabian. The woman was a platinum blond and did not seem to be involved or even interested in the conversation. She was neatly dressed in a pale pink tailored suit, long jacket, short skirt, her hair fastened behind her head with a clip.

The third photo was the most disturbing. The woman looked menacingly at Tony with her right hand under her jacket, while the other man in the picture stood next to her, arms folded, face expressionless. Tony looked frightened, holding his hands up in front of him, as if in defence. The place where the woman's hand disappeared under her jacket showed a shadow indicating there was a big bulge under her left arm. Hein, in the letter, explained that bulge as being the presence of a fire arm.

Anita did not notice the young man at the table behind her, just to her left, leaving the coffee shop seconds after her detective. She did not notice the older man at the same table now moving in her direction until he stood next to her asking permission to sit down. Before she could react, he made himself at home, smiled and acted as if he was a long lost friend who just happened to be at the right time at the right place.

"Excuse me, do we know each other?" she asked, the photos still lying on the table in front of her.

"Nice photos, who is your photographer?" Shocked, she quickly covered them with the envelope.

"It's none of your business. Who are you and what do you want?" Fear tied her insides in a knot. The man recognised the feelings reflected in her eyes. He smiled and in a gentle voice, said:

"Relax, lady, I'm not the enemy. Lucky for you. Now, please tell me what your interest is in the people in those photographs."

"And I am telling you again it is none of your business."

"May I see them? Please, hand them over to me and let me see."

"Absolutely not! Look, if you don't leave me alone I'm going to scream and you will be arrested. Don't think I won't. I'm serious, I shall." Apart from the fear in her eyes, the man also saw courage and determination. He had no reason not to believe she will do what she threatened. He is also convinced now that she is not on the side of those scoundrels in the pictures.

"My name is Anton. I have reason to believe anyone involved with the people in those pictures of yours, are in danger. So, dear lady, I'm trying to help you. I told you I am not the enemy."

"Well, what are you then, and how do I know you are telling the truth."

"You simply have to trust me. The Nigerian in the picture is a well-known drug smuggler. The Puerto Rican was imported to set things up, because he speaks Cape Afrikaans, among many other languages, fluently. He's been all over the world, lived and studied in the UK, lived in the Cape for several years, then went back to Venezuela to secure new contacts in the under-world. The woman is the South-African connection. The frightened young man is a local who was recruited as a dealer. He messed up and is about to be eliminated. Now, lady, I ask you again. What is your interest in these people?"

"How do you know all this?"

"It is my business to know. And to wipe out everyone who dares to bring their junk into our country to destroy our youth. I am waiting for your reply. Where do you fit in?" Anita's resistance crumbles. This man looks like he can, and at this point, should be trusted.

"Mister, err, it is personal. And it is very difficult for me to discuss it with a total stranger."

"I'm sorry. I should have checked you out before approaching you, but there was no time. Yesterday we saw your PI watching them and taking pictures, then followed him here to see whom he works for. Are you involved with the young man, Tony Benson?"

"Yes. I've known him for some months now. At first he would not let me do anything for him. Later he told me about a business deal, he needed money and accepted my offer. That was the first of many 'investments' I made. The amounts grew larger, as did the promised dividends, which of course never materialised."

"I see. Please call me Anton; your name is?"

"I'm Anita. And you are Anton who?"

"Sorry. Surname's not important."

"Those amounts you gave him, how large were they?"

"The last amount was three million. I was shocked and didn't want to give him one cent more, but there was such a menace in his expression and I could not find a way out. I got scared. But that was what made me decide to hire a private detective to find out what was going on."

"That money was supposed to pay for a shipment of cocaine. He shouldn't have let you transfer the money. All deals are supposed to be handled with cash for merchandise. Now there is a paper trail that leads not only to him, but to you as well. Our lady in your picture won't tolerate such a blunder."

"Do you mean I can be implicated?"

"It depends. If the police get hold of it, surely you will be implicated and convicted with the rest of them." Anita's face was drained from all colour.

"You are not in the police? Who are you working for? Show me some identification."

"I told you to relax. I don't work for the government. I don't carry any form of identification that reassures the good guys and intimidates the bad ones. We're just a few okes who don't like injustice and do something about it."

"Like what? Assassination?" Anton could not help smiling.

"No, nothing that harsh. Let's just say the perpetrators end up in an eastern country that deals harshly with drug smugglers, with their pockets full of their own stuff planted on them. Let someone else deal with them. Why should we bother to put up with our less than competent judicial system to handle these cases?"

"Do you believe all cops are corrupt? Don't you trust anyone?"

"No. There are many good cops in the force. A number of good judges too. The problem is not all at street-cop level, but just as much higher up. It's not always so clear whom you can trust. Running

risks with matters this serious is just not our way of dealing with it."
Anita sat back in her chair. This is unbelievable. How do these people
operate? Who are they? Who is this man sitting in front of her? Why
is he telling her all these things?

"What should I do? If I can be implicated, how do I protect myself?"

"Now we're getting to the point. This is the reason why I approached
you in the first place. From our side we will do all we can to keep the
case away from the police. But the bad guys must know about you by
now. Is there some place where you can stay that Tony Benson does
not know about?"

"You mean I can't go home?"

"That is exactly what I mean. I don't think you will be safe. They will
do everything they deem necessary to wipe out any tracks that might
lead to them. They might be waiting for you at this moment."

"You scare me. If I had my passport I'd get on a plane and go to my
brother in Australia."

"If you had your passport I'd strongly have recommended it. The
best you can do now is to stay with someone where you will be safe."

"I'll stay with one of my brothers, or my sister. But won't they be
endangered?"

"If there is a way to find them, it might be better to book into a hotel
in a densely populated area with many tourists coming and going. You
also might want to change your appearance, just a little bit."

"I've already done that. I don't normally look like this."

"Excellent! Now, let your family know you will be away for a while.
Tell them not to worry about your dog and your pot plants, they're
taken care of."

"I don't have a dog and no pot plants either."

"Perfect. Buy yourself a toothbrush and pj's and stay put till you hear
from me." He took out his cell phone:

"Give me your number; we'll have to stay in contact. And get in
touch with your PI. Tell him the matter has been settled, no more
snooping around. For his own safety, naturally. But be sure not to tell
him anything else. He does not have to know more. Case is closed as
far as he is concerned. Pay him and drop him." He did not tell her his
young assistant and protégé was at that moment at Hein Hoffman's
office busy convincing him to stop any further investigation in this
matter. Anton gave her his number and made her understand she was

not to call him except in a life and death situation. They said goodbye and went their separate ways. Anita's mind spun round the outcome of this day's little appointment with her detective, ending in a dangerous situation that kept her from returning to her own home.

Anita left the Honda where she parked it. She took a bus and bought a ticket to Table View, but got off at Milnerton. She crossed the street, walked over the bridge, passed the light house and went on to the beach where she pulled off her shoes. She walked barefoot on the sand in the direction of Blouberg, the icy Atlantic water lapping at her feet. She walked for half an hour, sat down against a dune and just stared at the water without seeing.

Five big ships were lying seemingly motionless on the calm waters waiting to be escorted into the harbour. Anita hardly noticed them. Her thoughts tried to make sense of all that happened in the past two hours. Yesterday all was going normal, a little uneasy with Tony, but things were normal. Now everything has changed. Her life might never be the same again. Yesterday felt like light-years ago.

She got up, dusted herself and walked back to the lighthouse. At the nearest coffee shop close to the lighthouse she chose a table in a dark corner and ordered a scone and coffee. Toying with the scone, she had a second cup of coffee, then left and started uphill toward the shopping centre. A toothbrush and a pyjama suit is what Anton suggested. She bought a few necessities and set out to find a place to stay.

Guesthouses and bed-and-breakfasts are not difficult to find in any city by the sea. In less than half an hour, Anita was booked in at a B&B close to the shops. Hot and tired from walking she took a shower, dressed in her new, unwashed night suit, and sat down on the bed with her cell phone. Time to make a few calls to let everyone know not to go to her house. She chose her words carefully not to arouse suspicion. No one needed to know the truth. No one needed to worry.

That done, she called an estate agent. A change of address will soon have to take place, she told herself. Life in Bantry Bay will never be the same again. Next she called Mister Wheels and ordered a used Toyota Tazz to be delivered to the B&B the next day. After a supper of coffee and rusks in her room, she got into bed and fell asleep with all the day's happenings still scrambling her mind.

Early the next morning she got up, dressed in the clothes she bought at Zep Stores and walked to the shopping centre. She was the first customer at the hairdresser. The treatment took longer than expected, so she called Mister Wheels and asked them to deliver the car at the coffee shop next to the hairdresser. An hour later Anita left the centre, hair cut short, coloured light brown, dressed in simple everyday T-shirt and jeans, driving an old, everyday car. A woman on the run, she thought with a smirk.

Anton did not call for three days. To keep busy and to keep herself from losing her mind, Anita found another place to stay, a guesthouse where she could unpack all her luggage for as long as it took. By now she had a small bag full of Zep Stores and Mr. Dice clothes, two pairs of sandals and a pair of canvas shoes, a straw hat and a huge pair of sunglasses. She went to the beach and walked miles at a time, had coffee and a scone or salad, all the while waiting for Anton's call.

****

Tony was flattered when he was invited to a party on a boat after being scolded for his negligent handling of the last transaction. He thought he was going to be cut out of the organisation and not see a penny of the money he invested. He was so eager to get his fingers on Anita's money that he did not think straight. But now he was invited back into the inner circle, partying with the important people. Wonderful what the drug trade can do for a man if you keep your cool. They probably now realise his value and the doors he can open for them. With his ego inflated he strutted on deck in his swimming trunk to join the others for drinks.

It is late afternoon, the sun low over the horizon and the temperature still in the late twenties. Amazing weather, far out on the ocean, great life. Fish playing in the water deep below the surface, shark fins in the distance, but they are all safely on the boat enjoying what might become his future. This is it, he thought. The Puerto Rican, whom he only knew by the name of Ronaldo, handed him a drink: "Cheers, my friend. Drink up."

"Cheers, partner," he replied and Ronaldo smiled a mysterious smile. He sipped the strong alcohol and quickly the blond woman appeared with another bottle to fill up his glass. She appeared to be a bit unstable on her feet, and not only because of the swells lifting and dropping the boat. As she leaned closer to Tony she lost her balance, smashed her glass against the railing and, as she regained her footing, bumped into

Tony with the broken glass cutting a nasty gash in his arm. Ronaldo is at his side in an instant. But not to take care of his wound. Before Tony realised what was happening, he flew over board and landed in the water with a big splash. While still trying to reach the surface, he heard the motors of the boat roaring away from him. He knew in an instant it was the End. Wounded, bleeding profusely in shark-infested waters left no chance for survival.

****

The call came late on the fourth day.

"Anton?"

"Yes, it's me. Can we meet tomorrow?"

"Sure. Where and what time?"

"Where are you?"

"Milnerton."

"Okay. Meet me at the coffee shop in Floral's, just up the road from Paddocks Centre. Let's say ten-thirty."

"Sure. See you there." The conversation was over and so was her prospect of a good night's sleep. Bleary eyed and pale faced she set out the next morning to meet Anton with the hope that he had good news for her.

"What news do you have for me?" she asked before she was even seated. Anton helped her into her chair and took his seat before answering her question.

"Good and bad news. All the bad guys involved in this matter have been dealt with."

"What do you mean 'been dealt with'?"

"Sometime soon *Ernestôôô* (and he pinched his nose as he pronounced the name to produce a nasal sound,) will deliver fried chicken to them." He smiled at her and she giggled, nervously: "I didn't take you for someone who watched TV, let alone the ads."

"It happens once in a while. Don't worry about the details. I told you we have our ways and means to handle these cases. Suffice to say you are safe and you can go home. Now, the bad news is we found Tony's car. We followed him, lost him, then found his car abandoned. No sign of him. What I don't understand is why did he have to borrow money from you if he could afford to drive a Ferrari? Or was it perhaps the only thing he owned?"

"The Ferrari is mine. It does not belong to him. He has the use of it while he is with me. When he leaves he won't take the car with him."

"If he returns."

"You don't think he will?"

"I told you he was about to be terminated."

"Do you think they … ?" Anita's face turned ashen.

"Afraid so. I believe they got to him before we could step in. Another problem you have to face now is the car. If the police finds it, it will be very awkward for you if you cannot explain how the car got abandoned in a parking lot behind the Crown Park Hotel."

"Oh God, what a mess."

"Yes. And pray is all you can do now." Anita looked at him as if he was speaking Greek.

"Pray! Are you a Christian?"

"You may not believe it, but yes. I am." Now I've seen everything, she thought.

"My sister, Francine and her husband, Gerald are Christians; my youngest brother, Terrence too." Anita is not sure why she told him this. She did not notice his slight hesitation, the momentary surprise on his face.

"Do you have any suggestions what to do about the car?"

"There are a few options. The best I can recommend is go to the hotel, get your car as if nothing is wrong. If anyone asks, just say you were at the hotel last night, too drunk to drive and took a taxi home. So you simply came to collect what was yours."

"You're a Christian and you want me to tell a lie?" Anton looked away, then replied: "Sorry. All right, if anyone asks, tell him to mind his own business. Since you have a key, no one is to question your ownership. You do have a spare key, don't you?"

"Yes, but not with me. I'll have to go home to get it."

"Would you like me to help you get your car back?"

"If you don't mind, yes, please. I don't want to involve friends or family in this mess."

Anton followed Anita home, checked out the house to see if anything is out of the ordinary and found nothing. He returned to his car and waited for her to get the keys to the Ferrari, then drove her to the Crown Park Hotel in Llandudno. No one paid attention when Anita unlocked the Ferrari, got in and drove off. Anton followed her home again to make sure all was well. She invited him in for coffee or something stronger to say thanks, but he declined. With a handshake and an encouraging touch on her shoulder, he said goodbye and left, never to see her again. Scoundrels where they belonged, damsel saved, mission accomplished. Pity they could not save Tony, but one cannot save them all.

Two days later there was a small piece in the newspaper telling of the partially shark eaten body of a man found on a deserted beach on the peninsula.

The body had been identified as Anthony Benson.

CHAPTER 25

Beginning of the End

Enid was unhappy about her children straying so far from the principals with which she brought them up. She became depressed and withered. She died before Debra-Ann married the worthless leach she was engaged to. Andrew flew us all over to Australia for the funeral in his Lear Jet. We did not know it at the time, but this trip would be the last for Andrew in his own jet. The money was already running out. Shortly after we arrived home, he put the plane up for sale.

Anita's daughter was the only one of the children who wanted to attend the funeral, but she was in her last month of pregnancy with her third baby and considered it too risky to fly for so many hours. So, of the children it was only Stevie and my two youngsters who went with us. It was Anita; Andrew and Marie; Terrence and Stacy and Gerald and I who went over. It was heart-warming for Edwin to see how we all joined in unison to comfort and support him.

It was one thing after another eating the millions Andrew, Edwin and Anita received from Dad's estate. To record it all would fill a small library. Edwin lost money on one scheme after another, his children doing their part on the fast lane. Andrew, at some point, realised he had to do something that could bring in money so that he could resume flying around the world, get his children educated and still have a home to go to when he needed a change of clothing, proverbially. He started trying his hand at playing the stock market with disastrous results.

When the amount of his total liquid value had dwindled to five million, he tried to start a business again (and again), but failed miserably. Edwin was even worse. He spoiled his children rotten and bought friendships as much as everything else. And Dad expected me to help them! Sorry, Dad, I promised to run your business, but taking care of those brats? Not me. I never promised I'd do it and I am not planning to.

Now, a few more years after I joined the company, my brother Andrew, having squandered his fortune, was employed by me to save him from bankruptcy. He has been with us for nineteen months. At first, he was rebellious and demanded a senior position. Higgins and I formed a united front to keep him in a place where he could advance, but only if he did his part. Eating so much humble pie is finally paying off. It looks as if he might qualify for promotion soon.

It happened like this. Andrew realised his money was running out. He sold the jet, retrenched the pilots with generous severance packages and used the money to pay off his house. Then he sold the house, retrenched the housekeeper and the gardener but kept the cleaner. He bought a smaller house and Marie had to start cooking again. Hired garden services took care of the small garden once a week.

Andrew, convinced he could easily get himself back on track, started a new business. It did not go well. In the years passed, he lost most of his business contacts and those he still saw on and off socially, did not trust his business sense anymore. He struggled along for some time, gave up and tried again on Marie's insistence. Each attempt cost him money he could not afford to lose. But he tried again, adamant not to end up in bankruptcy.

I got the call just after my mid-morning tea:

"Francine, I have something I wish to discuss with you. Can I come over?"

"I'm free in a couple of hours. I'll be in my office."

"On second thought, can I meet you at Luigi's for lunch? My treat."

"All right. But I can only get away by three, three-thirty. Would that suit you?"

"That would not be lunch. It would be more of a kind of lupper?"

"What? What is a 'lupper'?"

"Since a late breakfast-early-lunch is called brunch, a late lunch-early-supper should be called lupper. Don't you think that makes sense?" Laughing out loud, I compliment him on his creativity. This was unexpectedly original for my brother who loved to play copycat.

"Sure, let's make it lupper at three-thirty."

"Perfect. See you then."

So I went to meet with Andrew and was quite surprised at the reason he wanted to see me. Apart from taking me to lunch, something that never happened before, he had a business proposal. Actually, it was a request presented in the form of a proposal. Point blank he wanted me to invest money in his newest venture – precisely one hundred per cent of the financing was what he wanted from me.

"No. Sorry Andrew, but I will not finance your business." He was speechless for a moment, staring blankly at me.

"I don't understand. Why on earth not?"

"Your history. Somehow you managed to lose your wisdom and business sense. You don't make sensible decisions. Frankly, I think you've lost your skill to do business altogether."

"Now look, Francine, nobody will give me a chance. I thought you of all people would see things differently. You're my sister."

"Oh. I see. Because I am your sister I'm supposed to be willing to throw money down your drain? Is that it?"

"Is that your final answer? You will not help me, your own brother?"

"I didn't say I will not help you. I said I shall not throw money at you."

"I didn't ask for charity. I am presenting a business proposal to you."

"A proposal I will not consider. Look, Andrew, I can help you in many other ways. I will not enter into business with you. You have proven yourself capable to lose more money than you can generate. If you have shown any success lately, I might have considered it. But you've run one venture down the mud slope after the other. Come now. Let's at least enjoy the meal. You know how to choose your restaurants." With this compliment, I tried to soften the blow. After desert, he attempted one more time to convince me.

"Absolutely not, Andrew. I said no and I won't change my mind. I told you I can help you in other ways which has nothing to do with charity. Phone me if you want to know more."

"I wanted to ask you this long ago, but it was never my business. I just want to know why don't you make Dad's company a public one, you know, go on the stock market and sell shares? Don't you think you will do better?" Andrew had a way of changing a subject if things did not go the way he wanted.

"I don't feel comfortable with that idea. There are various reasons why I will not go that way." Some more chit-chat followed while finishing our meal. He tried to hide his feelings, but as we went our separate ways, I could not help notice the way his shoulders slumped just a little.

The big surprise call came about a month later. Marie invited me to lunch. My insides churned because I knew something was coming. Something bad. We met at a restaurant neither she nor I have ever been to. Marie was already sitting at a table in a corner of the restaurant when I entered. She was wearing a royal blue pantsuit with a silky-soft blue and cream coloured blouse that was becoming and very feminine. It also made her appear vulnerable. She looked pale and distraught. I noticed that she must have lost weight. She had always been well built and took care of herself, but she was not skinny. That seemed to have changed. We cheek kissed, sat down and placed our orders as the waiter was ready and waiting. When I insisted to pay for myself, she looked relieved. I waited for her to say something, but she kept fiddling with her napkin. As soon as the waiter brought our coffee and taken our orders, I prompted her to start talking, realising how difficult it must be for her. The situation must be lower than carpet level.

My sister-in-law told me she was worried about my brother:

"In the past Andrew always lifted his head after a setback. This time he seems unable to do so. Our situation is bad and Andrew does not know what to do. We are about to lose our house. Everything else is on the brink of being repossessed. He says all kinds of strange things. Things that scare me."

"What does he say, Marie?"

"Yesterday he told me I am young and good-looking enough to find someone who can take better care of me. I asked him what he meant by that. His reply was that perhaps it was time for him to move on. He can live modestly if he had to, but he can no longer give me what I'm used to, what I need and deserve." At this point Marie started dabbing her eyes. I knew it was not crocodile tears and she was not trying to play my emotions. Marie did not cry easily, especially in public. The churning in my insides intensified and my heart cried for her sake. No one might ever understand what it had cost Marie to come to me and share this with me, how deep her anguish must have been to take such an unthinkable step.

"What do you want me to do?"

"Is there any way you can help him, Francine?" Her lips quivered and she struggled to look me in the eyes. Our food came and we were quiet for a few minutes until the waiter left.

"Marie," I said, "Andrew came to me some weeks ago asking me to invest in a business he wanted to open. With his history, I told him I cannot do it. I offered help in some other way. He was not interested and that was the last I heard from him. My offer still stands. I can help him, but not on his terms."

"He is so stubborn. He thinks you want to pour charity on him and he won't have it."

"Yes, a real Hammond, isn't he?" Marie gave a little smile at this.

"I think we should pray about this. Then you go home and talk to him. Try to convince him to come and see me in my office. Tell him I am waiting for him." I reached over the table and took both her hands in mine, closed my eyes and started praying:

"Dear Father, you know this situation, you know our hearts. And you know Andrew. Break down the pride and stubbornness in him and give him the courage to except the help that you yourself has made available. I also ask you to bring peace to my sister's heart. Thank you that she loves Andrew, that she has always been willing and able to support him. In the name of Yeshua we pray. Amen." Marie looked strangely at me, half-smiling. She has never done anything remotely like this before, praying in public. And such a simple, conversational prayer she had never heard of before. She told me this, years later. For the moment, she looked relieved and greatly encouraged. This meeting brought us closer together and an amicable relationship between Marie and myself was born.

Andrew came to my office like any bigger brother who does his sister the honour of visiting her. The façade was thin and the visit quickly turned into a job interview. He argued with me about the position I offered him, the salary and then just to play tough guy. I phoned Higgins, who entered the conversation with authority telling Andrew exactly how it will be. Andrew accepted our offer outwardly frowning, but inside he was grateful and relieved. Just as Dad predicted, the first of his children have finished the full circle. At least he had the sense to come for help before he lost everything. Andrew now works in our dad's company as an ordinary employee.

****

Two years and five months after Enid's death Edwin arrived in Table-bay harbour with only two bags of clothing and personal belongings. Beard and hair sun-bleached, skin brown and leathery, hands calloused, he looked like a stranger when he knocked on my front door. My heart almost broke in two when I saw him, hunched shoulders, almost begging to come in as if I might refuse him. What he did not lose, he sold. He was back in Cape Town to stay. His children refused to come with him; their lives, they told him, was in Australia. He sold his yacht at a ridiculously low price with the condition that the new owner gave him a free lift to South-Africa on his way to Rio de Janeiro.

The money for the boat was all Edwin had left of his inheritance. Even though he had no problem living modestly - now that he did not have to provide for Enid anymore - he still needed some form of income. The money he got for the boat would not last long. He needed to do something to keep busy and at the same time earn a living. How could I not help him?

Fulfilling Dad's request I offered Edwin a job in one of the daughter companies of the business. It was a pharmaceutical outfit that could use Edwin's knowledge of chemistry. He was grateful and started at his new job two weeks after his arrival, promising to find accommodation of his own as soon as possible. Gerald told him we had no problem with him staying with us in the meantime

Both my elder brothers had squandered their fortune, both worked for me now, directly or indirectly. I was not hoping, but waiting for Anita's crash to come. I did not have to wait long. The crash happened more than a year ago, we just did not know about it. Anita was too proud to admit that her move to a smaller place, inland, had anything to do with becoming broke.

The last of her lovers not only borrowed huge amounts from her, he stole much more to pay his debts. He ordered on-line things like luxury items, from furniture to household appliances to jewellery, on her credit cards without her knowing and have them delivered to his ex-wife. Things that could be sold for cash, all to pay his gambling debts. She met him at a get-together at a friend's house. He set up a meeting to present to these fine ladies a fool-proof retirement scheme where their money will grow at a toadstool-rate; unheard of anywhere in the world. At the first signs of suspicion from one of the ladies a few months later, he simply took all he could gather and disappeared with the investments of all the ladies who were foolish enough to trust him.

Things went from bad to worse for Anita. After selling her multi-million-rand townhouse in Bantry Bay at a pittance, she also scaled down on her wheels. She sold the Ferrari as well as the Lamborghini and got herself a sporty BMW. The Honda was sold to Mister Wheels for a measly three thousand Rand. Anita lost big on those deals. With no male companion to keep her entertained, she followed the same way Donny and his girls went. Casino's welcomed them until they had to start borrowing to pay their debt. She mortgaged her house, lost it, sold the BMW and gambled away the money within a week. The impressive collection of jewellery went the same way. It was a good thing that she kept the Tazz. The car had sentimental value for her. It reminded her of Anton. So she drove her Tazz, rented a flat in an old building in Parow, ate take-away food and struggled along for months.

All her young male companions had sucked her bank accounts dry and left her. Her son Donny had a big hand in helping the process along. He was becoming increasingly like his father every day. He lost money gambling, never to return a cent to Anita on the rare occasions when he won a little. In the beginning of Anita's financial crash her daughter offered help, but Anita could not get along with the son-in-law. She was almost penniless before she turned to me.

No employment, no home, she parked her nine year old Tazz in the circular driveway one Saturday morning and walked thought the front door without knocking. It was, after all the house where she grew up in, so what need was there to knock? We sat down in the family room for a sisterly chat. Katrina brought coffee and pastries and Anita did not worry much about any kilos piling up. She was starved for something more homely to eat than take-away food. With her 'formula one' metabolism, she would never be fat or even moderately plump, but she worried about it no longer. There were more important things to concern herself with.

"Since both Andrew and Edwin work in Dad's company now, I want you to find me something too." Anita jumps in with a request in the form of a command.

"If you have your C.V. ready, I will see where we can fit you in. I never thought you would want to work again, not in Dad's company anyway." I cannot resist teasing her a little, but not without compassion. Her situation must be desperate.

"I simply am bored. I need to keep busy, but where would I a 'whitey' and middle aged get a job. If I knew you needed a C.V. I'd have brought one. Can I fax it through tomorrow?"

"Tomorrow is Sunday. Don't worry about it. I'll see what I can do and phone you on Monday. I'm sure I will find something suitable." She studies her shoes. After a moment's silence, she lifts her head just a bit and without looking at me, she says:

"Thank you, Sis."

"Welcome." Anita takes another pastry and without any gesture that she wants to leave, she says: "I suppose I have to get going."

"Why don't you spend the weekend with us?" I ask on impulse.

"No, well...err. *Ag* why not. Yes, all right."

"I'm sure I can lend you something to sleep in. And there are always new toothbrushes in the cabinet."

"It's fine, I have an overnight bag in the car." Saying this she does not look me in the eyes.

"You packed a bag?"

"I was going to visit a friend, but I changed my mind. I'd rather stay here if it's OK with you." She lies almost convincingly.

"I recall inviting you ..."

"That's right. Will it be OK with Gerald?"

"Of course my dear. I'll get Ephraim to get your bag out of the car."

"I do miss old Simon. Have you heard from him lately?"

"We visit him once in a while. He's fine, enjoying his retirement immensely."

"Say hello for me when you go again."

"You're welcome to come along if you want to. He's getting old and frail"

"I'll think about it."

That Sunday Anita, subdued and humbled, went with us to church. On Monday, she fetched the rest of her sparse belongings at Chanté's house where it was stored for her and moved, on my insistence, back to her room where she lived as a child in the house of our parents. With Edwin also in his old room, our numbers were halfway full. Andrew would never move back. He is doing well. If divorce were not looked upon with contempt, Marie would have divorced him as soon as she realized their money had run out. But she loved him and chose to stay being caught between the stigma of divorce and the humiliation of near bankruptcy. She endured and now things are well on track for them again.

Terrence will never be forced to move back or come knocking at my door hat in hand. He is doing great with his music recording - owning four more studio's and music schools in different parts of town - and more than one band, all in the 'less privileged' areas where there is so little hope for the young ones to improve their lives. Stacy keeps an eye on the guesthouse, but she mainly makes a home for her own family. Stevie is a happy, well-balanced boy and already a deeply committed Christian. His dad made sure he takes advantage of growing up in a musical environment. Stevie plays several instruments well and sings like a professional. A very successful family living a satisfied, fulfilled life, always seeking to remain in the Father's will for their lives.

Not only would Terrence never have to come to me for financial help. He created work in other fields outside the music scene. Stacy could do with more help in the guest house. Who better than her own sister? Terrence made an offer to his brother in law. After careful consideration Arnold accepted the offer and became head of security to protect Terrence's studios. The day Amelia and Arnold with Sammy and Jimmy, their two boys arrived in Cape Town was a happy reunion.

CHAPTER 26

Starting Over

Half the Hammond clan started over. Edwin was back on his feet four months after Anita moved back in with us. He found a nice place to stay close to his work place. I loaned him the money to pay a deposit to buy a simplex town house and helped him furnishing it. After that, we did not see him often. He became a kind of recluse after Enid's death.

Andrew's financial downfall turned him into a sour person, still in need of social acceptance, but now without most of his friends. Marie managed to keep up appearances of wealth and success, but all their new 'ex-friends' knew the truth, and many of their old friends talked about them behind their backs. Only a few stuck by them, proving to be sincere and reliable friendships.

****

Andrew's son Justin was expected to take a respectable job at a respectable company and live far above his income for appearance's sake. He refused and agreed to study if he was allowed to stay with Terrence and give a hand where necessary and go to church with him. Terrence encouraged him never to give up his studies, while cultivating in him a love of every aspect of the music business. That way Justin manages also to earn a living on a small scale, loving every minute of it.

Sadly he had to give up his dream of flying commercial. The purchase of the gyrocopter was cancelled, the training terminated, and the little white and yellow Cessna had to be sold. At least Andrew gave him a small amount from the money the Cessna brought in, to pay a deposit on an old Volkswagen. Justin painted the car white and yellow and named it Cessna II. He made the monthly payments with money that he earned working for Terrence and wherever he could find something to do on a casual basis all through his study years.

In the social circles where they grew up it was never expected of Delia to work. She followed in her mother's footsteps, doing good works for organizations with good intentions. She sings in the church choir, joins the right clubs and is seen at the right social events spending the right amounts of money as she went, but only after she was reeled in from her wanderings. During her teen years, Delia retained friendships with some undesirable girls from her old school. They were involved in a 'black clothing' cult and fascinated her with their life style, they almost managed to pull her in. Marie put a stop to these friendships and all was well for the time being. Delia was forbidden to see those girls again. Lacking her brother's courage and determination to do what she wanted, she complied with her mother's wishes. However, it did not keep her from rebelling against her parent's authority.

When at university, she nagged her parents to let her live in a student apartment. Again, she came under the influence of undesirable people. Never prepared to cope with pressure from outside, never learned to take a stand, she let herself be carried along with the trends of students who had no interest in their studies. Substance abuse and promiscuity became a lifestyle. Until Marie paid a surprise visit one sunny day. She knocked on the door with a basket full of homemade snacks. When the door flew open, Marie nearly fainted. A girl – or is it a girl? – stuck her head through the door opening.

"Mom! What are you doing here? You should have phoned … " She recognised her daughter's voice coming from the face of this apparition in front of her.

"What in the name of Saint Peter is going on here?!" The head disappeared, the safety chain was unhooked and the *apparition* stood aside to let Marie enter. But Marie was too stunned to move. When she eventually got a grip on herself, she asked?

"What in the name of the Farther have you done to yourself?" A half-naked man came out of a bedroom to see what was going on, followed by a half-naked girl. Marie did not pay attention. She kept on staring at Delia, who stood undecided in the entrance hall. Marie looked her up and down, from her hair, coloured pitch black and cut very short – except for a fringe that was partially covering her face – down to her ringed toes; toe nails painted black like her finger nails; no shoes. She was wearing black underwear under a see-through lace blouse that ended inches above her studded navel, and a wide full length black skirt made of something like cheese cloth. The face was covered with the palest foundation she could find while the eyes were ringed with thick black eyeliner. The lashes were extended about an inch and thickened almost solid. From each ear dangled about half a dozen silver ornaments; too big to be called earrings. Some more studs lined the edge of the ears right up to the top.

Anger rose up in Marie worse than she had ever felt. Ignoring the staring eyes of half a dozen onlookers that had appeared from the other rooms, Marie grabbed the longest of the earrings on Delia's left ear and started walking towards her car. Delia had no choice but to follow or have the earring torn from her flesh. Screaming from pain and protesting this harsh treatment she trotted along as Marie dragged her and bundled her into the car without saying a word, slamming the door shut. As soon as Marie took her seat behind the wheel, Delia launched a weak attack in her own defence:

"Mom, what has gotten into you? I have never known you to behave like this. Have you been spending time with Aunt Anita lately?" Getting herself under control, she replied:

"Just keep quiet, girl, just keep quiet."

"Oh, so now I'm not allowed to speak anymore?"

"I was not talking to you, Delia. I was talking to myself. But now that you mention it, yes. You are to shut up until we get home, clean yourself up, get dressed and be summoned. You will have all the opportunity in the word to defend yourself. If you think you have any defence worth listening to."

"Mom, I ... "

"Quiet! I said you can talk when we get home." In silence they drove home and Delia did as it was expected of her. Half an hour later she came down stairs wearing little make-up, a decent outfit, but the fringe still covering her face.

"Take that hair out of your face or I will pull it off of your scalp."

"Mom, you really sound like Aunt Anita." She protested, but obeyed.

"Quiet! I did not give you permission to speak. Now. You will have to make some decisions. Number one. Decide whether you want to study and qualify yourself, or stay ignorant for the rest of your life. Two. Do you prefer to look like some demon from hell, or do you plan to grow into the decent human being you were born to be. Three. Do you want me to trust you again in the distant future – because it will take quite a while before you can manage to earn my trust again – or shall I just lock you up in a room?"

"You cannot do that. It's not practically possible."

"If I send you to a convent in the mountains of Italy, it is quite possible."

"We're not Catholic."

"That's no problem. We can always convert if we have to. At least you can if I say you must." Delia wanted to argue, but thought better of it. She knew her mother would have an answer for every argument she might come up with. She knew she had just run out of options.

"I want you to take your time and think about your life. When you are ready, come back down and we will discuss your future. It is in your hands now. You are dismissed."

Finally by threatening to cut her out and send her away, Marie managed to pull Delia back into her circle of protection and made her live the life she was 'meant to live,' doing all the nice and respectable things her mother expected of her. She finished her studies while staying at home with the warning that if she ever get involved in anything funky or freaky, whatever the youngsters called it, it is over for her. She was encouraged to befriend the son of a club member friend of Marie's, to whom she is now engaged to be married. All is well that ends well.

****

Anita was deeply concerned about Edwin. She visited him often and invited him over to the house just as often. He appreciated her calling on him, but seldom accepted an invitation until Anita found a cure. She kept on going to church with us. One Sunday she bumped into an old friend of earlier years, renewed the friendship and learned that this friend, Valerie, became a widow five years before. Valerie agreed to go with Anita on a visit to Edwin.

At first, he was reluctant to crawl out of his shell. Again, Anita manipulated the situation. She bought three theatre tickets and asked Edwin to pick them up, since her car was in for repairs. On the night, she suddenly developed a severe attack of flu or something undefined. It was Valerie and Edwin off to the theatre, to a restaurant for a late dinner afterwards and a cheek kiss to say goodnight at Val's front door. There was a ray of hope for Edwin. And it lifted our spirits; all of us.

Five months later, after an intimate wedding reception at our house, Edwin took her to a mountain resort for a short honeymoon and then moved into her spacious house while letting his townhouse. My brother, thanks to our sister, was once more his old outgoing, tolerable if not pleasant self. Only once did he mention, half-jokingly, his concern over his financial status. Now that he had a wife to take care of again, how will he provide after retirement?

Now everyone started looking at Anita, trying to match her up with some nice, wealthy gentleman. But Anita had no use for this. She vowed years ago she would not marry again and stuck by her decision.

"I did meet a man some time ago," she told me one day.

"And?"

"And nothing. I think he was married."

"Was he younger than you?" I can't stop myself from asking.

"No, about the same age."

"Where did you meet him and what happened?"

"Nothing happened. He just helped me out of a jam. His name was Anton. I can't help it, but I think of him sometimes. I wish I could get to know him better. If I ever met a man like that again, I ... "

"Would you consider marrying then?"

"*Ag*, it's no use daydreaming. He was probably married. He never even gave me his surname." My curiosity was tickled.

"What kind of jam were you in?" Anita told me the story of Tony, just the basics. She gave no details. Just that the Ferrari was found abandoned. Anton told her Tony disappeared a day before.

"Why did Anton not give you his surname?"

"He said it was not important. I got the impression he lived a very secretive kind of life. Told me he and some other guys work on their own. They are not involved in any formal form of law enforcement. They live to seek out injustice and put things right. Especially concerning the drug trade. He had no tolerance for drug dealers whatsoever."

"What did he look like?" Anita described him as well as she could remember.

"A really nice man, gentle, compassionate, yet strong and unmovable, purpose driven."

I did not tell her, but the more she told me about the man, Anton, the more I became convinced I knew him. It must be Anton Joubert, the man in my old home cell back in Linden. Lara mentioned to me how much her dad despised the drug trade, how he used to fight against it, but she could give no details. I'd better give her or Lindie a call and find out how they were doing. I thought Anton was retired from that life. It just shows you, you can take the man out of the job, but not the job out of the man. He must have gone back to doing his part in fighting the drug trade. I hope he gets them all. 'Lord, help him and protect him for his beautiful family,' I pray in my mind.

Anita changed the focus to me, saying:

"Funny that I often think about you and Gerald. You never told me how you met each other. I can't even recall you dating anyone before him. Did you even have a boyfriend before him? You never said anything about a boyfriend before. You just came home one day announcing you are engaged to be married. You could have struck me down with a straw."

"You're right. I never had a boyfriend before Gerald. Never even dated anyone."

"Why not? How did you know he is the right man for you if you never knew any other men? How could you compare if there never was anyone to compare him with?"

"What need was there to compare? I knew what I wanted, what I didn't want and when I met Gerald, I knew this was the man I wanted. What need was there to date if I knew it would not lead any further? Dating is such a waste of time."

"That's where you're wrong. Dating is exciting, it is fun, it is a learning process."

"What do you learn from dating? That the man you want is somewhere out there but in the mean time you entertain yourself with anyone that's available?"

"No. You learn about different types of men so you can choose better." I doubt that she saw the irony of her own words about choosing a man.

"I didn't have to know different kinds of men to know what I want. I knew all along what it was that I wanted. So when I met Gerald, I knew he was what I wanted. Simple as that. No need to check them out. What if you fall in love with the wrong man and he breaks your heart? Or someone falls in love with you and you break his heart? Just a waste of emotions, creation of bad, sad memories and totally unnecessary. After every heartbreak you have to pick yourself up and start all over carrying baggage from one relationship to the next for the rest of your life."

"*Ag* no man. You're just trying to be difficult again. What's wrong with falling in love more than once?"

"One or more than one broken hearts, that's what." I told her about Enrique and Jonathan and how I handled their efforts to date me.

"Francine, are you serious? You turned down a smouldering Spaniard, and a doctor on top of it?"

"Doctors' wives don't have it easy, you know. They have to make an appointment to have dinner with their husbands."

"You're exaggerating. I know it's not as glamorous as people make it out to be, but they are rich and they give free medical treatment to the whole family."

"May be so, but there is more to a marriage than that."

"Sure. Now tell me about Jonathan. Where did you meet him and what did he do for a living?"

"Well, you know how everybody always tries to set spinsters like me up with some nice guy who can make their lives less lonely."

"You were not a spinster. Spinsterism is all in the head."

"Spinsterism? Good heavens, where did you get that word? Are you sure it's in the dictionary?"

"No, I just made it up. Now, go on, tell me about Jonathan."

"Edwin is a party man like he has always been. And whether it was his idea or Enid's, I don't know. But every time I was there, except when Debra-Ann was a baby, they had a party. And guess who did they invite?"

"Some nice, eligible young man, I guess?"

"Not some, but a room full. So there was this very attractive blond guy from the same faculty as Edwin. He tried to convince me that chemistry is the most interesting thing in the world. When he learned I was a painter he lectured me on the chemical composition of all different kinds of paint."

"Oh, boy, what a bore."

"Well, it was quite useful to learn how certain colours react with each other and why certain results could be expected. I didn't learn that in my art classes. At least not in depth. So when he asked me out, I agreed on the condition that we visit an art gallery or two so that he could tell me more about the paint used by the artists. I expected him to know it all, and he did. Well, not all, but a lot. Afterwards over coffee I told him thank you, it was very informative, but that was it, I was not in the market for another date and cheerio. It was not long after that episode that I started dating my heartthrob. Gerald was a gentleman. It was difficult for him, especially since he had been married before, but he respected me right up to our wedding day."

"Don't tell me you were a virgin when you got married."

"All right, so I won't tell you. You won't believe me anyway. But relax. I'm not trying to convince you and you'll never convince me. So let's talk about something else." So we talked about the family picnic on the beach that we have mentioned but not discussed. Time now to do some planning to make it happen. With such lovely weather we were having lately we should get serious about it.

****

Soon Anita felt it was time to live her own life again. She earned enough to make a good living, bought a small place in a secure complex and moved out of the big house in Pinegrove. I made the same offer of helping with a loan as I did for Edwin, but she declined. She had regained her self-respect and was adamant to make her own way in future.

To my surprise, she asked me to accompany her when she went to buy curtains, cushions and all kinds of items for decoration. She needed my sense of colour and composition, she told me. Afterwards when we went for lunch, Anita insisted on paying the bill. For the first time since Dad moved out, we were friends again. She did not need me, she wanted me beside her; wanted me to be a real sister to her and she wanted to be a real sister to me.

****

My life with Gerald and our two Crompton blessings - Robert and Gwen - goes so smoothly, it might have been lacklustre. If it was not for our love deepening, our relationship with the Lord growing more intimate as time goes by and our children growing up to be individuals with opposite kinds of talents and personalities, life could become monotonous; even boring. I am greatly thankful that the Lord spared us trouble and blessed us with peace in our home.

Robert showed early talent for the arts. He is always drawing something and it always has to do with some experience he has had. It is his way of processing new information or experience. He is forever around whenever I spent time in my 'paint room' as I like to call it, very eager to learn everything he can.

Other times he would stay quietly in his room writing poems and short stories, reflecting on his most recent experiences. He is an even-tempered boy, always sure of himself and what he liked or did not like; sure of what he wants to do or not. And he looks like me, mostly: big grey-green eyes, reddish brown hair. He is built like his father, well proportioned, but it looks as if he is going to be taller.

Gwen, a darling bubbling, giggling girl with her father's dimples, dark brown hair and her granddad's bright blue eyes, is often the centre of attraction and loving it. She is sporty, outgoing and always ready to help wherever necessary. Always ready to take action. While those around her indecisively stand assessing a situation, she would already have summed up what needed to be done and start doing it.

We are blessed parents: Both our children love the Lord and are determined to discover His will for their lives and stay in it. No parent could wish for more. When all is well with our children, then all is well.

CHAPTER 27

Closure

Another five years have passed. Contrary to worldwide 'prophecies,' we all survived twenty-first December twenty twelve and more. Aunt Emma is no longer with us. We buried her two weeks ago. It was a sad time for us all. She was a part of the household and the family for so long, the gap her passing has left, is enormous. Her children, my cousins expressed yet again their gratitude towards us for taking so well care of her. Of course, we consider it a privilege to have had her.

Old Simon is also gone. Anita and I attended his funeral. All his children were happy to see us. They all were well educated and established in good careers. Except Ephraim, who mentally could not manage to finish school and became his father's successor as our butler when Simon retired.

Andrew, grouchy about his situation, but realizing he has little choice, pushed on and became one of the best supervisors; was then promoted to manager and then became a district manager in the company. He is now esteemed again and has slowly regained his confidence, but never to be the overconfident and prideful man he used to be. There is now room and understanding in his life for people less fortunate than the privileged upper class. Retirement and a way to maintain a lifestyle satisfactory to Marie's standards, was what worried him most.

Edwin and his new wife, Valerie, make a good living. Both work hard, but also make time for relaxation and do good things that used to be strange for Edwin. I could never imagine him feeding poor people, yet there he is, every Sunday morning doing his part next to Valerie in the feeding scheme of their church. I am overwhelmed with gratitude to the Lord for what He is doing in the Hammond-family.

We received good news from Australia, and bad. The bad news was Debra-Ann's fiancé dropped her like a hot potato the moment he realized the money well had dried up. Actually, it was not such bad news after all. Her life would have been one of great misery, had she married him. Tamsin drifted from job to miserable job to support herself and her addiction. At first she tried to live off the generosity of her brother and sister, but found they were not so generous to people who tries to abuse the situation.

Now, the truly good news: Howie had a friend whose little brother was killed in a speedboat accident. This friend turned to God in anguish over the death of his younger brother. He first invited; then dragged a very reluctant Howie with him to this church called Mountain Melody that he discovered in his search for truth and the meaning of life. From the first moment Howie entered the building, he felt the Lord gripping his heart. He walked out a new creation and set on finding Father Abba's will for his life. It will be an uphill struggle, but if he hangs in there, he will get where he needs to be.

Anita was remorseful for spoiling her son. She knew unlimited cash would take him down, yet she gave him whatever he asked for. After she received her inheritance, Donny never bothered to get a job. Anita, living in a small flat in a less expensive part of town earlier; Donny - like his mother warned him so many years ago - had nowhere to go but a homeless shelter. Not even his sister was willing to help him after he ignored hundreds of warnings. Chanté believes he deserves what he is getting and it is time for him to grow up and learn his lesson the hard way.

Once again we had good news out of Australia. After Howie became a follower of Christ, he took pity on his little sister. Tamsin had become a full-blown drug addict. Howie bundled her into a rehab centre where she was converted when a youth outreach from a nearby church came visiting to witness. After kicking the bad habit, she joined the church, became a missionary and is preparing to go to China on a mission trip of two years.

My sister, always a hard worker, is now more focused. Now, for the first time she excelled in her job, the one I gave her. Retirement was of some concern to her. They, my brothers and sister, are all nearing the age where they will have to step out. Building a proper retirement fund in such a short period is impossible. It is time for a family gathering again.

****

As soon as they are all seated round the dining table in my house in Pinegrove, I take my place at the head of the table just like many years ago when I informed them about Dad's letter to me. Now is the time to show them the part of the letter I left out. I hand them each a copy of the letter, then read it out loud to them, ending with the words: "Be good to my children." Stunned silence filled the room.

Edwin speaks first:

"He knew." Then Andrew:

"Yes. He knew we would mess up." Then Terrence:

"Come on guys, don't beat yourselves up. So he knew, but still made provision for us."

"That's right. He did not have to, but he did," Andrew again.

Anita had to let her voice be heard: "He loved us. If we only knew how much he loved us".

"And we treated him like dung," Edwin replies.

"We did not know." Anita.

"No, we did not," answers Andrew.

"So, what now, Francine? Why did you decide to tell us at this stage? To torture us?"

"No, Edwin, on the contrary. I have watched you all closely. You have all learned from this experience. Retirement is lurking and no one wants to work till he is ninety years old. You are welcome to do so if you wish, but you should have the option to retire sooner. Therefore, I have decided it was time for me to share the company profits with you. Before Dad retired, he gave me the larger percentage of ownership, which was all he held at the time. I have now decided to hand over to each of you twelve per cent of my part. The company is doing well. This will ensure you a good future and a peaceful worry free old age if you hang on to it".

"Is that why you refused to take the company public?"

"Yes, Andrew. It would have been impossible, or at least very complicated to share ownership with you all if it was a public company. Now it is merely a formality."

I hand them the documentation for the transfer of shared ownership. In the presence of Daniel Denton junior, they all signed the documents. No handshake from anyone. Hugs and kisses instead. The mood around the room is not festive, like at the reading of Dad's will, but rather subdued, relieved and grateful. Gerald pops a cork and pours sparkling wine. They all lift their glasses:

"To partnership!" This time they ate slowly of the delicacies provided by Katrina and her daughter, Angie, who is being trained to take over as housekeeper from her mother. They seem reluctant to leave, so unlike that day when our dad's will was read.

As I watched them it was as if I could almost audibly hear the Lord's voice saying to me:

"Last time I heard your thoughts you said you shall not help them. What happened to make you change your mind?"

"Lord, they are my brothers and my sister. Even though I was so angry with them, they still are my blood. And what would the purpose of my taking charge of Dad's business be, if it was not to help them? That's exactly why I had to do it. To be able to help them and do what Dad expected of me instead of keeping the company and all its profits for myself. Is that not what Your will is for my life in the first place?"

As soon as they are all gone, Gerald, who was quietly observing the procedures, puts his arm around me, hugging me tightly:

"Well done. I'm glad you did it. But why didn't you tell them that you and I still hold the majority even if theirs are put together?"

"I did not think it was necessary. They will find out soon enough. And you know Edwin. He might not make trouble - he is not in a position to do so - but he is a born complainer and I did not want to give him any reason to argue."

"I'm sure he learnt his lesson thoroughly."

"Yes, I think so too, but still. He loves to quarrel and argue just for the sake of arguing. I am just grateful to Trevor for selling you his part when he retired." Gerald gives me a hug again and together we go out onto the back patio to watch the shadow of the mountain crawling over the lawn while the birds start to return to their nests for the night. Dad's will was done, and I could only do it by remaining in the Will of the Father who abundantly poured out his mercy and grace over me.

www.ingramcontent.com/pod-product-compliance
Lightning Source LLC
Chambersburg PA
CBHW052036090426
42739CB00010B/1930